Good Housekeeping

light & healthy
COOKING

250 Delicious, Satisfying,
Guilt-Free Recipes

Shrimp Kabobs with Asian BBQ Sauce (recipe page 124)

Good Housekeeping

light & healthy
COOKING

250 Delicious, Satisfying, Guilt-Free Recipes

HEARST BOOKS

New York

HEARST BOOKS
New York

An Imprint of Sterling Publishing
387 Park Avenue South
New York, NY 10016

GOOD HOUSEKEEPING

Rosemary Ellis	*Editor in Chief*
Courtney Murphy	*Creative Director*
Susan Westmoreland	*Food Director*
Samantha B. Cassetty, MS, RD	*Nutrition Director*

Book Design: Anna Christian
Cover Design: Jon Chaiet
Project Editor: Sarah Scheffel

Photography Credits on page 291

Library of Congress Cataloging-in-Publication Data

Good housekeeping light & healthy cookbook : 250 delicious, satisfying, guilt-free recipes.
    p. cm.
  Includes indexes.
  ISBN 978-1-58816-836-8
1. Cooking. 2. Cooking, American. 3. Low-fat diet—Recipes. 4. Low-calorie diet—Recipes. I. Good housekeeping. II. Title: Good housekeeping light and healthy cookbook. III. Title: Light & healthy cookbook.
  TX714.G6496 2011
  641.5'6384—dc23
                        2011015932

10 9 8 7 6 5 4 3 2 1

The Good Housekeeping Cookbook Seal guarantees that the recipes in this cookbook meet the strict standards of the Good Housekeeping Research Institute. The Institute has been a source of reliable information and a consumer advocate since 1900, and established its seal of approval in 1909. Every recipe has been triple-tested for ease, reliability, and great taste.

Published by Hearst Books
A division of Sterling Publishing Co., Inc.
387 Park Avenue South, New York, NY 10016

Good Housekeeping is a registered trademark of Hearst Communications, Inc.
www.goodhousekeeping.com

For information about custom editions, special sales, premium and corporate purchases, please contact Sterling Special Sales Department at 800-805-5489 or specialsales@sterlingpublishing.com.

Distributed in Canada by Sterling Publishing
c/o Canadian Manda Group, 165 Dufferin Street
Toronto, Ontario, Canada M6K 3H6

Distributed in Australia by Capricorn Link
(Australia) Pty. Ltd.
P.O. Box 704, Windsor, NSW 2756 Australia

Manufactured in China

Sterling ISBN 978-1-58816-836-8

Basil-Orange Chicken with Couscous (recipe page 157)

Orange Pork and Asparagus Stir-Fry (recipe page 206)

Contents

Honeyed Hot Fruit Salad (recipe page 270)

Foreword

Welcome to *Good Housekeeping*'s collection of our favorite light and healthy recipes.

We all want to eat nutritious meals. But sometimes it's hard finding easy, healthy recipes that everyone in your family will love. That's why we're so pleased to present this cookbook. Not only did we fill it with delicious recipes your family will want to eat, we created many dishes that are ready in less than 30 minutes to please the cook, too. Icons throughout the book indicate these quick-and-easy dishes, plus high-fiber, heart-healthy, and make-ahead options. (See Index of Recipes by Icon, page 300, for a complete list.)

The 250 salads, soups, main dishes, sides, and desserts in this book are sure crowd pleasers, whether you're making Tuesday night family dinner or entertaining a group of friends on the weekend. Each recipe has been triple-tested by the pros in the *Good Housekeeping* Test Kitchens, so you can be sure they'll come out great. Many feature whole

grains, which fill you up with wholesome fiber and other essential nutrients, too.

In every recipe, 30 percent or fewer of the calories come from fat. That's right in line with the USDA's dietary guidelines for healthy eating. We also offer info about healthy ingredients to include in your diet plus cooking tips from our expert team to help make your everyday food preparation as easy and healthy as can be!

You'll quickly discover that cooking with an eye toward good health doesn't mean sacrificing taste or familiar foods you know your family will eat. Stir fries, pastas, burritos, burgers, and even luscious desserts like brownies and carrot cake? Yes, all of these can be light and nutritious.

Here's to happy, healthy cooking for you and your family!

—Susan Westmoreland
Food Director, *Good Housekeeping*

Eating Well, the Light and Healthy Way

Providing healthy, low-calorie (not to mention low-fat) meals that are satisfying and easy to prepare is a big concern for all of us today. As the relationship between diet and health hits the headlines repeatedly, we all want to do our best to produce meals for our families and ourselves that meet today's nutritional guidelines. But figuring out how to do it isn't always easy. The latest USDA Dietary Guidelines (healthierus .gov/dietaryguidelines) and Choose My Plate

(ChooseMyPlate.gov) have revised the rules based on current medical research, but the goal is the same: to encourage us all to eat a diet that will lead to a long life of good health.

Over the years, *Good Housekeeping* has been a trusted source for making the latest information on health and nutrition a part of your daily life. As the rules change, *Good Housekeeping* editors translate the underlying research and provide the tools you need to make it work for you. Our *Light & Healthy Cookbook* follows that tradition by bringing you this collection of delicious, triple-tested recipes that meet the latest USDA dietary guidelines. The recipes selected emphasize whole grains, an abundance of fruits and vegetables, and fat-free or low-fat dairy products. They include fish, lean poultry, and meat, as well as beans, eggs, and nuts, but limit total fat to 30 percent of calories or less (the USDA cap is 35 percent), and also saturated fat, trans fat, cholesterol, and added sugar. Recipes keep tabs on sodium, too.

Calories Count

We hear a lot about America's obesity epidemic and the "flavor-of-the-day" diets that everyone is trying—but very little about counting calories. Calories aren't an old-fashioned enemy; they are simply a way of measuring the amount of energy produced when food is used by the body. Keeping an eye on them is still the most promising method to ease into a lifetime of weight control. In fact, one of the USDA's key recommendations is to manage body weight by controlling total calorie intake. It's just a matter of balance: Food calories in must equal energy calories out. For people who are overweight or obese, this will mean consuming fewer calories and increasing physical activity.

For centuries, our bodies have been stocking up during times of plenty to insure survival during times of scarcity, so we are naturally programmed to tuck away all excess food calories as those potential energy calories we know as fat. And that is not likely to change any time soon. You might try the latest diet fad and enjoy short-term success, but pretty soon your body will think the famine it has been planning for has arrived and will steadfastly hang on to those stored calories in case things get worse.

When it comes to light and healthy meal planning, instead of fad diets, *Good Housekeeping* recommends that you follow the "three, four, five" rule: Breakfast should be no more than 300 calories, lunch no more than 400 calories, and dinner no more than 500 calories, plus two optional snacks of 100 to 200 calories apiece. These simple guidelines will help you gauge

how your consumption is measuring up day by day. (For more precise calorie recommendations based on gender, age, and activity level, visit healthierus.gov/dietaryguidelines.)

Lifetime weight maintenance requires setting reasonable weight goals for yourself and enjoying just enough of today's bounty to provide the energy you need for all you do. Make balance a habit; eat healthy food that pleases you and do exercises that you enjoy.

Focus on Flavor

While controlling the calories and total fats in the recipes you prepare is a primary concern, providing mealtime satisfaction is also essential to achieving and maintaining a healthy weight. A diet of low-cal, low-fat foods that aren't delicious and satisfying will soon be abandoned. If your family members are found foraging for their favorite snacks an hour after dinner (or make excuses to go out to dinner to avoid your cooking altogether), then you need to rethink your meal plans. The recipes you'll find in our *Light & Healthy Cookbook* have been triple-tested and tasted in our kitchens with flavor and satiety in mind. We want you to discover how enjoyable healthy foods can be, so you and those you love will want to make them a long-term part of life.

We know there are many responsibilities competing for your time every day, so as we developed these light and healthy recipes to provide great taste and satisfaction, we never forgot that *quick and easy* is important when you have to get dinner on the table after a busy day. The recipes that made the cut require very little hands-on time. They can either be prepared quickly and served, or mind themselves in the oven or on the stovetop while you do other things. Some can also be prepared ahead and simply reheated when the dinner hour strikes.

We believe a collection of easy and nutritious recipes that your family enjoys is worth a place in your kitchen, and we hope that the healthy eating patterns that they encourage will become a family tradition. You'll see: Light and healthy cooking is not only guilt-free—it can be habit forming.

The Nutrients You Need: The Big Three

Our bodies need three essential nutrients: carbohydrates, proteins, and fats.

CARBOHYDRATES: The right kind of carbohydrates is the mainstay of a well-balanced diet. "Good" carbohydrates include fruits, vegetables, beans, legumes, and whole grains. Carbohydrates can be made up of dietary fiber, starch or sugar, or a combo of the two. Those who follow a diet rich in dietary fiber have been shown to have a reduced risk of coronary heart disease, among other benefits, and research indicates that whole-grain eaters are thinner than people who eat few whole-grain foods. According to the latest USDA recommendations, at least half of your grains should be whole grains. Unfortunately, it is not always easy to tell if a product is a whole grain–rich food. For label-reading tips, see "How Do You Know It's Whole Grain?," opposite.

The starch and sugar in carbohydrates supply the body with the energy it needs for normal functions. When carbohydrates are digested, they become blood sugar (glucose),

HOW DO YOU KNOW IT'S WHOLE GRAIN?

Searching your supermarket for whole-grain foods can be confusing—so how do you separate the wheat from the chaff?

+ **LOOK FOR THE WORD** *WHOLE* **IN THE INGREDIENTS LIST.** Even though breads and crackers may be labeled *multigrain, nine-grain*, or *100 percent wheat bread*, that's no guarantee that any of them are whole grain. If an item is whole grain, the word *whole* will typically precede the grain's name in the ingredients panel: *whole-wheat flour* or *whole rye flour*, for example.

+ **NOTE WHERE THE WHOLE GRAIN FALLS IN THE LIST OF INGREDIENTS.** Ingredients are listed in order of their weight: If a whole grain is listed first and is the only grain, there is a lot of whole grain in the product. If the first ingredient is *wheat flour* (which is really white flour), followed by some sort of sweetener, then whole-wheat flour is not the dominant grain.

+ **BUY WHOLE GRAINS PACKAGED OR IN BULK.** The best way to ensure you are eating whole grains is to prepare them yourself. Throughout this book, we provide easy, satisfying recipes featuring a wide variety of whole grains, from barley and brown rice to wheat berries and oats. Give them a try!

+ **THE AMOUNT OF DIETARY FIBER WON'T HELP YOU IDENTIFY WHOLE GRAINS.** Different whole grains vary widely in fiber content: A full serving of whole grains—16 grams—will contain from just over a half gram of fiber to around 3 grams of fiber. And, in order to earn the label "High in Fiber" (5 grams of fiber or more), most foods contain added fiber (extra bran, resistant starch, or other fibers). For further information, visit wholegrainscouncil.org.

which is then used as fuel in our bodies. In general, the less added sugar you eat, the better. However, this doesn't include the naturally occurring sugar found in fruit, milk, or yogurt. The real culprit is the added sugar that comes from sweeteners, including white sugar, high-fructose corn syrup, brown rice syrup, dextrose, sucrose, fruit juice concentrate, and other sweeteners.

PROTEINS: The body needs protein to produce new body tissue. Proteins are also great for weight loss, as they help keep you feeling full for hours after eating. Too much protein, however, is unhealthy; it can stress the kidneys, and if it comes from fatty meat, it is also filling you with saturated fat. For optimum health, you should eat a variety of protein-containing foods, including seafood, lean meat and poultry, eggs, beans and lentils, soy products, and unsalted nuts and seeds. The latest USDA guidelines suggest that you eat more fish and nonmeat protein; try increasing the amount and variety that you consume by substituting seafood (or beans, lentils, tofu, or another soy product) in place of some of the meat and poultry you would typically eat. Whatever protein you prepare for dinner, ideally, your plate should look like this: half-filled with vegetables and/or fruits, a quarter with starches, and another quarter with protein-rich foods (and a little fat).

FATS: The USDA guideline for fat consumption is 20 to 35 percent of your total daily calories, which is a wide range. However, much more important than the total fat is the amount of saturated and trans fat in your diet. Here's what you need to know about these fats.

When an excess of saturated fat is consumed, it raises your blood cholesterol level, increasing your risk of heart disease and stroke. Saturated fat is found naturally in foods, but it is especially concentrated in fatty animal-based foods, such as fatty red meat, butter, and chicken skin, and in some oils, such as palm and coconut. Even "good" oils like olive and canola contain a little saturated fat, so you can't avoid it entirely. For a heart-healthy diet, you should derive less than 10 percent of your total calories from saturated fat, which is a maximum of 15 grams of saturated fat daily, based on a 1,500-calorie diet. Throughout the book, we have indicated heart-healthy recipes, containing 5 grams or less of saturated fat per serving, with the following icon: ♥. Our heart-healthy recipes also limit cholesterol and sodium; for specifics, see our guidelines on page 301.

Even worse than saturated fat is trans fat, which not only raises the LDL ("bad cholesterol") but also lowers the HDL ("good cholesterol"). It is formed by a process called hydrogenation, which turns oils into semisolids like margarine and shortening. The good news: The government is requiring manufacturers to list trans-fat amounts on labels, and many companies are removing the fat as a result. Still, trans fats are used in some packaged foods. On the ingredients list, these oils appear as *partially hydrogenated oils* or *shortening* and are reflected in the trans-fat total on the Nutrition Facts label. To keep your intake of trans fat low, use canola or olive oil whenever possible and "0 trans" or "trans-fat-free" spread. Eliminate processed foods made with partially hydrogenated oils, and limit those high in saturated fat.

Choose Your Plate

The USDA's My Plate icon is a simple visual representation of the foods that you should eat each day to achieve a healthy, balanced diet. It shows a dinner plate with quadrants for the four basic food groups: fruits and vegetables on one-half,

grains and protein on the other plus a circle off to the side that denotes dairy. My Plate shows the relative importance of the different food groups. It replaces the USDA's Food Pyramid, which represented the food groups in colorful vertical bands with a staircase on the side that emphasized the importance of regular exercise in maintaining good health.

The My Plate icon is meant to serve as a reminder that helps you think about your food choices. It's paired with tips and suggestions, beginning with this commonsense advice that's right in line with GH's light and healthy eating guidelines: Enjoy your food, but eat less, avoiding oversized portions.

The My Plate plan advises on foods you should increase, so we've included lots of recipes in our *Light & Healthy Cookbook* to support these efforts.

✦ **Make half your plate fruits and vegetables.** Vary your vegetables and don't forget fruits, whether they're fresh or frozen, canned (without added sweeteners) or dried.

✦ **Make at least half your grains whole grains.** Bread, pasta, oatmeal, breakfast cereals, and tortillas all provide opportunities to eat more whole grains.

✦ **Switch to fat-free (skim) or low-fat (1%) milk, yogurt, and cheese.** Note that calcium-fortified soymilk can meet your dairy requirements, too.

✦ **Go lean with protein.** Choose from lean cuts of meat and skinless poultry; fish and seafood; beans and peas; and soy products like tofu.

The plan also advises on foods to reduce. It notes that currently, many of the foods and beverages Americans eat and drink contain empty calories—solid fats and added sugars—that pack on the calories but deliver few or no nutrients. Limit the empty calories you consume from "junk food" like soda, candy, cakes, cookies, and pastries. Also limit foods high in saturated fat—like pizza and cheese—and especially those high in saturated fat and sodium—such as sausages, hot dogs, and bacon. Drink water instead of sugary drinks like sodas, sports drinks, and fruit drinks.

Because your food and physical activity choices each day affect your long-term health, the USDA has included interactive features on its website that help you customize and keep track of your diet and exercise: Visit myplate.gov to get started.

Interpreting Nutrition Information on Packages

While the Nutrition Facts label can tell you a lot about a food, you need to check the ingredients list to see what you're really eating. For example, is your breakfast cereal made with whole grains, or does your favorite salad dressing contain oil that is high in saturated fat?

UNDERSTANDING FOOD LABELS

Food labels help you make informed choices about the foods to include in your diet. The Percent Daily Values reflect the percentage of the recommended daily amount of a nutrient based on 2,000 calories daily. First, note the serving size. Sometimes even a small package holds multiple servings. Then budget your intake of nutrients by adding up calories and percentages. For example, this label shows that you get 27 percent of the daily value of saturated fat from one serving. If the next food you eat contains 25 percent of the recommended daily limit for saturated fat, then you have already consumed more than 50 per-

Nutrition Facts

Serving Size 2 pieces (29g)
Servings Per Container 15

Amount Per Serving	
Calories 150	Calories from Fat 80

	% Daily Value*
Total Fat 8g	13%
Saturated Fat 5g	27%
Cholesterol 25mg	8%
Sodium 115mg	5%
Total Carbohydrate 18g	6%
Dietary Fiber 0g	0%
Sugars 6g	
Protein 2g	

Vitamin A 0%	•	Vitamin C 0%
Calcium 2%	•	Iron 2%

* Percent Daily Values are based on a 2,000 calorie diet.

cent of your total saturated fat allowance for that day.

When it comes to fat, saturated fat, sodium, and cholesterol, it's a good idea to keep the daily values under 100 percent. Fiber, vitamins A and C, calcium, and iron are listed, too, because diets often fall short; aim for 100 percent or more of these nutrients. (Other vitamins and minerals may also appear on food labels.)

The Daily Values footnote (not shown) includes a chart with some daily values for 2,000- and 2,500-calorie diets. Use these numbers as a guide. Your own daily values may be lower, depending on your calorie needs.

By law, ingredients lists must be ordered by weight. The heaviest ingredient goes first, followed by the next-heaviest ingredient, and so on. It is not a good sign if sugar is among the first three ingredients listed in a cereal, or when bad fats like partially hydrogenated soybean and cottonseed oils are the third ingredient listed on a can of biscuit dough. Below is an explanation of common phrases found on many food packages:

"CHOLESTEROL FREE": Naturally cholesterol-free foods, by FDA regulations, can't be labeled "cholesterol free" unless they also say something like "Peanut butter, a cholesterol-free food," indicating that all peanut butters are, in fact, free of cholesterol. If you find this confusing just remember: Only foods of animal origin contain cholesterol. So, cookies made with butter or eggs will list cholesterol on the label, while crackers made with olive oil will not—unless they contain some other animal-derived product, like cheese.

"LIGHT": This word is used to describe fat content, taste, color, or consistency. If the manufacturer is describing the fat content as "light," the product has at least 50 percent less fat than the original. The label must also say "50% less fat than our regular product." "Light" olive oil, on the other hand, describes the oil's color. The oil is as caloric as regular olive oil but has been processed to remove some of its flavor. A muffin mix can say "light and fluffy" as a way to describe its texture or consistency.

"LOW-FAT" OR "FAT-FREE": Low-fat products must contain 3 grams or less fat per serving, and fat-free products must have less than 0.5 grams of fat per serving. But check the number of calories—that number could be very high. It is easy to gain lots of weight eating fat-free cookies because they are loaded with sugar.

"LOW SODIUM" OR "LIGHT IN SODIUM": This means that the sodium was cut by at least 50 percent compared to the original product. Be careful when using a "low-sodium" version of a super-high-sodium food such as soy sauce or soup. You can still end up consuming a lot of sodium. Check the numbers on the Nutrition Facts label.

"SUGAR-FREE," "NO ADDED SUGARS," "WITHOUT ADDED SUGARS": A sugar-free chocolate candy may not contain a speck of sugar, but it's still got plenty of fat and calories. Be sure to check out the Nutrition Facts label to know how many calories and grams of saturated fat you're consuming.

"SWEETENED WITH FRUIT JUICE," "FRUIT JUICE SWEETENER," OR "FRUIT JUICE CONCENTRATE": These sweeteners are made by reducing fruit juice—usually grape juice—into a sticky sweetener. These sweeteners are not nutritious; they are just like sugar.

Easy Changes You Can Make Right Now

Enjoying the benefits of a healthy lifestyle might require some changes, but they don't have to be painful. In fact, giving up your favorites forever should never be part of the program. There are actually a lot of small changes you can make that will be a big step in the right direction. Here are some of our favorites:

✦ **Go whole grain.** There are now more whole-grain choices than ever. In addition to the readily available bulk grains—from bulgur to millet to wheat berries—there's a multitude of whole-grain packaged foods available. Start with whole-wheat or multigrain pasta and whole-grain breads. Be sure to check bread labels to see how much of the rich brown color actually comes from whole grains rather than from coloring agents, cocoa, or molasses. (See "How Do You Know It's Whole Grain?," page 13, for more helpful pointers.)

✦ **Snack from the produce department.** Even if you are in a hurry, there are a lot of ready-to-eat fruit and vegetable choices in the produce department these days. If you don't see anything prepackaged that you want, go to the salad bar and select your own snack (then choose a reduced-fat or fat-free dressing and use it as a veggie dip).

✦ **Gradually switch to low-fat or fat-free milk and yogurt.** You'll be amazed how easy it is to downsize from whole to fat-free milk and yogurt if you do it in stages. Go to 2% for a few weeks, 1% for a while, and you are there. We'll bet you don't ever want to go back.

✦ **Explore reduced-fat, low-sodium options.** Many reduced-fat and low-sodium products will work well in your favorite family recipes. Grandma's lasagna might be just as delicious with reduced-fat cheeses and low-sodium toma-

LIGHT AND HEALTHY SHOPPING

Healthy lifestyle changes start in the supermarket; if you make the right selections there, your time in the kitchen will be easy. Here are some strategies for filling your cart and your cupboards with light, healthy, natural choices.

✦ Select a week's worth of recipes from our *Light & Healthy Cooking* and make a list of ingredients you will need for the planned meals.

✦ Discard high-fat items from your cupboards and add low-fat versions of your favorites to the list.

✦ Add one item from the snack aisle to the list so you won't feel deprived; make it the small size.

✦ Head for the market, but not until you have a healthy breakfast, lunch, or dinner. If you aren't hungry, you're not as likely to be tempted by unhealthy choices from the supermarket aisles.

✦ Check sell-by dates of groceries and select produce that is the freshest, even if it means adjusting your menu to make use of the best ingredients available.

✦ Compare Nutrition Facts labels among similar products and select those that best meet your dietary goals.

✦ Buy only what's on your list; don't be tempted by the end-of-aisle specials.

✦ Select the candy-free checkout lane; treat yourself to a magazine instead.

toes. In fact, if they had been in her local market, she probably would have used them to produce healthy meals for her family.

✦ **Always read the Nutrition Facts labels.** It doesn't take a lot of time and you can learn a lot. Sometimes those packages with the biggest fat-free, low-fat, or low-salt labels are very high in sugar and calories. (See "Understanding Food Labels," page 16).

✦ **Break high-calorie combos.** Discover bread with a little hummus (instead of butter), baked potatoes with herbs (try nonfat Greek yogurt instead of sour cream), dessert without whipped cream (or ice cream)—you'll enjoy the food's flavor even more.

✦ **Take control of salt.** The latest USDA guidelines recommend reducing your daily sodium intake to less than 2,300 milligrams; they recommend further reducing it to 1,500 milligrams for people who are 51 and older and those of any age who have hypertension, diabetes, or chronic kidney disease. That's a tall order, especially if you like to cook with prepared sauces and seasoning packets and spice mixtures. These products are convenient, to be sure, but watch out for the hidden salt. Look for reduced-sodium versions and add only as much as you need.

✦ **Remember, liquid calories count.** The number of calories in beverages might shock you. Fruit juice, alcoholic drinks, sweetened lemonade and iced tea, soda, and especially lattés and other gourmet coffee drinks are loaded with empty calories. And, on a warm day, you might go ahead and have a refill.

✦ **Walk to your local ice cream store**—or drive if it is really too far to walk. Just don't keep that half-gallon in the freezer. You don't need to deny yourself your favorite treat, but if enjoying a bowl of ice cream requires a trip, you have to think about it—and it becomes a special occasion. Or dip into some frozen yogurt or sorbet for a lower-calorie treat.

Light and Healthy Cooking Techniques

Often, great flavor comes as much from how a food is prepared as from the food itself. We use the following high-flavor, low-fat cooking techniques in recipes throughout the book. Some are slow, others fast, but all can be low maintenance. Make them a part of your light and healthy cooking repertoire.

BRAISING AND STEWING: Few dishes satisfy as much as a long-simmered stew or braised pot roast. Braising is usually done in a Dutch oven or heavy-bottomed pot with a tight-fitting lid and a handle at each side. For the richest flavor, brown the meat or poultry (first cut into chunks if you're making stew), add vegetables and a small amount of stock or water, cover tightly, and simmer. Patience is key: Even the toughest cuts of meat will become meltingly tender through this moist-heat method, but it takes a long time for the collagen in meat to break down. Tip: Do not let the liquid cook at more than a slow simmer or the meat will end up dry and tough.

ROASTING: Slow-cooking meat, poultry, whole fish, vegetables, and even fruits in the oven intensifies their natural flavors. The interior of the food becomes succulent and tender, while the exterior develops a delightfully caramelized crust. You'll need a heavy, shallow roasting pan; place it, uncovered, on a rack in the center of the oven so the hot air can circulate freely. When you're roasting vegetables or fruit, spread them out in a single layer or they will steam instead of caramelizing. Tip: The only way to guarantee that meat or poultry is roasted to the desired doneness is a meat thermometer. To ensure an accurate reading, always insert the thermometer into the center or thickest part of the roast without touching any bone or fatty sections.

BAKING: Meat, poultry, and seafood can be baked in covered cookware with a little liquid, which ensures that items like chicken breasts and fish won't dry out during cooking. Or fill packets made from aluminum foil or parchment paper with the ingredients (potatoes or other root vegetables work nicely) and seal tightly; the packets keep moisture and flavor in—and require a minimum of cleanup. Tip: Before sealing the packets, toss in some lemon slices or sprigs of fresh herbs, such as rosemary or thyme, for added flavor.

GRILLING: Whether you grill outdoors on a gas or charcoal grill or indoors in a ridged grill pan, the intense heat caramelizes the crust and lends delicious smoky flavor to whatever meat, poultry, seafood, or vegetable you're grilling. Much of the fat drips away during the process, making this quick and easy method an excellent choice for those looking to lighten up. Tip: To intensify flavor, use a dry rub or marinade. Use the leftover marinade to baste the food as it cooks.

STIR-FRYING: The fastest of cooking methods, stir-frying yields quick, tasty results and requires only a small amount of oil. Small pieces of food are cooked over high heat in a wok or skillet, stirred constantly to keep the food from sticking or burning. Vegetables should be sliced or chopped to roughly the same size to ensure even cooking; the fastest-cooking ingredients should be the last items you add to the pan. Lean cuts of meat should be sliced very thinly across the grain or cubed. Shrimp can be stir-fried with their shells on or off. Tip: When a recipe calls for soy sauce, use the reduced-sodium kind or dilute regular soy sauce with water.

STEAMING: Cooking vegetables in a steamer basket over simmering water is a smart choice for light and healthy cooking. Steaming preserves the veggies' natural color, flavor, and nutritional value, and it doesn't require any added fat. Tip: You can also steam vegetables in the microwave. For instructions and cook times for individual vegetables, see "Easy Microwave-Steamed Vegetables," page 246.

ABOUT THE RECIPES

◔ = 30 MINUTES OR LESS   ♥ = HEART HEALTHY   ⚘ = HIGH FIBER   🍲 = MAKE AHEAD

We've selected the recipes in this book according to our light and healthy guidelines. With a few exceptions, they are low calorie. At *Good Housekeeping*, that means a maximum of 450 calories per serving for main dishes that include a starch or fruit and 300 calories for main dishes without. All other courses should be 150 calories or less. The handful of breakfast, side, and dessert recipes that contain more than 150 calories per serving can easily be incorporated into meals or snacks that meet our "three, four, five" calories guidelines; see page 11.

Since eating less saturated fat should be on the agenda for all of us, we've included heart-healthy recipes that not only limit saturated fat, but also limit cholesterol and sodium. (For a breakdown, see Index of Recipes by Icon, page 300). And, because fiber provides a host of health benefits, from promoting good digestion and weight loss to quelling hunger, we've also called out main and side dishes that are high in fiber (contain 5 grams of fiber or more per serving).

If keeping track of this nutritional information seems labor-intensive, don't worry: We do the work for you. At the end of every recipe, you'll find complete nutritional information that lists the approximate calories (and percentage of calories from fat), protein, carbohydrates, total and saturated fat, fiber, cholesterol, and sodium content per serving. The nutritional information is followed by the colorful icons shown above to help you quickly identify recipes by your category of choice, from 30-minute or make-ahead meals to heart-healthy and high-fiber options.

Our nutritional calculations do not include any optional ingredients or garnishes, and when alternative ingredients are listed (such as margarine instead of butter), our calculations are based on the first item listed. Unless we note low-fat or reduced-fat dairy products, whole-fat milk, yogurt, and cheese has been used. But we invite you to swap in reduced-fat or nonfat products to create even lighter meals. If you're keeping tabs on your sodium intake, you should also feel free to substitute low-sodium broths, no-salt-added beans, and reduced-sodium soy sauce. In fact, we could all make this a habit!

Breakfasts & Brunches

You've heard it before but we'll say it again: A good breakfast is the foundation of any healthy diet. And, because, nothing kickstarts your day like a serving of fill-you-up fiber, we've provided an assortment of high-fiber offerings. If mornings are hectic at your house, try our multigrain cereal—it takes just five minutes to prepare. Or bake our reduced-fat granola ahead of time and, come morning, layer it with berries and vanilla yogurt for a sweet and satsifying parfait. For more on the benefits of fiber, see "Fiber: The Fabulous Fat Fighter" (page 25).

If you want to take breakfast on the go, bake up a batch of our low-fat carrot muffins, apple-oat muffins, or banana bread. Grab a muffin or a slice and a piece of fruit and you have a healthy breakfast you can pack in your purse. We offer two equally tempting options for those of you who like preparing breakfast in a blender: One includes strawberries, mango or apricot nectar, and yogurt, the other gives bananas, peanut butter, and soy milk a whirl.

We also provide light and healthy options just right for leisurely mornings or weekend brunches, including an assortment of egg dishes. Eggs are a high-quality source of protein—especially the egg white. Thus, our omelet, frittata, and soufflé recipes are made with a combination of eggs and egg whites—and loaded with veggies—so you can eat them without guilt. And, because everyone needs a little sweetness in their life, we've shared healthier whole-grain takes on brunch favorites like French toast and pancakes.

Granola-Yogurt Parfaits (recipe page 27)

Mango-Strawberry Smoothie

A healthy and colorful morning lift off! Either way you make it—with mango or with apricot nectar—this is a wonderful combination. If you use frozen strawberries, skip the ice cubes.

TOTAL TIME: 5 minutes

MAKES: 2 ½ cups or 2 servings

1	cup fresh or frozen unsweetened strawberries
1	cup mango or apricot nectar, chilled
½	cup plain or vanilla yogurt
4	ice cubes

In blender, combine strawberries, mango nectar, yogurt, and ice and blend until mixture is smooth and frothy. Pour into 2 tall glasses. Serve with straws, if you like.

EACH SERVING: About 125 calories (7 percent calories from fat), 4g protein, 27g carbohydrate, 1g total fat (0g saturated), 0g fiber, 3mg cholesterol, 44mg sodium ❤️ ♥

EAT YOUR STRAWBERRIES

These days, strawberries are easy to find all year long, but they are at their sweet, juicy peak in spring. Delicious and nutritious, twelve medium berries weigh in at 45 calories, 3 grams fiber, and about 135 percent of the daily recommended requirement for vitamin C.

Banana-Peanut Butter Smoothie

For a thicker, colder smoothie, cut peeled banana into chunks and freeze up to one week in a self-sealing plastic bag.

TOTAL TIME: 5 minutes

MAKES: 1 ½ cups or 1 serving

1	small ripe banana, cut in half
½	cup soy milk
1	teaspoon creamy natural peanut butter
3	ice cubes

In blender, combine banana, soy milk, peanut butter, and ice cubes; blend until mixture is smooth and frothy.

EACH SERVING: About 165 calories (22 percent calories from fat), 6g protein, 28g carbohydrate, 4g total fat (2g saturated), 2g fiber, 5mg cholesterol, 85mg sodium

Five-Minute Multigrain Cereal

Get a great-grains start to your day with a hot and tasty serving of three kinds of grains in five minutes. For photo, see page 11.

TOTAL TIME: 5 minutes

MAKES: 1 serving

2   tablespoons quick-cooking barley
2   tablespoons bulgur
2   tablespoons old-fashioned oats, uncooked
2/3 cup water
2   tablespoons raisins
pinch ground cinnamon
1   tablespoon chopped walnuts or pecans
low-fat milk or soy milk (optional)

In microwave-safe 1-quart bowl, combine barley, bulgur, oats, and water. Microwave on High 2 minutes. Stir in raisins and cinnamon; microwave 3 minutes longer. Stir, then top with walnuts and, if you like, milk.

EACH SERVING: About 265 calories (20 percent calories from fat), 8g protein, 50g carbohydrate, 6g total fat (1g saturated), 7g fiber, 0mg cholesterol, 5mg sodium

FIBER: THE FABULOUS FAT FIGHTER

Switching to a high-fiber diet can be like taking a magic weight-loss pill. But how exactly does fiber work?

+ **IT'S FILLING.** It swells a little in the stomach, quelling hunger. So, a 100-calorie portion of Kellogg's All Bran (18 grams fiber) will make you feel a lot fuller than a 100-calorie portion of Kellogg's Corn Flakes (1 gram fiber).

+ **IT LOWERS BLOOD SUGAR.** Many high-fiber foods (think oatmeal) help moderate your blood sugar level and keep your insulin level normal. Lower insulin has been linked to lower body fat and a lower risk of diabetes.

+ **IT FLUSHES OUT FAT.** Some types of fiber, particularly those in fruits and vegetables, can sweep out fat before the body absorbs it.

+ **IT'S LOW CAL.** Pure fiber itself has virtually no calories. Your body can't break it down, so it runs right through your digestive system, providing only bulk. That's why high-fiber foods are usually lower in calories than low-fiber foods. For example, a cup of apple juice has no fiber and 117 calories; a cup of sliced, unpeeled apple has 34 grams fiber and 74 calories.

GOOD SOURCES OF FIBER: Fruits, vegetables, legumes, brans, breads, cereals, pasta, and starchy foods made with whole grains. (See "How Do You Know It's Whole Grain?," page 13, and "Get Your Grains" boxes throughout the book.)

Apple-Fig Compote

Try this breakfast compote warm or chilled, spooned over a bowl of oatmeal or topped with plain yogurt. It's nice as a dessert sauce, too: Try it on sorbet.

ACTIVE TIME: 15 minutes
TOTAL TIME: 35 minutes

MAKES: 6 cups or 12 servings

1   lemon
2   pounds (4 to 6 medium) Rome Beauty or Jonagold apples, peeled, cored, and cut into 8 wedges
1½ cups apple cider
1   package (8 ounces) dried Calimyrna figs, each cut into quarters
½   cup dried tart cherries
⅓   cup sugar
1   stick cinnamon

1. From lemon, remove peel with vegetable peeler in 1-inch-wide strips, then squeeze 2 tablespoons juice.

2. In 4-quart saucepan, combine lemon peel and juice, apples, cider, figs, cherries, sugar, and cinnamon; cover and heat to boiling over high heat. Reduce heat to medium-low; simmer, covered, 20 minutes or until apples are tender, stirring occasionally.

3. Pour fruit mixture into bowl; serve warm or cover and refrigerate to serve within 4 days.

EACH ½-CUP SERVING: About 65 calories (0 percent calories from fat), 0g protein, 17g carbohydrate, 0g total fat, 2g fiber, 0mg cholesterol, 0mg sodium
♥ 🍱

Lower-Fat Granola

We baked oats, almonds, quinoa, wheat germ, and sesame seeds with apple juice instead of oil.

ACTIVE TIME: 10 minutes
TOTAL TIME: 45 minutes
MAKES: 6 cups or 12 servings

4	cups old-fashioned oats, uncooked
½	cup honey
½	cup apple juice
1½	teaspoons vanilla extract
¾	teaspoon ground cinnamon
½	cup natural almonds
½	cup quinoa, thoroughly rinsed
¼	cup toasted wheat germ
2	tablespoons sesame seeds
½	cup dried apricots, cut into ¼-inch dice
½	cup dark seedless raisins

1. Preheat oven to 350°F. Place oats in two 15½″ by 10½″ jelly-roll pans. Bake until lightly toasted, about 15 minutes, stirring twice.

2. In large bowl, with wire whisk, mix honey, apple juice, vanilla, and cinnamon until blended. Add toasted oats, almonds, quinoa, wheat germ, and sesame seeds; stir well to coat.

3. Spread oat mixture evenly in same jelly-roll pans; bake until golden brown, 20 to 25 minutes, stirring frequently. Cool in pans on wire rack.

4. When cool, transfer granola to large bowl; stir in apricots and raisins. Store at room temperature in air-tight container up to 1 month.

EACH ½-CUP SERVING: About 350 calories (21 percent calories from fat), 12g protein, 64g carbohydrate, 8g total fat (2g saturated), 8g fiber, 0mg cholesterol, 10mg sodium

Granola-Yogurt Parfait

A healthy breakfast doesn't get any easier than this. For photo, see page 22.

TOTAL TIME: 5 minutes
MAKES: 1 serving

½	cup fresh or frozen (partially thawed) raspberries or other favorite berry
¾	cup vanilla low-fat yogurt
2	tablespoons Lower-Fat Granola (left)

Into parfait glass or wineglass, spoon some of the raspberries, vanilla yogurt, and granola. Repeat layering until all ingredients are used.

EACH SERVING: About 255 calories (11 percent calories from fat), 10g protein, 47g carbohydrate, 3g total fat (2g saturated), 5g fiber, 12mg cholesterol, 160mg sodium

EAT YOUR YOGURT

Need to fit more calcium and protein into your diet? This creamy, tangy snack is the way to go. Any low-fat or nonfat all-natural brand has health benefits (it contains bacteria that aids in digestion, for starters), but we really love Greek-style yogurt. This special, strained yogurt has a dense texture and rich flavor—even the nonfat versions. Perk up plain yogurt with add-ins like fresh fruit, honey, reduced-fat granola, and nuts. Or, swap mayo or sour cream for yogurt to create low-fat dips and dressings. Greek yogurt is so creamy, it can even be used in some sauces to replace butter or cream.

Garden Vegetable Omelet

This is a mostly egg-white omelet with two whole eggs (and even a little feta) added for richness. Fill 'er up with red potatoes, onion, pepper, zucchini and fresh basil, and you have a healthy and flavorful start to your day.

ACTIVE TIME: 30 minutes
TOTAL TIME: 45 minutes

MAKES: 4 servings

8	ounces red potatoes, cut into ½-inch pieces
1	onion, finely chopped
1	red pepper, cut into ½-inch pieces
1	green pepper, cut into ½-inch pieces
1	small zucchini (8 ounces), cut into ½-inch pieces
¾	teaspoon salt
¼	teaspoon coarsely ground black pepper
¼	cup water
4	tablespoons chopped fresh basil leaves
6	large egg whites
2	large eggs
½	cup crumbled feta cheese (2 ounces)

1. In small saucepan, heat potatoes and enough *water* to cover to boiling over high heat. Reduce heat to low; cover and simmer until tender, about 10 minutes. Drain.

2. Spray 12-inch nonstick skillet with cooking spray. Add onion and cook over medium heat until golden, about 5 minutes. Add red and green peppers, zucchini, salt, and black pepper and cook, stirring frequently, until vegetables are tender-crisp. Stir in water and heat to boiling. Reduce to low; cover and simmer until vegetables are tender, 10 minutes. Remove skillet from heat; stir in potatoes and 1 tablespoon basil.

3. Preheat oven to 375°F. In medium bowl, with wire whisk or fork, mix egg whites, eggs, ¼ cup feta, and remaining 3 tablespoons basil.

4. Spray oven-safe 10-inch skillet with non-stick cooking spray. Pour egg mixture into pan and cook over medium-high heat until egg mixture begins to set, 1 to 2 minutes. Remove skillet from heat. With slotted spoon, spread vegetable mixture over egg mixture in skillet; sprinkle with remaining ¼ cup feta. Bake until omelet sets, 10 minutes. If you like, broil 1 to 2 minutes to brown top of omelet.

EACH SERVING: About 185 calories (29 percent calories from fat), 13g protein, 20g carbohydrate, 6g total fat (3g saturated), 3g fiber, 119mg cholesterol, 860mg sodium

Breakfast Tortilla Stack

Looking for a breakfast that will keep you full all morning long? Top a whole-wheat tortilla with fluffy eggs, fat-free refried beans, and salsa.

ACTIVE TIME: 25 minutes
TOTAL TIME: 30 minutes
MAKES: 4 main-dish servings

¼	cup chopped red onion
2	ripe medium tomatoes, chopped
¼	cup loosely packed fresh cilantro leaves, chopped
4	large eggs
4	large egg whites
⅛	teaspoon salt
⅛	teaspoon ground black pepper
1	cup fat-free refried beans
¼	teaspoon chipotle chile powder
4	(7-inch) whole-wheat tortillas

1. Prepare salsa: In cup of *ice water*, soak onion 10 minutes; drain well. In small bowl, combine onion, tomatoes, and cilantro; set aside.

2. In medium bowl, with wire whisk or fork, beat whole eggs, egg whites, salt, and pepper until blended.

3. Spray 10-inch nonstick skillet with cooking spray; heat on medium 1 minute. Pour egg mixture into skillet; cook, stirring occasionally, about 5 minutes or until egg mixture is set but still moist.

4. Meanwhile, in microwave-safe small bowl, mix beans and chile powder. Cover with vented plastic wrap; heat in microwave on High 1 minute or until hot.

5. Place stack of tortillas between damp paper towels on microwave-safe plate; heat in microwave on High 10 to 15 seconds to warm. To serve, layer each tortilla with eggs, beans, and salsa.

EACH SERVING: About 200 calories (18 percent calories from fat), 13g protein, 29g carbohydrate, 4g total fat (1g saturated), 13g fiber, 160mg cholesterol, 635mg sodium

South-of-the-Border Vegetable Hash

To create a skinnier hash with a new flavor twist, we replaced the meat with kidney beans and added fresh lime and cilantro.

ACTIVE TIME: 20 minutes
TOTAL TIME: 50 minutes

MAKES: 4 main-dish servings

- 3 large Yukon Gold potatoes (1½ pounds), cut into ¾-inch chunks
- 1 tablespoon plus 1 teaspoon olive oil
- 1 large onion (12 ounces), cut into ¼-inch dice
- 1 red pepper, cut into ¼-inch-wide strips
- 3 garlic cloves, crushed with garlic press
- 2 teaspoons ground cumin
- ¾ teaspoon salt
- 1 can (15 to 19 ounces) red kidney or black beans, rinsed and drained
- 2 tablespoons chopped fresh cilantro
- plain yogurt, lime wedges, salsa, and warmed corn tortillas (optional)

1. In 3-quart saucepan, place potato chunks and enough *water* to cover; heat to boiling over high heat. Reduce heat to low; cover and simmer until potatoes are almost tender, about 5 minutes; drain well.

2. Meanwhile, in nonstick 12-inch skillet, heat oil over medium heat until hot. Add onion, red pepper, garlic, cumin, and salt, and cook 10 minutes, stirring occasionally. Add drained potatoes and cook, turning occasionally, until vegetables are lightly browned, about 5 minutes longer. Stir in beans and cook until heated through, 2 minutes longer. Sprinkle with cilantro.

3. Serve vegetable hash with yogurt, lime wedges, salsa, and tortillas, if you like.

EACH SERVING: About 340 calories (14 percent calories from fat), 12g protein, 63g carbohydrate, 6g total fat (1g saturated), 15g fiber, 0mg cholesterol, 618mg sodium

California Frittata

Mexican-style salsa, a medley of vegetables, including crisp jicama, and tortillas contribute California flavor to this substantial frittata. An egg substitute may be used instead of eggs, if you prefer.

ACTIVE TIME: 30 minutes
TOTAL TIME: 1 hour 5 minutes

MAKES: 4 main-dish servings

2 to 3 small potatoes (6½ ounces)

1 tablespoon olive oil

1½ cups thinly sliced onions

1 zucchini (6 ounces), thinly sliced

1 cup thinly sliced cremini mushrooms

2 plum tomatoes (6½ ounces), cored, halved, and thinly sliced

½ teaspoon kosher salt (optional)

½ teaspoon freshly ground black pepper

1 cup shredded spinach or Swiss chard

1 tablespoon slivered fresh basil leaves (optional)

2 large eggs

3 large egg whites

½ jicama (8 ounces), peeled and cut into 2" by ¼" matchstick strips

2 teaspoons lemon juice

2 tablespoons chopped fresh flat-leaf parsley

¾ cup bottled salsa

4 (6-inch) corn tortillas

1. Preheat oven to 350°F. In saucepan, heat potatoes and enough *water* to cover to a boil over high heat. Reduce heat to low; cover and simmer until fork-tender, 15 to 20 minutes. Drain and cool. Cut into ¼-inch-thick slices.

2. In cast-iron or another heavy oven-safe skillet, heat oil over medium heat. Add onions and cook until softened, about 5 minutes. Add potatoes, zucchini, mushrooms, and tomatoes; cook, stirring gently, until zucchini begins to soften, 2 to 3 minutes. Add spinach and, if using, basil, and cook until spinach wilts, 1 to 2 minutes.

3. In medium bowl with wire whisk, mix eggs and egg whites. With spatula, stir vegetables while pouring eggs into skillet. Transfer skillet to oven and bake until eggs are set, 3 to 5 minutes.

4. While frittata bakes, sprinkle jicama sticks with lime juice; set aside.

5. When frittata is done, scatter parsley on top. Cut into 4 pieces and serve with salsa, tortillas, and jicama sticks.

EACH SERVING: About 265 calories (24 percent calories from fat), 11g protein, 38g carbohydrate, 7g total fat (1g saturated), 8g fiber, 106mg cholesterol, 140mg sodium ♥ ⊛

EAT YOUR TOMATOES

Tomatoes are an excellent source of vitamin C, which enhances the body's ability to absorb iron. They also contain lycopene and other substances associated with lowering the risk of certain cancers. If you're not a fan of fresh tomatoes, you may just not have met the right one: Sample some firm and flavorful heirloom tomatoes from your farmer's market. Come late summer, there's a tomato to suit every taste.

Huevos Rancheros

Fast and flavorful, these Mexican-inspired baked eggs are ideal for brunch. Baking rather than frying the tortilla cups keeps this dish low-fat.

ACTIVE TIME: 15 minutes
TOTAL TIME: 30 minutes

MAKES: 4 main-dish servings

4	(6-inch) corn tortillas

nonstick cooking spray

1	jar (16 ounces) mild low-sodium salsa (see Tip)
1	cup canned black beans, rinsed and drained
1	cup frozen corn kernels
3	green onions, sliced
1	teaspoon ground cumin
4	large eggs
½	cup loosely packed fresh cilantro leaves, thinly sliced
½	avocado, sliced into thin wedges
1	lime, sliced into wedges

1. Preheat oven to 350°F. In 15 ½″ by 10 ½″ jelly-roll pan, invert four 6-ounce custard cups. With kitchen shears, make four evenly spaced 1-inch cuts, from edge toward center, around each tortilla. Lightly spray both sides of tortillas with cooking spray and drape each over a custard cup. Bake tortilla cups 8 minutes or until golden and crisp. Set aside to cool.

2. Meanwhile, in nonstick 12-inch skillet, combine salsa, beans, corn, green onions, and cumin; heat to boiling over medium heat. Cover and cook 3 minutes to blend flavors. With large spoon, make four indentations for the eggs in salsa mixture, spacing them evenly around skillet. One at a time, break eggs into cup and gently pour into an indentation in salsa mixture. Cover and simmer 8 to 10 minutes or until eggs are set or cooked to desired doneness.

3. To serve, set each tortilla cup on a plate. Spoon an egg with some salsa mixture into each tortilla cup. Spoon any remaining salsa mixture around and on eggs in cups. Sprinkle with cilantro; serve with avocado and lime wedges.

EACH SERVING: About 290 calories (26 percent calories from fat), 12g protein, 40g carbohydrate, 10g total fat (2g saturated), 11g fiber, 213mg cholesterol, 630mg sodium 🟢 🟣

TIP: Check salsas for the lowest-sodium option available, such as Newman's Own, which contains less than half the sodium of many bottled salsas.

Spinach Soufflé

Even though this recipe requires about 40 minutes total, only 20 minutes is active prep. During the remaining time, while the soufflé bakes, you can relax!

ACTIVE TIME: 20 minutes
TOTAL TIME: 40 minutes

MAKES: 4 main-dish servings

3   tablespoons plain dried bread crumbs
nonstick cooking spray
1½ cups low-fat (1%) milk
⅓   cup cornstarch
2   large eggs, separated
1   package (10 ounces) frozen chopped spinach, thawed and squeezed dry
3   tablespoons grated Parmesan cheese
½   teaspoon salt
¼   teaspoon coarsely ground black pepper
½   teaspoon cream of tartar
4   large egg whites

1. Preheat oven to 425°F. Spray 10-inch quiche dish or shallow 2-quart casserole with cooking spray and sprinkle with bread crumbs to coat. Set aside.

2. In 2-quart saucepan, with wire whisk, beat milk with cornstarch until blended. Heat milk mixture over medium-high heat until mixture thickens and boils, stirring constantly. Boil 1 minute. Remove saucepan from heat.

3. In large bowl, with rubber spatula, mix egg yolks, spinach, Parmesan, salt, and pepper until blended; stir in warm milk mixture. Cool slightly (if spinach mixture is too warm, it will deflate beaten egg whites when folded in).

4. In another large bowl, with mixer at high speed, beat cream of tartar and egg whites until stiff peaks form. Gently fold egg-white mixture, one-third at a time, into spinach mixture.

5. Spoon soufflé mixture into quiche dish. Bake 20 minutes or until top is golden and puffed. Serve immediately.

EACH SERVING: About 195 calories (23 percent calories from fat), 15g protein, 23g carbohydrate, 5g total fat (2g saturated), 2g fiber, 114mg cholesterol, 590mg sodium

Whole-Grain Pancakes

Have a stack of pancakes without a side of guilt. These flapjacks contain healthy oats and whole-wheat flour. Plus they're topped with delicious fresh fruit.

ACTIVE TIME: 15 minutes
TOTAL TIME: 30 minutes

MAKES: 12 pancakes or 4 main-dish servings

2	ripe peaches, pitted and chopped
½	pint raspberries (1½ cups)
1	tablespoon sugar
½	cup all-purpose flour
½	cup whole-wheat flour
½	cup quick-cooking oats, uncooked
2	teaspoons baking powder
½	teaspoon salt
1¼	cups skim milk
1	large egg, lightly beaten
1	tablespoon vegetable oil

1. In medium bowl, combine peaches, raspberries, and sugar. Stir to coat; set aside.

2. Meanwhile, in large bowl, combine flours, oats, baking powder, and salt. Add milk, egg, and oil; stir just until flour mixture is moistened; batter will be lumpy.

3. Spray 12-inch nonstick skillet with cooking spray; heat on medium 1 minute. Pour batter by scant ¼ cups into skillet, making about 4 pancakes at a time. Cook until tops are bubbly, some bubbles burst, and edges look dry. With wide spatula, turn pancakes and cook until undersides are golden. Transfer pancakes to platter. Cover; keep warm.

4. Repeat with remaining batter, using more nonstick cooking spray if necessary.

5. To serve, top with fruit mixture.

EACH SERVING: About 275 calories (20 percent calories from fat), 10g protein, 46g carbohydrate, 6g total fat (1g saturated), 6g fiber, 55mg cholesterol, 545mg sodium ♥ ☺

Healthy Makeover French Toast

Our slimmed-down take on this Sunday-morning favorite is practically saintly. Subbing in low-fat milk and egg whites gives it half the fat and a third less cholesterol than traditional French toast. Plus, it's a cinch to whip up.

ACTIVE TIME: 15 minutes
TOTAL TIME: 25 minutes

MAKES: 4 main-dish servings

2	large egg whites
1	large egg
¾	cup low-fat (1%) milk
¼	teaspoon vanilla extract
⅛	teaspoon salt
2	teaspoons butter or margarine
8	slices firm whole-wheat bread

maple syrup and fresh blackberries, raspberries, and blueberries (optional)

1. Preheat oven to 200°F. In pie plate, with whisk, beat egg whites, egg, milk, vanilla, and salt until blended. In 12-inch nonstick skillet, melt 1 teaspoon butter over medium heat.

2. Dip bread slices, one at a time, in egg mixture, pressing bread lightly to coat both sides well. Place 3 or 4 slices in skillet, and cook 6 to 8 minutes or until lightly browned on both sides.

3. Transfer French toast to cookie sheet; keep warm in oven. Repeat with remaining butter, bread slices, and egg mixture. Serve French toast with maple syrup and berries, if you like.

EACH SERVING: About 300 calories (27 percent calories from fat), 12g protein, 46g carbohydrate, 9g total fat (2g saturated), 6g fiber, 56mg cholesterol, 755mg sodium

Spiced Apple Pancake

This simple pancake makes delightful brunch fare. For the puffiest pancake, use a cast-iron skillet. If you don't have one, choose a heavy 12-inch skillet with a bottom that is at least 10 inches in diameter and an oven-safe handle.

ACTIVE TIME: 5 minutes
TOTAL TIME: 35 minutes

MAKES: 8 main-dish servings

2   tablespoons butter or margarine
2   tablespoons water
½   cup plus 2 tablespoons sugar
1½ pounds Granny Smith apples
    (3 to 4 medium), peeled, cored,
    and cut into 8 wedges
3   large eggs
¾   cup milk
¾   cup all-purpose flour
1   teaspoon pumpkin pie spice or
    ½ teaspoon ground cinnamon
¼   teaspoon salt

1. Preheat oven to 450°F. In 12-inch cast-iron skillet, heat butter, water, and ½ cup sugar over medium-high heat to boiling. Add apple wedges; cook 12 to 15 minutes or until apples are golden and sugar mixture begins to caramelize, stirring occasionally.

2. Meanwhile, in blender or food processor with knife blade attached, place eggs and milk. Add flour, pumpkin pie spice, salt, and remaining 2 tablespoons sugar. Blend until batter is smooth.

3. When apple mixture in skillet is deep golden, pour batter over apples. Place skillet in oven; bake 15 to 17 minutes or until puffed and lightly browned. Serve immediately.

EACH SERVING: About 210 calories (26 percent calories from fat), 5g protein, 36g carbohydrate, 6g total fat (3g saturated), 2g fiber, 91mg cholesterol, 140mg sodium ♥

Low-Fat Banana Bread

We used egg whites and unsweetened applesauce to slim down everyone's favorite quick bread without sacrificing moisture. For a whole-grain variation, substitute ½ cup whole-wheat flour for the same amount of all-purpose flour.

ACTIVE TIME: 20 minutes
TOTAL TIME: 1 hour
MAKES: 1 loaf, 16 slices

1¾ cups all-purpose flour
½   cup sugar
1   teaspoon baking powder
½   teaspoon baking soda
½   teaspoon salt
1   cup mashed very ripe bananas (2 medium)
⅓   cup unsweetened applesauce
2   large egg whites
1   large egg
¼   cup pecans, chopped

1. Preheat oven to 350°F. Grease 9" by 5" metal loaf pan. In large bowl, combine flour, sugar, baking powder, baking soda, and salt. In medium bowl, with fork, mix bananas, applesauce, egg whites, and egg until well blended. Stir banana mixture into flour mixture just until flour mixture is moistened.

GO NUTS!

Dieters have long viewed nuts as the enemy. Sure, they're high in fat and calories—but eaten in moderation (2 tablespoons daily), nuts can do wonders. By adding a bit of fat to a fat-free meal like cereal and skim milk, nuts can slow down the emptying of your stomach, making you feel fuller longer. In addition, nuts may suppress the appetite longer than other fatty foods do. Buy nuts roasted and unsalted for big flavor without the sodium. Or spread a little peanut butter—or almond or cashew butter—on your morning toast.

2. Pour batter into prepared pan; sprinkle with chopped pecans. Bake until toothpick inserted in center comes out almost clean, 40 to 45 minutes. Cool in pan on wire rack 10 minutes; remove from pan and cool completely on wire rack.

EACH SERVING: About 120 calories (15 percent calories from fat), 3g protein, 23g carbohydrate, 2g total fat (0g saturated), 1g fiber, 13mg cholesterol, 155mg sodium ♥ ▦

Skinny Carrot Muffins

Moist muffins studded with raisins and carrots—perfect for breakfast on the go!

ACTIVE TIME: 15 minutes
TOTAL TIME: 45 minutes

MAKES: 12 muffins

2¼ cups all-purpose flour

½ cup granulated sugar

1 teaspoon ground cinnamon

1 teaspoon salt

1 teaspoon baking soda

½ teaspoon baking powder

¼ teaspoon ground ginger

3 carrots, peeled and finely shredded (1½ cups)

1 container (8 ounces) vanilla nonfat yogurt

½ cup egg substitute

½ cup unsweetened applesauce

½ cup dark seedless raisins

⅓ cup packed light brown sugar

1 teaspoon vanilla extract

1 teaspoon confectioners' sugar

1. Preheat oven to 350°F. Spray 12 standard muffin-pan cups with nonstick cooking spray. Place the prepared brioche pans in a 15 ½″ by 10 ½″ jelly-roll pan for easier handling.

2. In medium bowl, combine flour, granulated sugar, cinnamon, salt, baking soda, baking powder, and ginger. In large bowl, with wire whisk or fork, mix carrots, yogurt, egg substitute, applesauce, raisins, brown sugar, and vanilla until well blended. Stir flour mixture into carrot mixture just until flour is moistened.

3. Spoon batter into muffin cups. Bake until toothpick inserted in center of muffins comes out clean, about 30 minutes. Let muffins sit in pans on wire racks for 10 minutes; remove from pans and cool on wire racks. Sprinkle with confectioners' sugar while muffins are still warm.

EACH SERVING: About 190 calories (0 percent calories from fat), 5g protein, 43g carbohydrate, 1g total fat (0g saturated), 1g fiber, 1mg cholesterol, 337mg sodium

Apple-Oat Muffins

These muffins are wholesome and *delicious.*

ACTIVE TIME: 15 minutes
TOTAL TIME: 45 minutes
MAKES: 12 muffins

2   cups old-fashioned oats, uncooked
1¼   cups all-purpose flour
½   cup packed brown sugar
2   teaspoons baking powder
¾   teaspoon baking soda
¾   teaspoon salt
½   teaspoon ground cinnamon
1   cup buttermilk
2   tablespoon vegetable oil
1   large egg, lightly beaten
1   cup shredded Golden Delicious or
      Granny Smith apples (1 to 2 medium)
½   cup walnuts, chopped

1. Preheat oven to 400°F. Grease 12 standard muffin-pan cups. In large bowl, combine oats, flour, sugar, baking powder, baking soda, salt, and cinnamon.

2. In medium bowl, with fork, beat buttermilk, oil, and egg until well blended; stir in apples. Add apple mixture to flour mixture, and stir just until flour mixture is moistened; batter will be very thick and lumpy. Stir in chopped walnuts.

3. Spoon batter into prepared muffin-pan cups. Bake 23 to 25 minutes or until muffins begin to brown and toothpick inserted in center of muffin comes out clean. Immediately remove muffins from pan. Serve warm, or cool on wire rack to serve later.

EACH SERVING: About 210 calories (24 percent calories from fat), 5g protein, 33g carbohydrate, 7g total fat (1g saturated), 3g fiber, 18mg cholesterol, 320mg sodium

GET YOUR GRAINS: OATS

Oatmeal is touted as a healthy breakfast choice, and for good reason. Oats contain a type of fiber, beta-glucan, that studies have shown to be effective in reducing levels of "bad" (LDL) cholesterol. Their regular inclusion in a diet can help regulate blood sugar. Steel-cut oats are the whole-grain kernels cut into pieces. They are very chewy, but have a wonderfully sweet nutty flavor that's tasty as a breakfast cereal. Rolled oats are whole oats that have been toasted, hulled, steamed, and flattened with rollers; use them in granolas and baked goods.

2

Salad Makes the Meal

Salad, in its most familiar guise, is composed of cool, crisp greens tossed with a piquant dressing. But, as the recipes in this chapter demonstrate, a winning salad can be created from a seemingly endless array of ingredients: beans, grains, or a combination; rice noodles or pasta; fresh veggies, fruits, and herbs—all bolstered with chicken, meat, or seafood to create a salad that's a meal in a bowl.

Since high-fat dressings are often the downfall of otherwise healthy salads, we offer five recipes for skinny salad dressings that contain 15 calories or less and zero grams of fat per serving. Citrus juice and zest, ginger and fresh herbs keep the vinaigrettes flavorful, while a little reduced-fat buttermilk and low-fat mayo are responsible for the creamy dressings. Try them on our black bean and avocado chopped salad, or on mixed greens of your choosing.

Since salads and light and healthy eating go hand-in-hand, we offer an assortment of main dish salads perfect for lunch or a light dinner. Our Tex-Mex-style cobb salad and tuna salad with a trio of beans bring new life to garden-variety classics. Grilled shrimp and pineapple dress up a simple mix of basil and baby greens, while stir-fried Korean steak in lettuce cups delivers salad you can eat out of hand.

From warm wheat berry and farro to six-bean salad and tabbouleh, our grain and bean salads can be served as nourishing main dishes, too. Or prepare an assortment and create a colorful platter: Our barley, corn, and tomato salad pairs nicely with our spring-green snap pea and low-fat potato salads, as shown on page 63.

Curried Chicken Salad with Cantaloupe Slaw (recipe page 50)

Pasta Salad with Lemon and Peas

Small shell or bow-tie pasta is dressed in a light, lemony mayonnaise made even more flavorful with the addition of green onions and basil.

ACTIVE TIME: 15 minutes
TOTAL TIME: 20 minutes

MAKES: 16 side-dish servings

1   pound bow-tie or small shell pasta
1   package (10 ounces) frozen baby peas
2   lemons
2/3 cup low-fat (1%) milk
1/2 cup light mayonnaise
1/4 teaspoon coarsely ground black pepper
1   cup loosely packed fresh basil leaves, chopped
4   green onions, thinly sliced
1   teaspoon salt

1. In large saucepot, cook pasta as label directs, adding frozen peas during last 2 minutes of cooking time. Drain pasta and peas; rinse under cold running water and drain well.

2. Meanwhile, from lemons, grate 1 tablespoon peel and squeeze 3 tablespoons juice. In large bowl, with wire whisk, mix lemon peel and juice with milk, mayonnaise, pepper, basil, green onions, and salt until blended.

3. Add pasta and peas to mayonnaise dressing; toss to coat well. Cover and refrigerate up to 2 days if not serving right away.

EACH SERVING: About 160 calories (18 percent calories from fat), 4g protein, 28g carbohydrate, 3g total fat (0g saturated), 2g fiber, 3mg cholesterol, 210mg sodium 🟢 🟫

Rice Noodles with Many Herbs

Whip up this summery main (or side) dish with fast-cooking noodles, cucumber, carrots, herbs, and our delicious Asian dressing.

ACTIVE TIME: 20 minutes
TOTAL TIME: 30 minutes

MAKES: 5 main-dish or 10 side-dish servings

3   small carrots, peeled and cut into 2" by 1/4" matchstick strips (1 1/3 cups)
1/3 cup light seasoned rice vinegar
1   package (16 ounces) 1/2-inch-wide flat rice noodles
5   quarts water
1/3 English (seedless) cucumber, unpeeled and cut into 2" by 1/4" matchstick-thin strips
1   cup loosely packed fresh cilantro leaves
1/2 cup loosely packed fresh mint leaves
1/3 cup loosely packed small fresh basil leaves
1/3 cup snipped fresh chives
2   teaspoons Asian sesame oil

1. In small bowl, stir carrots with rice vinegar. Let stand while preparing noodles.

2. In 8-quart saucepot, heat water to boiling over high heat. Add noodles and cook 3 minutes or just until cooked through. Drain noodles; rinse under cold running water and drain again.

3. Transfer noodles to large shallow serving bowl. Add carrots with their liquid, cucumber, cilantro, mint, basil, chives, and sesame oil; toss to mix well.

EACH MAIN-DISH SERVING: About 370 calories (5 percent calories from fat), 2g protein, 87g carbohydrate, 2g total fat (0g saturated), 2g fiber, 0mg cholesterol, 248mg sodium 🟢 🖤

Skinny Salad Dressings

These flavor-packed drizzles are so good, you'll forget you're eating low fat.

Honey-Lime Vinaigrette

TOTAL TIME: 5 minutes

MAKES: ½ cup or 8 servings

⅓   cup fresh lime juice (from 2 to 3 limes)
4   teaspoons honey
1   tablespoon rice vinegar
⅛   teaspoon salt

In small bowl, with wire whisk, mix lime juice, honey, vinegar, and salt until blended. Cover and refrigerate up to 3 days.

EACH TABLESPOON: About 15 calories (0 percent calories from fat), 0g protein, 4g carbohydrate, 0g total fat, 0g fiber, 0mg cholesterol, 37mg sodium ♥ ♥

Tomato-Orange Vinaigrette

TOTAL TIME: 5 minutes

MAKES: ½ cup or 8 servings

½   cup tomato juice
1   tablespoon balsamic vinegar
¼   teaspoon grated orange peel
¼   teaspoon sugar
¼   teaspoon ground black pepper

In small bowl, with wire whisk, mix tomato juice, vinegar, orange peel, sugar, and pepper until blended. Cover and refrigerate up to 3 days.

EACH TABLESPOON: About 5 calories (0 percent calories from fat), 0g protein, 1g carbohydrate, 0g total fat, 0g fiber, 0mg cholesterol, 55mg sodium ♥ ♥

Orange-Ginger Dressing

TOTAL TIME: 5 minutes

MAKES: 1 cup or 16 servings

½   cup seasoned rice vinegar
½   cup orange juice
½   teaspoon grated, peeled fresh ginger
½   teaspoon soy sauce
⅛   teaspoon Asian sesame oil

In small bowl, with wire whisk, mix vinegar, orange juice, ginger, soy sauce, and sesame oil until blended. Cover and refrigerate up to 5 days.

EACH TABLESPOON: About 10 calories (0 percent calories from fat), 0g protein, 3g carbohydrate, 0g total fat, 0g fiber, 0mg cholesterol, 110mg sodium ♥ ♥

Buttermilk-Chive Dressing

TOTAL TIME: 5 minutes

MAKES: ¾ cup or 12 servings

½   cup reduced-fat buttermilk
2   tablespoons distilled white vinegar
2   tablespoons chopped fresh chives
1   tablespoon low-fat mayonnaise
¼   teaspoon salt
¼   teaspoon ground black pepper

In small bowl, with wire whisk, mix buttermilk, vinegar, chives, dressing, salt, and pepper until blended. Cover and refrigerate up to 3 days.

EACH TABLESPOON: About 6 calories (0 percent calories from fat), 0g protein, 1g carbohydrate, 0g total fat, 0g fiber, 0mg cholesterol, 65mg sodium ♥ ♥

Creamy Ranch Dressing

TOTAL TIME: 5 minutes

MAKES: 1 cup or 16 servings

¾ cup plain nonfat yogurt

¼ cup low-fat mayonnaise

1 green onion, minced

1 tablespoon cider vinegar

2 teaspoons Dijon mustard

¼ teaspoon dried thyme

¼ teaspoon coarsely ground black pepper

In small bowl, with wire whisk, mix yogurt, mayonnaise, green onion, vinegar, mustard, thyme, and pepper until blended. Cover and refrigerate up to 5 days.

EACH TABLESPOON: About 15 calories (0 percent calories from fat), 1g protein, 2g carbohydrate, 0g total fat, 0g fiber, 0mg cholesterol, 60mg sodium ● ♥

GIVE IT A LIFT WITH CITRUS

Grated peel or a splash of juice can perk up almost anything sweet or savory—without adding fat. Just a sprinkle or squeeze before serving can make the difference between a plain dish and a memorable one. Try these simple, flavor-boosting ideas.

GRATED PEEL

✦ Stir any citrus peel into rice pilaf to transform it from simple to sumptuous.

✦ Toss orange peel with lightly buttered carrots or roasted sweet potatoes.

✦ Sprinkle lime peel over coconut sorbet for a zesty fresh flavor.

JUICE

✦ Squirt some lemon, lime, or orange juice over steamed shellfish or grilled chicken just before eating.

✦ Add some lemon juice to bottled low-fat salad dressing to give it a sprightly homemade taste.

✦ Stir some lime juice into canned black bean or lentil soup to add zip before serving.

GRATED PEEL AND JUICE

✦ Stir grated lemon peel and juice into a tablespoon of low-fat mayonnaise for a tangy sandwich spread or dressing for steamed asparagus.

✦ Grate any citrus peel into a bowl with a tablespoon of butter or margarine, and add a squirt of juice plus a pinch of dried herb to make a citrus butter. Toss with cooked vegetables.

✦ Combine grated lime peel and juice with minced fresh ginger. Stir into a fruit salad (bananas, cantaloupe, and blueberries would be a nice match).

Peaches and Greens

Try this cool, refreshing alternative to a classic green salad.

ACTIVE TIME: 25 minutes

MAKES: 12 side-dish servings

1	large lime
2	tablespoons honey
1	tablespoon olive oil
1	tablespoon chopped fresh mint leaves
½	teaspoon Dijon mustard
¼	teaspoon salt
¼	teaspoon coarsely ground black pepper
2	bunches watercress (4 ounces each), tough stems discarded
2	pounds ripe peaches (6 medium), peeled and cut into wedges
1	large jicama (1¼ pounds), peeled and cut into 1½" by ¼" sticks

1. Prepare dressing: From lime, grate ¼ teaspoon peel and squeeze 2 tablespoons juice. In large bowl, with wire whisk, mix lime peel, lime juice, honey, oil, mint, mustard, salt, and pepper.

2. Just before serving, add watercress, peaches, and jicama to dressing in bowl; toss to coat.

EACH SERVING: About 55 calories (16 percent calories from fat), 1g protein, 11g carbohydrate, 1g total fat (0g saturated), 3g fiber, 0mg cholesterol, 55mg sodium ♥ ♥

TASTE THE RAINBOW

The vibrant colors of fruits and vegetables do more than add visual appeal to a drab dinner. Natural pigments in produce, called phytochemicals, keep your body healthy too. Scientists are still learning about the wide range of phytochemicals in nature, so don't expect to get these helpers from a pill. Instead, eat a colorful diet filled with reds, yellows, oranges, and greens. For instance, salad greens offer a wide variety of phytochemicals, so be sure to enjoy an assortment of types. Watercress or arugula add peppery notes to salad, mâche offers a delicious mild flavor and tender leaf, while a baby spinach tastes as great on a sandwich as it does in a bowl.

Black-Bean and Avocado Salad

A satisfying combination of summer veggies, romaine lettuce, and black beans tossed with a creamy buttermilk dressing. This salad would also be good with our Creamy Ranch Dressing or Honey-Lime Vinaigrette (pages 46–47).

TOTAL TIME: 20 minutes

MAKES: 4 main-dish servings

Buttermilk-Chive Dressing (page 46)

1   small head romaine lettuce (about 1 pound), cut into ¾-inch pieces (about 8 cups)

2   medium tomatoes, cut into ½-inch pieces

2   Kirby cucumbers (about 4 ounces each), unpeeled, each cut lengthwise into quarters, then crosswise into ¼-inch-thick pieces

1   ripe avocado, cut into ½-inch pieces

1   can (15 to 19 ounces) black beans, rinsed and drained

1. Prepare Buttermilk-Chive Dressing.

2. In large serving bowl, combine romaine, tomatoes, cucumbers, avocado, and beans. Add dressing and toss until evenly coated.

EACH SERVING: About 235 calories (23 percent calories from fat), 11g protein, 36g carbohydrate, 6g fat (1g saturated), 15g fiber, 0mg cholesterol, 521mg sodium ☑ ⊕

Tex-Mex Turkey Cobb Salad

Warm Southwestern accents give this classic a new attitude.

TOTAL TIME: 30 minutes

MAKES: 4 main-dish servings

¼   cup fresh lime juice

2   tablespoons chopped fresh cilantro leaves

4   teaspoons olive oil

1   teaspoon sugar

¼   teaspoon ground cumin

¼   teaspoon salt

¼   teaspoon coarsely ground black pepper

1   medium head romaine lettuce (1¼ pounds), trimmed and leaves cut into ½-inch-wide strips

1   pint cherry tomatoes, each cut into quarters

12 ounces cooked skinless roast turkey meat, cut into ½-inch pieces (2 cups)

1   can (15 to 19 ounces) pinto beans, rinsed and drained

2   small cucumbers (6 ounces each), peeled, seeded, and sliced ½ inch thick

1. Prepare dressing: In small bowl, with wire whisk, combine lime juice, cilantro, oil, sugar, cumin, salt, and pepper.

2. Place lettuce in large serving bowl. Arrange tomatoes, turkey, beans, and cucumbers in rows over lettuce and present the salad. Just before serving, toss salad with dressing.

EACH SERVING: About 310 calories (20 percent calories from fat), 39g protein, 32g carbohydrate, 7g total fat (1g saturated), 13g fiber, 71mg cholesterol, 505mg sodium ☑ ⊕

Curried Chicken Salad with Cantaloupe Slaw

Here, curry, crystallized ginger, and crushed red pepper bring out the full sweet flavor of fresh fruit. For photo, see page 42.

ACTIVE TIME: 25 minutes
TOTAL TIME: 35 minutes plus marinating
MAKES: 4 main-dish servings

1 to 2 limes

1	container (6 ounces) plain low-fat yogurt
¾	teaspoon curry powder
¼	cup chopped crystallized ginger
1	teaspoon salt
¼	teaspoon crushed red pepper
4	medium skinless, boneless chicken breast halves (about 1¼ pounds)
½	small cantaloupe, rind removed, cut into julienne strips (2 cups)
1	large mango, peeled and cut into julienne strips (2 cups)
½	cup loosely packed fresh cilantro leaves, chopped
1	head Boston lettuce

lime wedges (optional)

1. Prepare outdoor grill for covered direct grilling over medium heat.

2. From limes, grate ½ teaspoon peel and squeeze 2 tablespoons juice. In large bowl, with wire whisk, combine 1 tablespoon lime juice and ¼ teaspoon lime peel with yogurt, curry powder, 2 tablespoons ginger, ¾ teaspoon salt, and ⅛ teaspoon crushed red pepper. Add chicken, turning to coat with marinade. Cover and let stand 15 minutes at room temperature or 30 minutes in refrigerator, turning occasionally.

3. Meanwhile, prepare slaw: In medium bowl, with rubber spatula, gently stir cantaloupe and mango with cilantro, remaining 2 tablespoons ginger, 1 tablespoon lime juice, ¼ teaspoon lime peel, ¼ teaspoon salt, and ⅛ teaspoon crushed red pepper; set aside. Makes about 4 cups.

4. Grease grill rack. Remove chicken from marinade; discard marinade. Place chicken on hot rack. Cover grill and cook chicken 10 to 12 minutes or until juices run clear when thickest part of breast is pierced with tip of knife, turning chicken over once. Transfer chicken to cutting board; cool slightly until easy to handle, then cut into long thin slices.

5. To serve, arrange lettuce leaves on four dinner plates; top with chicken and slaw. Serve with lime wedges, if you like.

EACH SERVING CHICKEN WITH LETTUCE: About 205 calories (18 percent calories from fat), 34g protein, 5g carbohydrate, 4g total fat (1g saturated), 1g fiber, 92mg cholesterol, 330mg sodium ♥

EACH ½ CUP SLAW: About 50 calories (0 percent calories from fat), 1g protein, 13g carbohydrate, 0g total fat, 1g fiber, 0mg cholesterol, 150mg sodium ♥

Grilled Chicken Taco Salad

A great way to prepare this Mexican favorite during the summer. Spicy chicken breasts are first grilled and then served over black-bean salsa, shredded lettuce, and crisp corn tortillas.

ACTIVE TIME: 25 minutes
TOTAL TIME: 35 minutes

MAKES: 4 main-dish servings

1	can (15 to 19 ounces) low-sodium black beans, rinsed and drained
¾	cup medium-hot salsa
1	tablespoon fresh lime juice
1	cup loosely packed fresh cilantro leaves, chopped
2	tablespoons chili powder
1	teaspoon ground cumin
1	teaspoon ground coriander
1	teaspoon brown sugar
½	teaspoon salt
¼	teaspoon cayenne (ground red) pepper
1	tablespoon olive oil
1	pound skinless, boneless chicken breast halves
4	corn tortillas
4	cups thinly sliced lettuce

lime wedges, avocado slices, and reduced-fat sour cream (optional)

1. Prepare outdoor grill for direct grilling over medium-high heat.

2. In medium bowl, mix beans, salsa, lime juice, and half of cilantro; set aside.

3. In cup, stir chili powder, cumin, coriander, brown sugar, salt, cayenne, and oil until evenly mixed (mixture will be dry).

4. If necessary, place chickn breast halves between two sheets of plastic wrap and pound to uniform ¼-inch thickness. With hands, rub chicken with chili-powder mixture.

5. Place chicken on hot grill over medium-high heat and grill until juices run clear when thickest part of breast is pierced with tip of knife, 8 to 10 minutes, turning over once. Place tortillas on grill with chicken and cook until lightly browned, 3 to 5 minutes, turning over once.

6. Transfer chicken to cutting board. Place tortillas on four dinner plates. Cut chicken into long thin strips. Top tortillas with lettuce, bean mixture, and chicken. Sprinkle with remaining cilantro. If you like, serve with lime wedges, avocado slices, and sour cream.

EACH SERVING: About 375 calories (19 percent calories from fat), 34g protein, 41g carbohydrate, 8g total fat (1g saturated), 11g fiber, 63mg cholesterol, 648mg sodium ☻

Asian Chicken Salad

This fast, easy chicken salad recipe is full of Asian-inspired flavors.

ACTIVE TIME: 20 minutes
TOTAL TIME: 30 minutes

MAKES: 6 main-dish servings

3	limes
4	medium boneless, skinless chicken breast halves (1½ pounds)
1	bag (16 ounces) frozen shelled edamame
⅓	cup reduced-sodium soy sauce
¼	cup loosely packed fresh cilantro leaves, chopped
1	tablespoon peeled fresh ginger, grated
2	teaspoons Asian sesame oil
1	pound napa (Chinese) cabbage (½ small head), sliced
1	bunch or 1 bag (6 ounces) radishes, trimmed and thinly sliced

1. Cut 2 limes into thin slices. From remaining lime, squeeze 2 tablespoons juice; set aside.

2. In covered 12-inch skillet, heat half of lime slices and *1 inch water* to boiling on high. Add chicken; cover, reduce heat to medium-low and cook 13 to 14 minutes or until chicken loses its pink color throughout. With slotted spoon or tongs, remove chicken from skillet and place in large bowl of *ice water;* chill 5 minutes. Drain chicken well; with hands, shred chicken into bite-size pieces.

3. Meanwhile, cook edamame as label directs; drain. Rinse with cold running water to stop cooking and drain again. In large bowl, whisk soy sauce, cilantro, ginger, sesame oil, and reserved lime juice. Add cabbage, edamame, radishes, and shredded chicken to bowl; toss to combine.

4. To serve, transfer to deep bowls and garnish with remaining lime slices.

EACH SERVING: About 285 calories (25 percent calories from fat), 39g protein, 14g carbohydrate, 8g total fat (1g saturated), 6g fiber, 66mg cholesterol, 560mg sodium ☯ ✿

Korean Steak in Lettuce Cups

Sliced round steak and shredded carrots are braised in a rich soy-ginger sauce and served in delicate Boston-lettuce leaves.

ACTIVE TIME: 15 minutes
TOTAL TIME: 20 minutes plus marinating
MAKES: 4 main-dish servings

3   tablespoons soy sauce
1   tablespoon sugar
2   teaspoons Asian sesame oil
1   teaspoon minced, peeled fresh ginger
¼   teaspoon cayenne (ground red) pepper
1   garlic clove, crushed with garlic press
1   beef top round steak (about 1 pound), trimmed, cut into ½-inch cubes
4   celery stalks with leaves, thinly sliced
½   (10-ounce) package shredded carrots (1¾ cups)
3   green onions, thinly sliced
1   tablespoon sesame seeds, toasted (see Tip)
1   head Boston lettuce, separated into leaves
green-onion tops for garnish

1. In medium bowl, stir soy sauce, sugar, oil, ginger, cayenne, and garlic until blended. Add beef, turning to coat with soy-sauce mixture, and marinate 15 minutes at room temperature, stirring occasionally.

2. In 12-inch skillet, heat celery, carrots, and *½ cup water* to boiling over medium-high heat. Cook 2 to 3 minutes or until vegetables are tender-crisp, stirring occasionally. Add beef with its marinade and cook 2 minutes or until meat just loses its pink color throughout, stirring quickly and constantly. Stir in green onions and sesame seeds; cook 1 minute, stirring.

3. To serve, let each person place some beef mixture on a lettuce leaf. Garnish with green-onion tops. If you like, fold sides of lettuce leaf over filling to make a package to eat out of hand.

EACH SERVING: About 300 calories (30 percent calories from fat), 28g protein, 12g carbohydrate, 10g total fat (3 g saturated), 3g fiber, 53mg cholesterol, 855mg sodium

TIP: *Toasting brings out the nutty flavor of sesame seeds. To toast, heat seeds in a small, dry skillet over medium heat, stirring constantly, until fragrant and a shade darker, 3 to 5 minutes.*

Shrimp and Pineapple Salad with Basil

No grill basket? Thread shrimp onto skewers instead. If you use wooden skewers, presoak them in hot water for at least 30 minutes to prevent them from burning.

ACTIVE TIME: 10 minutes
TOTAL TIME: 25 minutes

MAKES: 6 main-dish servings

3 to 4 limes
3   tablespoons olive oil
1½   cups loosely packed fresh basil leaves
½   teaspoon salt
¼   teaspoon coarsely ground pepper
1½   pounds large shrimp, shelled and deveined
1   pineapple (3 pounds)
12   corn tortillas
olive oil cooking spray
1   bag (5 to 6 ounces) baby greens
2   medium heads Belgian endive, sliced

1. Prepare outdoor grill for direct grilling over medium heat.

2. Prepare dressing: From limes, grate ½ teaspoon peel and squeeze ¼ cup juice. In blender, place lime peel and juice, oil, ½ cup basil leaves, salt, and pepper. Blend until pureed.

3. Spoon 2 tablespoons dressing from blender into medium bowl. Add shrimp to bowl and toss to coat with dressing.

4. Cut off crown and stem ends from pineapple. Stand pineapple upright and slice off rind and eyes. Cut pineapple lengthwise into 8 wedges, then cut off core from each wedge.

5. Place pineapple wedges on hot grill rack over medium heat and cook until lightly charred and tender, about 10 minutes, turning over once. Place shrimp in grill basket on same grill rack with pineapple wedges and cook until opaque throughout, 5 to 8 minutes, turning over once. Transfer shrimp to large bowl. Transfer pineapple to cutting board and cut into ½-inch chunks.

6. Lightly spray both sides of tortillas with cooking spray and place on hot grill rack. Cook until toasted, 4 to 5 minutes, turning over once.

7. To bowl with shrimp, add greens, endive, pineapple, and remaining 1 cup basil and dressing; toss to coat. Place 2 tortillas on each of six plates; top with salad.

EACH SERVING: About 350 calories (28 calories from fat), 23g protein, 43g carbohydrate, 11g total fat (2g saturated), 6g fiber, 140mg cholesterol, 420mg sodium ♥ ♥ ❀

Warm Eggplant and Wheat-Berry Salad

This salad serves up a rainbow of goodness—vitamins A, C, B$_6$, and K (to name just a few), as well as iron, protein, and antioxidants galore.

ACTIVE TIME: 35 minutes
TOTAL TIME: 2 hours and 40 minutes plus soaking
MAKES: 4 main-dish servings

1	cup wheat berries (whole-wheat kernels)
6 ¾	cups water
1	can (14 ½ ounces) low-sodium vegetable broth or 1 ¾ cups homemade (page 92)
2	tablespoons olive oil
1	teaspoon salt
1	teaspoon dried thyme
½	teaspoon coarsely ground black pepper
1	medium yellow pepper, cut into ¼-inch-wide strips
1	small zucchini (about 8 ounces), halved lengthwise and cut into ¾-inch chunks
1	package (8 ounces) mushrooms, each cut in half
1	small eggplant (about 12 ounces), cut lengthwise into quarters and sliced into ¾-inch chunks
1	cup frozen peas, thawed
1	small ripe tomato, cut into ½-inch chunks

1. In large bowl, soak wheat berries overnight in 5 cups water.

2. Drain wheat berries. In 2-quart saucepan over high heat, heat wheat berries, broth, and remaining 1 ¾ cups water to boiling over high heat. Reduce heat to low; cover and simmer until wheat berries are tender, about 2 ½ hours.

3. After wheat berries have cooked 1 ½ hours, preheat broiler as manufacturer directs.

4. Coat rack in broiling pan with nonstick cooking spray. In medium bowl, mix 1 tablespoon oil, ½ teaspoon salt, ½ teaspoon thyme, and ¼ teaspoon black pepper; add yellow pepper, zucchini, and mushrooms, tossing to coat. Arrange vegetables on rack in broiling pan. Place pan under broiler 5 to 7 inches from source of heat; broil vegetables until tender and browned, 10 to 15 minutes, stirring them occasionally and removing them to large bowl as they are done. Keep vegetables warm.

5. In same medium bowl, mix remaining 1 tablespoon oil, ½ teaspoon salt, ½ teaspoon thyme, and ¼ teaspoon pepper; add eggplant, tossing to coat. Arrange eggplant on rack in broiling pan; broil until tender and browned, 10 to 15 minutes, stirring occasionally. Remove to bowl with other vegetables.

6. About 5 minutes before end of wheat berry cooking time, add thawed peas to heat through. Drain any liquid from wheat-berry mixture. Add wheat berries and tomato chunks to bowl with vegetables; toss to mix well. Serve warm.

EACH SERVING: About 315 calories (23 percent calories from fat), 13g protein, 50g carbohydrate, 8g total fat (1g saturated), 12g fiber, 0mg cholesterol, 650mg sodium 🌱

Warm Farro Salad with Roasted Vegetables

If you've never tried farro, this hearty main-dish salad is the perfect opportunity to enjoy its nutty goodness. Try it as a side dish alongside grilled fish or chicken, or serve on a bed of lettuce for a main dish.

ACTIVE TIME: 25 minutes
TOTAL TIME: 1 hour 5 minutes
MAKES: 6 side-dish servings

2	large carrots, peeled and cut into ½-inch dice
2	small fennel bulbs, trimmed and cut into 1-inch pieces
1	red onion, halved and sliced through root end
3	tablespoons olive oil
1	teaspoon salt
¼	teaspoon ground black pepper
1	bunch radishes, cut into ½-inch dice
1	tablespoon red wine vinegar
2½	cups water
1	cup farro
3	tablespoons fresh lemon juice
2	teaspoons freshly grated lemon peel
1	cup lightly packed fresh basil leaves, chopped

1. Preheat oven to 400°F.

2. In large bowl, combine carrots, fennel, red onion, 1 tablespoon oil, ½ teaspoon salt, and ⅛ teaspoon pepper; toss. Turn onto 15 ½″ by 10 ½″ jelly-roll pan and spread evenly. Roast 20 minutes, stirring once. Stir in radishes and roast until vegetables are tender, about 10 minutes. Stir in vinegar.

3. Meanwhile, in medium saucepan, bring water, farro, and ¼ teaspoon salt to boiling over high heat. Reduce heat to medium-low; cover and simmer until farro is tender and water is absorbed, 25 to 30 minutes.

4. In large bowl, whisk lemon juice, lemon peel, remaining 2 tablespoons oil, ¼ teaspoon salt, and ⅛ teaspoon pepper. Add farro, roasted vegetables, and basil; toss to combine. Serve warm.

EACH SERVING: About 215 calories (29 percent calories from fat), 6g protein, 34g carbohydrate, 7g total fat (1g saturated), 6g fiber, 0mg cholesterol, 472mg sodium ⊙

GET YOUR GRAINS: FARRO

This ancient grain is also known as emmer wheat. It contains starch that is similar to the starch found in short-grain rices; try substituting it for Arborio rice the next time you make risotto. A good source of fiber and protein, farro has a nutty wheat flavor and chewy texture.

Six-Bean Salad with Tomato Vinaigrette

This salad is a tasty powerhouse of protein, iron, bone-building vitamin K, and a host of heart-healthy antioxidants.

ACTIVE TIME: 20 minutes
TOTAL TIME: 45 minutes plus chilling
MAKES: 18 side-dish servings

1½   teaspoons salt
8   ounces green beans, trimmed and cut into 1-inch pieces
8   ounces wax beans, trimmed and cut into 1-inch pieces
1   can (15 to 19 ounces) garbanzo beans
1   can (15 to 19 ounces) black beans or black soybeans
1   can (15 to 19 ounces) red kidney beans
1½   cups (half of 16-ounce bag) frozen shelled edamame, thawed
1   small ripe tomato (4 ounces), coarsely chopped
1   small shallot, coarsely chopped
¼   cup olive oil
2   tablespoons red wine vinegar
1   tablespoon Dijon mustard
¼   teaspoon ground black pepper

1. In 12-inch skillet, heat *1 inch water* with 1 teaspoon salt to boiling over high heat. Add green and wax beans; return water to a boil. Reduce heat to low; simmer until beans are tender-crisp, 6 to 8 minutes. Drain beans. Rinse with cold running water to stop cooking; drain again. Transfer beans to large serving bowl.

2. While green and wax beans are cooking, rinse and drain garbanzo, black, and kidney beans. Add canned beans and edamame to bowl with green and wax beans.

3. In blender, combine tomato, shallot, oil, vinegar, mustard, remaining ½ teaspoon salt, and pepper. Blend until smooth.

4. Add vinaigrette to beans in bowl. Toss until beans are evenly coated. Cover and refrigerate at least 1 hour to blend flavors or up to 8 hours.

EACH SERVING: About 130 calories (27 percent calories from fat), 7g protein, 18g carbohydrate, 4g total fat (0g saturated), 7g fiber, 0mg cholesterol, 360mg sodium ♥ ⊗ ▭

Shredded Beets with Celery and Dates

This simple salad features raw grated beets, which lends it high crunch appeal and showcases the rich garnet color of beets. For photo, see page 21.

TOTAL TIME: 10 minutes

MAKES: 4 cups or 8 side-dish servings

1	pound beets, peeled
3	stalks celery, thinly sliced
½	cup pitted dried dates, chopped
3	tablespoons fresh lemon juice
¼	teaspoon salt
¼	teaspoon coarsely ground black pepper

1. Cut beets into quarters. In food processor with shredding blade attached, shred beets; transfer to large bowl.

2. Stir in celery, dates, lemon juice, salt, and pepper. If not serving right away, cover and refrigerate up to 4 hours.

EACH SERVING: About 50 calories (0 percent calories from fat), 1g protein, 13g carbohydrate, 0g total fat, 2g fiber, 0mg cholesterol, 110mg sodium ♥ ♥ 📇

EAT YOUR BEETS

Just one cooked cup of this superveggie packs 34 percent of your daily need for folate (which can help lower levels of heart-threatening homocysteine), 15 percent of potassium (which reduces blood pressure levels), and 27 percent of manganese (which helps maintain your bones). To bring out beets' natural juices, peel and grate them. Then subdues the earthy flavor with lemon juice and sweet dates; see Shredded Beets with Celery and Dates, above. The celery slices add crunch. Or, for an easy side, try our Basil and Balsamic Beets, page 258. The fresh basil and vinegar bring out the veggie's sweetness.

Tomato and Mint Tabbouleh

Tabbouleh, the popular bulgur wheat and vegetable salad, is one of the best ways to enjoy tomatoes, cucumbers, and herbs.

TOTAL TIME: 20 minutes plus standing and chilling
MAKES: 12 side-dish servings

1½ cups boiling water
1½ cups bulgur
¼ cup fresh lemon juice
1 pound ripe tomatoes (3 medium), cut into ½-inch pieces
1 medium cucumber (8 ounces), peeled and cut into ½-inch pieces
3 green onions, chopped
¾ cup loosely packed fresh flat-leaf parsley leaves, chopped
½ cup loosely packed fresh mint leaves, chopped
1 tablespoon olive oil
¾ teaspoon salt
¼ teaspoon coarsely ground black pepper

1. In medium bowl, combine water, bulgur, and lemon juice, stirring to mix. Let stand until liquid has been absorbed, about 30 minutes.

2. To bulgur mixture, add tomatoes, cucumber, green onions, parsley, mint, oil, salt, and pepper, stirring to mix. Cover and refrigerate to blend flavors, at least 1 hour or up to 4 hours.

EACH SERVING: About 85 calories (21 percent calories from fat), 3g protein, 17g carbohydrate, 2g total fat (0g saturated), 4g fiber, 0mg cholesterol, 157mg sodium ♥ 🗑

Crunchy Carrot Coleslaw

A mix of shredded cabbage and carrots gives this slaw its crunch; cider vinegar and a little cayenne give it a bite.

TOTAL TIME: 10 minutes
MAKES: 10 cups or 8 side-dish servings

⅓ cup fresh orange juice
¼ cup cider vinegar
2 tablespoons sugar
2 tablespoons Dijon mustard
1 tablespoon vegetable oil
1 teaspoon salt
¼ teaspoon dried mint
⅛ teaspoon cayenne (ground red) pepper
1 bag (16 ounces) shredded cabbage (for coleslaw)
1 bag (10 ounces) shredded carrots

In large bowl, with wire whisk, mix orange juice, vinegar, sugar, mustard, oil, salt, mint, and cayenne until blended. Add cabbage and carrots; toss well. Serve slaw at room temperature, or cover and refrigerate until ready to serve.

EACH SERVING: About 65 calories (28 percent calories from fat), 1g protein, 12g carbohydrate, 2g total fat (0g saturated), 2g fiber, 0mg cholesterol, 385mg sodium ✓ 🗑

Barley, Corn, and Tomato Salad

Here the whole-grain goodness of pearl barley is combined with the fresh flavors of summer— corn cut from the cob, tomatoes off the vine, and the heady perfume of basil.

ACTIVE TIME: 15 minutes
TOTAL TIME: 40 minutes

MAKES: 12 side-dish servings

2½ cups water

1¼ cups pearl barley

5 medium ears corn, husks and silk removed

1 small bunch fresh basil

¼ cup rice vinegar

3 tablespoons olive oil

1 teaspoon salt

¼ teaspoon ground black pepper

2 large ripe tomatoes (about 8 ounces each), cut into ½-inch chunks

2 green onions

1. In 2-quart saucepan, heat water to boiling over high heat. Stir in barley; return to boiling. Reduce heat to low; cover and simmer until barley is tender, 30 to 35 minutes.

2. Meanwhile, place corn on plate in microwave. Cook on High 4 to 5 minutes, turning and rearranging corn halfway through cooking. Cool slightly until easy to handle. Chop enough basil leaves to equal ⅓ cup; reserve remaining basil for garnish.

3. With sharp knife, cut corn kernels from cobs. In large bowl, with fork, mix vinegar, oil, salt, and pepper; stir in corn, warm barley, tomatoes, green onions, and chopped basil until combined. If not serving right away, cover and refrigerate up to 4 hours. Garnish with basil leaves.

EACH SERVING: About 145 calories (25 percent calories from fat), 4g protein, 26g carbohydrate, 4g total fat (1g saturated), 5g fiber, 0mg cholesterol, 205mg sodium ♥ ⊛ ▭

GET YOUR GRAINS: BARLEY

Barley is one of the oldest grains in cultivation. In most grains, the fiber is concentrated in the bran, which is removed when the kernel is refined. But even when all of barley's tough bran is removed (as with pearl barley, the most refined type), at least half the original fiber remains. A half cup of cooked barley contains 3 grams of fiber, compared to white rice's one-third gram.

Snap Pea Salad

This yummy double-pea salad is easy to prepare and pretty to serve. Use any leftover fresh dill in your next mayonnaise-based salad.

ACTIVE TIME: 10 minutes
TOTAL TIME: 15 minutes
MAKES: 8 side-dish servings

1   pound sugar snap peas, strings removed
1   package (10 ounces) frozen peas
½   cup minced red onion
2   tablespoons white wine vinegar
2   tablespoons vegetable oil
2   tablespoons chopped fresh dill
1   tablespoon sugar
½   teaspoon salt
¼   teaspoon coarsely ground black pepper

1. In 5- to 6-quart saucepot, heat *2 inches water* to boiling over high heat. Add snap peas and frozen peas; cook 1 minute. Drain peas; rinse under cold running water to stop cooking. Drain again; pat dry between layers of paper towels.

2. In large bowl, stir onion, vinegar, oil, dill, sugar, salt, and pepper until mixed. Add peas; toss to coat. If not serving right away, cover and refrigerate up to 4 hours.

EACH SERVING: About 100 calories (27 percent calories from fat), 4g protein, 13g carbohydrate, 3g total fat (0g saturated), 4g fiber, 0mg cholesterol, 245mg sodium 🟢 ❤️ ▦

Zesty Potato Salad

Spicy mustard, onion, and cider vinegar lend this salad zip; light mayo keeps it skinny.

ACTIVE TIME: 15 minutes
TOTAL TIME: 30 minutes plus standing and chilling
MAKES: 6 cups or 10 side-dish servings

2   pounds red potatoes (about 8 medium), cut into 1-inch chunks
¼   cup minced onion
3   tablespoons cider vinegar
2   teaspoons spicy brown mustard
1   teaspoon salt
½   teaspoon ground black pepper
⅓   cup light mayonnaise
¼   cup low-fat (1%) milk
1   large stalk celery, finely chopped
½   cup loosely packed fresh parsley leaves, chopped

1. In 4-quart saucepan, place potatoes and enough *water* to cover by 1 inch; heat to boiling over high heat. Reduce heat and simmer 6 to 7 minutes or until potatoes are tender. Meanwhile, in large bowl, with whisk, mix onion, vinegar, mustard, salt, and pepper.

2. Drain potatoes well; add to dressing in bowl and gently stir with rubber spatula until evenly coated. Let stand 20 minutes to cool slightly.

3. In small bowl, whisk mayonnaise and milk. Add mayonnaise mixture, celery, and parsley to potato mixture; gently stir with rubber spatula until potatoes are well coated. If not serving right away, cover and refrigerate up to 1 day.

EACH SERVING: About 110 calories (23 percent calories from fat), 3g protein, 18g carbohydrate, 3g total fat (0g saturated), 1g fiber, 3mg cholesterol, 321mg sodium ❤️ ▦

Three-Bean Tuna Salad

This no-cook salad serves up heart-healthy omega-3 fats (the tuna) and nearly three-quarters of a day's worth of cholesterol-lowering fiber (the beans).

TOTAL TIME: 15 minutes

MAKES: 6 main-dish servings

1   lemon
2   tablespoons extra-virgin olive oil
3   stalks celery, thinly sliced
2   green onions, thinly sliced
¼   teaspoon salt
⅛   teaspoon coarsely ground black pepper
3   cans (15 to 19 ounces each) assorted low-sodium beans such as white kidney beans (cannellini), garbanzo beans, and pink beans, rinsed and drained
2   cans (6 ounces each) chunk light tuna in water, drained and coarsely flaked
6   large Boston lettuce leaves

1. From lemon, grate 1 teaspoon peel and squeeze 2 tablespoons juice.

2. In large bowl, mix lemon peel and juice, oil, celery, green onions, salt, and pepper. Stir in beans until coated, then gently stir in tuna.

3. Serve bean mixture in lettuce cups.

EACH SERVING: About 335 calories (19 percent calories from fat), 25g protein, 42g carbohydrate, 7g total fat (1g saturated), 11g fiber, 29mg cholesterol, 517mg sodium ✅ 🌱

Creamy Cucumber-Dill Salad

This creamy, cool, and crunchy salad is a summertime classic. Don't skip the salting step, or the cukes will be limp, not crisp.

TOTAL TIME: 35 minutes plus standing and chilling

MAKES: 5 cups or 10 side-dish servings

8	large (about 5 pounds) cucumbers
1	teaspoon salt
6	large radishes
1	container (8 ounces) plain low-fat yogurt
½	cup reduced-fat sour cream
½	cup loosely packed fresh dill, chopped
2	tablespoons fresh lime juice
¼	teaspoon ground black pepper
1	small garlic clove, crushed with garlic press

1. With vegetable peeler, remove several strips of peel from each cucumber. Cut each cucumber lengthwise in half; with teaspoon, scoop out seeds. With knife or in food processor fitted with slicing blade, thinly slice cucumber halves crosswise. In large bowl, toss cucumbers with salt; let stand 30 minutes.

2. Meanwhile, thinly slice radishes; transfer to serving bowl. Add yogurt, sour cream, dill, lime juice, pepper, and garlic. Stir until combined.

3. Transfer sliced cucumbers to a colander. Place colander in sink and, with hands, press cucumbers to remove as much liquid as possible. Pat cucumbers dry with paper towels.

4. Add cucumbers to bowl with yogurt mixture. Toss until evenly coated. Cover and refrigerate at least 1 hour or overnight to blend flavors.

EACH SERVING: About 60 calories (30 percent calories from fat), 3g protein, 9g carbohydrate, 2g total fat (1g saturated), 2g fiber, 6mg cholesterol, 180mg sodium ♥ 🍲

Nectarine and Berry Salad

Summer fruits need little adornment. Our Nectarine and Berry Salad gets a little boost from crystallized ginger and fresh lime juice.

TOTAL TIME: 15 minutes

MAKES: 8 side-dish servings

3	tablespoons fresh lime juice (from 2 limes)
2	tablespoons finely chopped crystallized ginger
1	tablespoon sugar
2	pounds nectarines (6 medium), pitted and chopped
2	half-pints blackberries

In large bowl, stir lime juice, ginger, and sugar until sugar dissolves. Add nectarines and berries, and toss until coated. If not serving immediately, spoon into storage container with tight-fitting lid and refrigerate for up to 4 hours.

EACH SERVING: About 85 calories (10 percent calories from fat), 1g protein, 21g carbohydrate, 1g total fat (0g saturated), 4g fiber, 0mg cholesterol, 0mg sodium ♥ ♥ ▤

Cantaloupe and Cucumber Salad

Juicy, ripe cantaloupes and crunchy English cucumbers are a tempting duo.

TOTAL TIME: 20 minutes

MAKES: 8 ½ cups or 10 side-dish servings

¼	cup fresh lime juice
¼	teaspoon salt
⅛	teaspoon freshly ground black pepper
1	large English (seedless) cucumber (1 pound), peeled in alternating strips and coarsely chopped
2	ripe cantaloupes, coarsely chopped
3	green onions, thinly sliced
½	cup loosely packed fresh cilantro leaves, chopped

In large bowl, whisk lime juice, salt, and pepper until blended. Add cucumber, cantaloupe, green onion, and cilantro; toss to coat.

EACH SERVING: About 45 calories (0 percent calories from fat), 6g protein, 25g carbohydrate, 5g total fat (1g saturated), 5g fiber, 0mg cholesterol, 160mg sodium ♥ ♥ ✿

Soups, Stews & Chilis

Whether you favor a stockpot or a slow cooker, soups, stews, and chilis are one-pot cooking at its finest. Here, we offer wholesome recipes that'll ensure you're filling that pot with fiber-rich grains and beans, vitamin-packed veggies, and lean poultry and meat.

We open with cool, refreshing soups that require little to no cooking, including a fresh pea puree and a chilly buttermilk and corn chowder. Then it's on to warm, soothing vegetable soups: Try puréed carrot and dill, a low-fat take on beet borscht, or any one of our easy creamy vegetable soups made from frozen veggies, canned stock, and skim milk to keep them light.

Soups and, of course, chilis are some of the best vehicles we know for beans. Our recipes take advantage of a wide range: There's a lentil stew with sweet butternut squash, a three-bean chili that features edamame, and a red bean chili made even redder through the addition of beets. See "Eat Your Beans," page 75, to learn more about the health benefits of incorporating more beans into your diet.

If you love chicken soup, we offer several options, from a south-of-the border recipe flavored with fresh cilantro and lime juice to a Thai chicken and rice noodle soup accented with basil and fresh ginger. Even beef stew can be on a healthy menu if it's made with lean beef and lots of hearty root vegetables like ours is. Recipes for homemade veggie and chicken broths provide alternatives to canned broths, which are typically high in sodium. Make a big batch and freeze it so you'll have a supply on hand whenever you want to fill up your soup pot.

Valentine's Day Red Chili (recipe page 83)

Chilled Tuscan-Style Tomato Soup

The lush summer flavors of Tuscany shine in this refreshing, easy-to-make cold tomato soup. We blend cubes of country bread in with the tomatoes, to achieve a thicker body and a velvety mouthfeel. For photo, see page 10.

TOTAL TIME: 15 minutes plus chilling

MAKES: 6 cups or 4 first-course servings

1	teaspoon olive oil
1	garlic clove, minced
2	cups cubed country-style bread (1-inch cubes; 3 ounces)
3	pounds ripe tomatoes, each cut into quarters
¼	cup loosely packed fresh basil leaves, chopped, plus additional basil leaves, for garnish
1	teaspoon sugar
½	teaspoon salt

1. In small skillet, heat oil over medium heat until hot. Add garlic and cook 1 minute, stirring. Remove skillet from heat.

2. In food processor with knife blade attached, pulse bread until coarsely chopped. Add tomatoes and garlic; pulse until soup is almost pureed. Pour soup into bowl; stir in chopped basil, sugar, and salt. Cover and refrigerate until well chilled, at least 2 hours or overnight. Garnish each serving with basil leaves.

EACH SERVING: About 145 calories (19 percent calories from fat), 5g protein, 28g carbohydrate, 3g total fat (1g saturated), 4g fiber, 0mg cholesterol, 445mg sodium

Chilled Buttermilk and Corn Soup

This refreshing refrigerator soup—with corn, tomatoes, cucumber, and basil—is both low in fat and satisfying.

TOTAL TIME: 20 minutes plus chilling

MAKES: 4½ cups or 6 first-course servings

1	quart buttermilk
4	ripe medium tomatoes (1½ pounds), seeded and chopped
1	small cucumber, peeled, seeded, and chopped
2	cups corn kernels cut from cobs (about 4 ears)
½	teaspoon salt
¼	teaspoon coarsely ground black pepper
10	fresh basil sprigs

1. In large bowl, combine buttermilk, tomatoes, cucumber, corn, salt, and pepper. Cover and refrigerate until very cold, at least 2 hours.

2. To serve, set aside 6 small basil sprigs; pinch 12 large basil leaves from remaining sprigs and thinly slice. Spoon soup into bowls; garnish with sliced basil and small basil sprigs.

EACH SERVING: About 135 calories (13 percent calories from fat), 8g protein, 24g carbohydrate, 2g total fat (1g saturated), 2g fiber, 6mg cholesterol, 365mg sodium

Carrot and Dill Soup

Combine sweet carrots with fresh orange, dill, and a touch of milk for a refreshing, creamy soup without the cream.

ACTIVE TIME: 25 minutes
TOTAL TIME: 1 hour 10 minutes
MAKES: 10 ½ cups or 10 first-course servings

1	tablespoon olive oil
1	large onion (12 ounces), chopped
1	stalk celery, chopped
2	large oranges
2	bags (16 ounces each) carrots, peeled and chopped
1	can (14 ½ ounces) vegetable broth or 1 ¾ cups homemade (page 92)
1	tablespoon sugar
¾	teaspoon salt
¼	teaspoon coarsely ground black pepper
4	cups water
1	cup milk
¼	cup chopped fresh dill
	dill sprigs for garnish

1. In 5-quart Dutch oven, heat oil over medium-high heat. Add onion and celery; cook until tender and golden, about 15 minutes, stirring occasionally.

2. Meanwhile, with vegetable peeler, remove 4 strips of peel (3″ by 1″ each) from oranges and squeeze 1 cup juice.

3. Add orange-peel strips to Dutch oven and cook 2 minutes longer, stirring. Add orange juice, carrots, broth, sugar, salt, pepper, and water; heat to boiling over high heat. Reduce heat to low; cover and simmer until carrots are very tender, about 25 minutes.

4. Remove strips of orange peel from soup. In blender, with center part of lid removed to allow steam to escape, blend soup in small batches until smooth. Pour pureed soup into large bowl after each batch.

5. Return soup to Dutch oven; stir in milk and chopped dill; heat just to simmering over medium heat. Spoon soup into bowls; garnish each serving with dill sprigs.

EACH SERVING: About 95 calories (28 percent calories from fat), 3g protein, 16g carbohydrate, 3g total fat (1g saturated), 3g fiber, 3mg cholesterol, 335mg sodium ♥

THE SKINNY ON SOUP

Looking to lose a few pounds? Embrace soup. Research shows that the best way to start a meal may be with a broth- or water-based soup. It fills you up—even more so than salad or other low-calorie foods—so you'll end up eating less at that meal.

Or make soup a meal in itself. Try our veggie- and grain-based soups; they provide fiber to keep you feeling fuller longer. Look for this icon ✿ to locate soup recipes that are high in fiber, containing 5 grams or more of fiber per serving.

Spring Pea Soup

Healthy, creamy, and full of flavor, this pea soup makes an excellent start to a spring dinner.

ACTIVE TIME: 12 minutes
TOTAL TIME: 35 minutes
MAKES: 10 first-course servings

2	tablespoons butter or margarine
2	large shallots, thinly sliced (¾ cup)
1	carton (32 ounces) reduced-sodium chicken broth (4 cups)
2	cups water
2	bags (16 ounces each) frozen peas, thawed
1	large all-purpose potato (8 ounces), peeled and cut into 1-inch chunks
½	cup loosely packed fresh mint leaves, chopped
¾	teaspoon salt
¼	teaspoon freshly ground black pepper
3	tablespoons fresh lemon juice
10	nasturtium flowers for garnish (see Tip)

1. In 4-quart saucepan, heat butter over medium-low heat until melted. Add shallots and cook 10 to 12 minutes or until very tender.

2. Add broth, water, peas, potato, half of mint, salt, and pepper; heat to boiling over high heat. Reduce heat to medium; simmer mixture 10 minutes, stirring occasionally.

3. Spoon half of mixture into blender; cover, with center part of lid removed to let steam escape, and puree until smooth. Pour puree into medium bowl. Repeat with remaining mixture. Return soup to saucepan and reheat over medium heat if necessary. Stir in lemon juice and remaining ¼ cup mint.

4. To serve, spoon soup into ten serving bowls; garnish with nasturtiums.

EACH SERVING: About 120 calories (23 percent calories from fat), 6g protein, 19g carbohydrate, 3g total fat (1g saturated), 5g fiber, 0mg cholesterol, 475mg sodium

TIP: *Nasturtiums and other edible flowers can be found in the produce section of supermarkets and at farmers' markets.*

Barley Minestrone with Pesto

Top this soup with a dollop of our homemade pesto, which you can make in a mini food processor or blender. In a hurry? Store-bought refrigerated pesto makes an excellent stand-in—although it's not as light as our version. For photo of soup, see page 15.

ACTIVE TIME: 50 minutes
TOTAL TIME: 1 hour 15 minutes
MAKES: 10½ cups or 6 main-dish servings

MINESTRONE

1   cup pearl barley
1   tablespoon olive oil
2   cups thinly sliced green cabbage (about ¼ small head)
2   large carrots, peeled, each cut lengthwise in half, then crosswise into ½-inch-thick slices
2   large stalks celery, cut into ½-inch dice
1   onion, cut into ½-inch dice
1   garlic clove, finely chopped
3   cups water
2   cans (14½ ounces each) vegetable broth or 3½ cups homemade (page 92)
1   can (14½ ounces) diced tomatoes
¼   teaspoon salt
1   medium zucchini (8 to 10 ounces), cut into ½-inch dice
4   ounces green beans, trimmed and cut into ½-inch pieces (1 cup)

LIGHT PESTO

1   cup firmly packed fresh basil leaves
2   tablespoons olive oil
2   tablespoons water
¼   teaspoon salt
¼   cup freshly grated Pecorino-Romano cheese
1   garlic clove, finely chopped

1. Heat 5- to 6-quart Dutch oven over medium-high until hot. Add barley and cook until toasted and fragrant, 3 to 4 minutes, stirring constantly. Transfer barley to small bowl; set aside.

2. Add oil to same Dutch oven, still over medium-high heat. When oil is hot, add cabbage, carrots, celery, and onion; cook until vegetables are tender and lightly browned, 8 to 10 minutes, stirring occasionally. Add garlic and cook until fragrant, 30 seconds. Stir in barley, water, broth, tomatoes with their juice, and salt. Cover and heat to boiling over high heat. Reduce heat to low and simmer 25 minutes.

3. Stir zucchini and green beans into barley mixture; increase heat to medium, cover, and cook until all vegetables are barely tender, 10 to 15 minutes longer.

4. Meanwhile, prepare pesto: In blender container with narrow base or in mini food processor, combine basil, oil, water, and salt; cover and blend until mixture is pureed. Transfer pesto to small bowl; stir in Romano and garlic. Makes about ½ cup pesto.

5. Ladle minestrone into six large soup bowls. Top each serving with some pesto.

EACH SERVING SOUP WITH 1 TEASPOON PESTO: About 230 calories (20 percent calories from fat), 7g protein, 42g carbohydrate, 5g total fat (0g saturated), 9g fiber, 1mg cholesterol, 725mg sodium

Black-Bean Soup

This simple but hearty soup is sure to become a standby. The cilantro and fresh lime juice add Latin flavor.

ACTIVE TIME: 15 minutes
TOTAL TIME: 45 minutes plus cooling
MAKES: 6½ cups or 6 main-dish servings

1	tablespoon olive oil
2	medium carrots, peeled and chopped
2	garlic cloves, finely chopped
1	large onion (10 to 12 ounces), chopped
1	medium red pepper (4 to 6 ounces), chopped
2	teaspoons ground cumin
¼	teaspoon crushed red pepper
½	teaspoon salt
2	cups water
2	cans black beans (15 to 19 ounces), rinsed and drained
1	can (14½ ounces) reduced-sodium chicken broth
¼	cup fresh cilantro leaves, chopped, plus sprigs for garnish
1	tablespoon fresh lime juice

EAT YOUR BEANS

Whether you choose black beans, garbanzos, pintos, or cannellini, beans are packed with protein and insoluble and soluble fiber. Insoluble fiber helps promote regularity and may stave off such digestive disorders as diverticulosis. Soluble fiber can reduce LDL cholesterol levels and help control blood-sugar levels in people with diabetes. Beans are also high in saponin, a cancer-fighting plant compound.

1. In 6-quart saucepot, heat oil over medium heat until hot. Add carrots, garlic, onion, and pepper; cook 12 to 15 minutes or until vegetables are lightly browned and tender, stirring occasionally. Add cumin, crushed red pepper, and salt; cook 1 minute.

2. Stir in water, beans, and broth; heat to boiling over medium-high heat. Reduce heat to low and simmer, uncovered, 15 minutes to blend flavors.

3. Ladle 3 cups soup into blender; cover, with center part of lid removed to allow steam to escape, and blend until pureed. Stir puree into soup in saucepot; heat through over medium heat. Stir in cilantro and lime juice, and garnish with cilantro sprigs to serve.

EACH SERVING: About 165 calories (16 percent calories from fat), 9g protein, 33g carbohydrate, 3g total fat (0g saturated), 11g fiber, 0mg cholesterol, 705mg sodium 🌿 🍲

Not Your Grandma's Borscht

It's impossible to peel beets without getting red all over your hands—unless you wear rubber gloves. For easy cleanup, peel beets in the sink.

ACTIVE TIME: 15 minutes
TOTAL TIME: 1 hour 15 minutes

MAKES: 5 main-dish servings

1	tablespoon olive oil
1	onion, chopped
1	garlic clove, crushed with garlic press
½	teaspoon ground allspice
1	can (14½ ounces) diced tomatoes
1	pound (not including tops) beets
6	cups sliced green cabbage (1 pound)
3	large carrots, peeled and cut into ½-inch chunks
4	cups water
1	can (14½ ounces) vegetable broth or 1¾ cups homemade (page 92)
1	bay leaf
¾	teaspoon salt
2	tablespoons red wine vinegar
¼	cup loosely packed fresh dill or parsley leaves, chopped

reduced-fat sour cream (optional)

1. In 5- to 6-quart saucepot, heat oil over medium heat until hot. Add onion and cook until tender, about 8 minutes. Stir in garlic and allspice; cook 30 seconds. Add tomatoes with their juice and cook 5 minutes.

2. Meanwhile, peel beets and shred in food processor (or on coarse side of box grater).

3. Add beets to onion mixture along with cabbage, carrots, water, broth, bay leaf, and salt; heat to boiling over high heat. Reduce heat to medium-low; cover and simmer until all vegetables are tender, about 30 minutes.

4. Remove bay leaf. Stir in vinegar and dill. Serve with sour cream, if you like.

EACH SERVING: About 160 calories (28 percent calories from fat), 5g protein, 27g carbohydrate, 5g total fat (1g saturated), 6g fiber, 5mg cholesterol, 920mg sodium ☘

EAT YOUR CABBAGE

Whether you choose savoy, green, or red, eating cabbage a few times a week can cut your risk of breast, lung, and colon cancers. In one study of three hundred Chinese women, those with the highest levels of cancer-fighting isothiocyanates—found in cabbage—had a 45 percent lower incidence of breast cancer than those with the lowest levels. Cabbage also delivers a good dose of vitamin C. If you find its flavor too pungent, try savoy or Chinese cabbages, which have a milder taste. Or mix it with raisins or chopped fruit and a little apple juice to help mask any musty flavor.

Hearty Fish Chowder

Cod, potatoes, and a sprinkling of crumbled bacon make every bite of this creamy chowder rich and satisfying.

ACTIVE TIME: 20 minutes
TOTAL TIME: 35 minutes
MAKES: 4 main-dish servings

4	slices center-cut bacon
1	large carrot, peeled and chopped
1	medium celery root (13 ounces), peeled and chopped
1	large all-purpose potato (12 ounces), peeled and chopped
2	tablespoons plus ½ cup water
2	small onions (4 to 6 ounces each), chopped
2	tablespoons all-purpose flour
1	cup bottled clam juice
1	pound skinless cod fillets, cut into 1-inch chunks
½	cup reduced-fat (2%) milk
¼	teaspoon salt
⅛	teaspoon freshly ground black pepper
	fresh flat-leaf parsley leaves, chopped, for garnish

1. In 6- to 7-quart saucepot, cook bacon over medium heat 5 to 7 minutes or until browned and crisp, turning occasionally. Drain on paper towels; set aside. Discard all but 1 tablespoon bacon fat. Keep saucepot with rendered bacon fat over medium heat.

2. While bacon cooks, in large microwave-safe bowl, combine carrot, celery root, potato, and 2 tablespoons water. Cover with vented plastic wrap and microwave on High 5 minutes or until vegetables are just tender.

3. Add onion to saucepot and cook 6 to 8 minutes or until tender, stirring occasionally. Add carrot mixture and cook 2 minutes, stirring.

4. Add flour and cook 2 minutes, stirring. Add clam juice and remaining ½ cup water and whisk until smooth. Heat to boiling, stirring occasionally. Add cod chunks, cover, and cook 4 to 5 minutes or until fish just turns opaque throughout.

5. Stir in milk, salt, and pepper. Cook 1 to 2 minutes or until hot but not boiling. Spoon chowder into shallow bowls; sprinkle with parsley and crumble 1 strip bacon over each serving.

EACH SERVING: About 310 calories (20 percent calories from fat), 27g protein, 35g carbohydrate, 7g total fat (3g saturated), 5g fiber, 64mg cholesterol, 595mg sodium ✿

Quick Cream of Asparagus Soup

Start with a package of frozen vegetables, a can of broth, and seasonings—in 25 minutes you'll have a luscious, creamy, lower-fat soup.

ACTIVE TIME: 5 minutes
TOTAL TIME: 25 minutes
MAKES: 3¾ cups or 4 first-course servings

1	tablespoon butter or margarine
1	onion, finely chopped
1	can (14½ ounces) fat-free chicken broth
1	package (10 ounces) frozen asparagus cuts or spears
¼	teaspoon dried thyme
¼	teaspoon dried tarragon
⅛	teaspoon salt
⅛	teaspoon ground black pepper
1½	cups skim milk
2	teaspoons fresh lemon juice
snipped fresh chives for garnish (optional)	

1. In 2-quart saucepan, melt butter over medium heat. Add onion and cook, stirring occasionally, until tender, 5 minutes. Add broth, asparagus, thyme, tarragon, salt, and pepper; heat to boiling over high heat. Reduce heat to low and simmer 10 minutes.

2. Spoon one-fourth of mixture into blender; cover, with center part of lid removed to let steam escape, and puree until smooth. Pour puree into bowl. Repeat with remaining mixture.

3. Return soup to saucepan; stir in milk. Heat through over medium heat, stirring often (do not boil, or soup may curdle). Remove saucepan from heat; stir in lemon juice. Garnish with snipped chives, if you like.

EACH SERVING: About 115 calories (24 percent calories from fat), 8g protein, 11g carbohydrate, 3g total fat (1g saturated), 2g fiber, 2mg cholesterol, 480mg sodium ☻

QUICK CREAM OF CAULIFLOWER SOUP: Prepare as directed but substitute *1 package (10 ounces) frozen cauliflower florets* for asparagus and *½ teaspoon curry powder* for dried tarragon. If you like, garnish with *chopped fresh apple.*

EACH SERVING: About 115 calories (24 percent calories from fat), 8g protein, 11g carbohydrate, 3g total fat (1g saturated), 2g fiber, 2mg cholesterol, 480mg sodium ☻

QUICK CREAM OF SQUASH SOUP: Prepare as directed but substitute *1 package (10 ounces) frozen winter squash* for asparagus. Add *¼ teaspoon pumpkin-pie spice* to onions at the end of cooking time and cook 30 seconds longer. Omit dried tarragon. If you like, garnish with *chopped ripe tomato.*

EACH SERVING: About 115 calories (23 percent calories from fat), 8g protein, 11g carbohydrate, 3g total fat (1g saturated), 2g fiber, 2mg cholesterol, 480mg sodium ☻

Lentil Stew with Butternut Squash

This hearty vegetarian option is packed with fiber and low in sodium. A slow cooker makes it a cinch to prepare.

ACTIVE TIME: 20 minutes
SLOW-COOK TIME: 8 hours on Low

MAKES: 11½ cups or 8 main-dish servings

3	large stalks celery, cut into ¼-inch-thick slices
1	large onion (12 ounces), chopped
1	large butternut squash (2½ pounds), peeled, seeded, and cut into 1-inch chunks
1	bag (1 pound) brown lentils
4	cups water
1	can (14 to 14½ ounces) vegetable broth or 1¾ cup homemade (page 92)
½	teaspoon dried rosemary
¾	teaspoon salt
¼	teaspoon freshly ground black pepper
1	ounce Parmesan or Pecorino-Romano cheese, shaved with vegetable peeler
¼	cup loosely packed fresh parsley leaves, chopped

1. In 4½- to 6-quart slow cooker bowl, combine celery, onion, squash, lentils, water, broth, rosemary, salt, and pepper. Cover slow cooker and cook on Low 8 hours.

2. To serve, spoon lentil stew into serving bowls, top with Parmesan shavings, and sprinkle with chopped parsley.

EACH SERVING: About 285 calories (68 percent calories from fat), 20g protein, 51g carbohydrate, 2g total fat (1g saturated), 20g fiber, 3mg cholesterol, 420mg sodium ♥ ⓥ ▤

Macaroni, Cabbage, and Bean Soup

A light yet chunky vegetable soup that's ready in less than half an hour.

ACTIVE TIME: 5 minutes
TOTAL TIME: 20 minutes

MAKES: 12 cups or 6 main-dish servings

1½	cups elbow macaroni or mini penne (pennette) pasta
1	tablespoon olive oil
1	onion, cut in half and thinly sliced
½	small head savoy cabbage (about 1 pound), thinly sliced
2	garlic cloves, crushed with garlic press
¼	teaspoon ground black pepper
3	cans (14½ ounces each) low-sodium chicken broth or 5¼ cups homemade (page 93)
2	cans (15 to 19 ounces each) white kidney beans (cannellini), rinsed and drained
1½	cups water
	freshly grated Parmesan or Pecorino-Romano cheese (optional)

1. Cook macaroni as label directs; drain.

2. Meanwhile, in 5- to 6-quart saucepot, heat oil over medium-high heat until hot. Add onion, cabbage, garlic, and pepper; cook, stirring often, until cabbage begins to wilt, 6 to 8 minutes. Stir in broth, beans, and water; heat to boiling.

3. Stir macaroni into cabbage mixture; heat through. Serve with Parmesan, if you like.

EACH SERVING: About 305 calories (11 percent calories from fat), 15g protein, 53g carbohydrate, 4g total fat (1g saturated), 11g fiber, 3mg cholesterol, 397mg sodium ⓥ ♥ ⓥ

Classic Beef Stew

Lean beef, winter vegetables, and a richly flavored sauce make this a candidate for family suppers or casual entertaining.

ACTIVE TIME: 30 minutes
TOTAL TIME: 1 hour 30 minutes

MAKES: 6 main-dish servings

1	pound lean beef for stew, trimmed and cut into 1-inch cubes
1	tablespoon vegetable oil
½	teaspoon salt
2	stalks celery, chopped
1	large onion (12 ounces), chopped
1	can (14½ ounces) stewed tomatoes
1	can (14½ ounces) beef broth
1	cup plus 2 tablespoons water
3	large potatoes (1½ pounds), peeled and cut into 1½-inch chunks
3	medium carrots (8 ounces), peeled and cut into ¾-inch chunks
3	medium turnips (12 ounces), peeled and cut into 1½-inch chunks
1	tablespoon soy sauce
2	tablespoons all-purpose flour
1	package (10 ounces) frozen peas
2	tablespoons freshly grated lemon peel

1. Pat beef dry with paper towels. In 5-quart Dutch oven, heat oil over medium-high heat until very hot. Add beef, sprinkle with salt, and cook, turning pieces occasionally, until beef is browned on all sides. Transfer beef to bowl.

2. Add celery and onion to drippings in Dutch oven and cook, stirring, until lightly browned. Return beef to Dutch oven; stir in stewed tomatoes, broth, and 1 cup water. Heat to boiling over high heat. Reduce heat to low; cover and simmer 25 minutes.

3. Add potatoes, carrots, turnips, and soy sauce; heat to boiling over high heat. Reduce heat to low; cover and simmer until meat and vegetables in pot are fork-tender, about 20 minutes longer.

4. In cup, with fork, mix flour and remaining 2 tablespoons water until blended. Stir flour mixture into meat mixture; cook over medium-high heat until mixture boils and thickens slightly. Stir in frozen peas; heat through. Sprinkle with lemon peel.

EACH SERVING: About 330 calories (19 percent calories from fat), 23g protein, 45g carbohydrate, 7g total fat (2g saturated), 7g fiber, 53mg cholesterol, 905mg sodium ⓥ ▥

Valentine's Day Red Chili

Beets and fire-roasted tomatoes color this vegetarian chili—and provide the inspiration for its name. For photo, see page 68.

ACTIVE TIME: 35 minutes
TOTAL TIME: 1 hour 30 minutes
MAKES: 9 cups or 6 main-dish servings

2   teaspoons ground cumin

1   teaspoon dried oregano

½   teaspoon chipotle chile powder

2   tablespoons vegetable oil

3   large beets (6 to 8 ounces each), trimmed, peeled, and chopped

1   jumbo red onion (1 pound), finely chopped

1   large red pepper (8 to 10 ounces), chopped

½   teaspoon ground black pepper

4   garlic cloves, crushed with press

1   can (28 ounces) fire-roasted diced tomatoes

1   can (15 ounces) low-sodium black beans, rinsed and drained

1   can (15 ounces) low-sodium red kidney beans, rinsed and drained

1   can (15 ounces) low-sodium pinto beans, rinsed and drained

1   cup water

1   cup reduced-fat sour cream

¼   cup fresh cilantro leaves

Double Cornbread, for serving (optional; page 253)

1. In 7- to 8-quart Dutch oven or heavy saucepot, combine cumin, oregano, and chile powder. Cook over medium heat 1 to 2 minutes or until toasted and fragrant. Transfer to sheet of waxed paper; set aside. In same Dutch oven, heat oil over medium heat until hot. Add beets, onion, red pepper, and ¼ teaspoon black pepper. Cook 15 minutes or until vegetables are tender, stirring occasionally.

2. Add garlic and reserved spice mixture. Cook 2 minutes, stirring constantly. Add tomatoes, all beans, and water. Heat to boiling over medium-high heat. Reduce heat to medium-low and simmer 30 minutes, stirring and mashing some beans occasionally. Season with remaining ¼ teaspoon black pepper. (Can be prepared up to this point up to 2 days ahead; transfer to airtight container and refrigerate. Reheat before serving.) Divide among serving bowls and top with sour cream and cilantro. Serve with cornbread, if you like.

EACH SERVING: About 345 calories (29 percent calories from fat), 15g protein, 52g carbohydrate, 10g total fat (3g saturated), 15g fiber, 13mg cholesterol, 540mg sodium 🌱 🍲

Three-Bean Vegetable Chili

This chili is so good we doubled the recipe. You can find edamame beans in the freezer case of most large supermarkets.

ACTIVE TIME: 35 minutes
TOTAL TIME: 1 hour 5 minutes
MAKES: 11½ cups or 8 main-dish servings

1	tablespoon vegetable oil
1	pound carrots, peeled and cut into ½-inch dice
2	large stalks celery, sliced
2	garlic cloves, crushed with press
1	jumbo onion (1 pound), chopped
4	teaspoons chili powder
1	tablespoon ground cumin
½	teaspoon ground cinnamon
¼	teaspoon cayenne (ground red) pepper
1	teaspoon salt
1	can (14½ ounces) diced tomatoes
1	can (14½ ounces) vegetable broth or 1¾ cups homemade (page 92)
1	cup water
2	cans (15 to 19 ounces) white kidney beans (cannellini), rinsed and drained
1	can (15 to 19 ounces) pink beans, rinsed and drained
2	cups frozen shelled edamame
¼	cup fresh cilantro leaves, chopped, plus additional leaves for garnish

reduced-fat sour cream (optional)

shredded reduced-fat Cheddar cheese (optional)

1. In 5- to 6-quart Dutch oven, heat oil over medium-high heat until hot. Add carrots, celery, garlic, and onion, and cook 10 to 12 minutes or until all vegetables are browned and tender, stirring occasionally.

2. Stir in chili powder, cumin, cinnamon, cayenne, and salt; cook 30 seconds, stirring. Add tomatoes and their juice, broth, and water; heat to boiling. Reduce heat to low; cover and simmer 15 minutes. Stir white kidney beans and pink beans into Dutch oven; cover and cook 10 minutes longer. Stir in edamame and cook, uncovered, 5 to 7 minutes or until edamame are just tender, stirring occasionally.

3. Stir chopped cilantro into chili. Spoon half of chili into serving bowls; garnish with cilantro leaves. Serve with sour cream and Cheddar, if you like. Spoon remaining chili into freezer-safe containers (see Tip).

EACH SERVING: About 345 calories (21 percent calories from fat), 19g protein, 51g carbohydrate, 8g total fat (1g saturated), 15g fiber, 0mg cholesterol, 945mg sodium 🌱 🍲

TIP: *To reheat on the rangetop after thawing, in a covered saucepan, heat the chili to boiling then simmer over medium heat, about 30 minutes, stirring occasionally. To use a microwave oven, place the chili in a microwave-safe bowl and heat, covered, on Low (30 percent) 10 minutes, stirring once or twice, then on High 5 to 10 minutes, stirring once.*

EAT EDAMAME

These sweet, nutty soybeans have gone by many names over the years—beer beans, sweet beans, garden soys—but the Japanese *edamame* is the one that stuck. Cultivated in ancient China for medicinal purposes, edamame are a nutritional powerhouse. Rich in calcium, iron, vitamins A and C, and fiber, they don't contain saturated fat and they are high in protein. Look for the precooked edamame in your supermarket's freezer or produce section. Try whole beans as a snack or enjoy them in recipes:

✦ Toss shelled beans into stir-fries, soups, stews, and salads.

✦ Puree shelled, cooked beans, roasted garlic, olive oil, and spices to make a creamy dip for pita chips or crackers.

✦ Add edamame to a succotash in place of lima beans.

Turkey and White Bean Chili

You can cut calories by a third and fat by half when you substitute ground turkey for beef chuck. The cannellini beans deliver an impressive 10 grams of fiber per serving— almost half your daily requirement.

ACTIVE TIME: 15 minutes
TOTAL TIME: 25 minutes

MAKES: 6 cups or 4 main-dish servings

1	tablespoon olive oil
1	pound ground turkey (93% lean)
½	teaspoon salt
1	onion, chopped
4	teaspoon chili powder
1	tablespoon ground cumin
1	can (28 ounces) whole tomatoes in juice, chopped
1	can (15 to 19 ounces) white kidney beans (cannellini), rinsed and drained
½	cup water
½	cup plain nonfat yogurt

1. In 12-inch skillet, heat oil over medium-high heat until hot. Add turkey and salt, and cook 6 to 8 minutes or until turkey loses its pink color throughout, stirring to break meat up with side of spoon. Add onion and cook 4 minutes. Stir in chili powder and cumin; cook 1 minute.

2. Add tomatoes with their juice, beans, and water; heat to boiling over high heat. Reduce heat to medium and cook, uncovered, 10 minutes, stirring occasionally. Ladle chili into serving bowls and top with a dollop of yogurt.

EACH SERVING: About 380 calories (30 percent calories from fat), 33g protein, 35g carbohydrate, 13g total fat (3g saturated), 10g fiber, 81mg cholesterol, 875mg sodium ● ● ▬

South-of-the-Border Chicken Soup

We give this rich chicken soup a Latin accent with lime and cilantro. Serve it with chunks of avocado and baked tortilla chips, if desired.

ACTIVE TIME: 25 minutes
TOTAL TIME: 1 hour 25 minutes
MAKES: 16 cups or 8 main-dish servings

8	medium all-purpose potatoes (2½ pounds)
1	chicken (4 pounds), cut into 8 pieces
3	large stalks celery, each cut into thirds
3	carrots, peeled and each cut into thirds
2	onions unpeeled, each cut into quarters
10	cups water
10	sprigs fresh cilantro, plus ¼ cup chopped
2	bay leaves
1	teaspoon whole black peppercorns
1	can (15¼ to 16 ounces) whole-kernel corn, drained
2	teaspoons salt
¼	cup fresh lime juice (3 large limes)
2	medium avocados, cut into ½-inch pieces

baked tortilla chips and lime wedges (optional)

1. Peel 3 potatoes. In 8-quart Dutch oven, combine chicken, peeled potatoes, celery, carrots, onions, water, cilantro sprigs, bay leaves, and peppercorns; heat to boiling over high heat. Reduce heat; cover and simmer until chicken loses its pink color throughout and vegetables are tender, 35 to 45 minutes. Transfer chicken and potatoes to separate bowls.

2. Strain broth through sieve into large bowl; discard vegetables. Skim and discard fat from broth; clean Dutch oven and return broth to pot. Mash cooked potatoes with 1 cup broth; stir potato mixture into broth in Dutch oven.

3. Peel and chop remaining 5 potatoes. Add to broth; heat to boiling over high heat. Reduce heat; cover and simmer until potatoes are tender, about 10 minutes.

4. Meanwhile, discard skin and bones from chicken; cut chicken into bite-size pieces. Stir chicken, corn, and salt into broth; heat through.

5. Just before serving, stir lime juice and ¼ cup chopped cilantro into soup. Top with avocado and serve with tortilla chips and/or lime wedges, if you like.

EACH SERVING: About 345 calories (29 percent calories from fat), 28g protein, 34g carbohydrate, 11g total fat (2g saturated), 6g fiber, 76mg cholesterol, 772mg sodium

Thai Chicken-Basil Soup

Fresh basil and lime juice give this easy Thai noodle soup its perky personality.

ACTIVE TIME: 5 minutes
TOTAL TIME: 60 minutes

MAKES: 15 cups or 8 main-dish servings

1	tablespoon vegetable oil
1	onion, chopped
1	medium poblano chile (3 ounces), seeded and chopped
4	teaspoons finely chopped, peeled fresh ginger
3	garlic cloves, thinly sliced
¼	teaspoon crushed red pepper
3	tablespoons reduced-sodium Asian fish sauce (see Tip)
2	cartons (32 ounces each) reduced-sodium chicken broth
3	cups water
½	cup packed fresh basil leaves, thinly sliced, plus basil sprigs for garnish
1½	pounds boneless, skinless chicken thighs, trimmed of fat, thinly sliced crosswise
1	package (14 ounces) linguine-style (¼-inch-wide) rice noodles (see box, opposite)
	3 to 4 large limes

1. In 6-quart Dutch oven, heat oil over medium heat. Add onion and poblano, and cook 10 minutes or until lightly browned and tender, stirring occasionally. Add ginger, garlic, crushed red pepper, and 1 tablespoon fish sauce; cook 1 minute.

2. Add broth, water, and half of sliced basil; heat to boiling over high heat. Reduce heat to low; cover and simmer 20 minutes. Uncover; increase heat to medium-high. Stir in chicken and uncooked noodles; heat to boiling. Boil 1 minute.

3. Remove Dutch oven from heat. Skim off fat. Cut 1 lime into wedges and set aside for garnish. Squeeze enough juice from remaining limes to make ¼ cup. To serve, stir in lime juice, remaining 2 tablespoons fish sauce, and remaining sliced basil. Garnish each serving with basil sprigs. Serve with additional fish sauce and lime wedges.

EACH SERVING: About 315 calories (17 percent calories from fat), 19g protein, 47g carbohydrate, 6g total fat (1g saturated), 1g fiber, 70mg cholesterol, 925mg sodium

TIP: *Highly pungent, Asian fish sauce is made from the liquid of salted fermented anchovies. That means a little goes a long way—happily it has an extended shelf life. If you don't have any on hand, substitute half the amount of reduced-sodium soy sauce.*

ASIAN NOODLE SAVVY

From rice vermicelli to udon, Asian noodles make stir-fries, soups, and salads feel new. The options below are available at supermarkets or Asian grocery stores, but if you can't locate them, we've provided pastas you can substitute for equally good results.

+ **BEAN THREAD** (also known as *cellophane*, *slippery*, or *mung bean noodles*): Chewy, translucent, threadlike noodles made from the starch of mung beans. Bean threads become slippery when softened in hot water and cooked. Their understated flavor lets them absorb the other good tastes in the pan. Try them in brothy soups. Substitute: Thin rice noodles, capellini, or vermicelli.

+ **CHINESE WHEAT NOODLES:** Made with wheat flour and water, these round or flat noodles come in varying thicknesses and are available fresh or dried. The flat, wide noodles are called *chow fun*. The thinnest noodles are called *Chinese somen*. Use thinner ones in delicate soups; thicker ones hold their own in stir-fries. (Wheat noodles made with eggs are called *mein*; they resemble spaghetti.) Substitute: Fresh or dried fettuccine.

+ **RICE NOODLES:** Round or flat, these thin, translucent white noodles are made from rice flour and water; their neutral flavor makes them a perfect foil for robust, meaty flavors. Rice noodles may be called *vermicelli* (extra thin), *thread* (fine), or *rice stick* (flat). However, the labeling is not standardized, so look at the noodle rather than the name. Vermicelli is also known as *mi fen* (Chinese), *bun* (Vietnamese), and *sen mee* (Thai). Rice sticks are known as *banh pho* in Vietnam and *jantaboon* in Thailand. Substitute: vermicelli, linguine, or fettuccine (depending on size of rice noodle called for).

+ **SOBA NOODLES:** Soba are thin, delicately textured Japanese noodles made of wheat flour and buckwheat, which lends them a brown color and nutty flavor. (See photo, below.) The more buckwheat these noodles contain, the more expensive they are. Soba noodles are often served cold with a dipping sauce or hot in soups, but they are versatile enough to be used in Chinese chicken salad or stir-fries too. Substitute: Whole-wheat spaghetti.

+ **UDON NOODLES:** These wheat-based Japanese noodles are available fresh or dried. Fat and bouncy in texture, delicate fresh udon noodles cook fast, which makes them a great option for soups. Dried udon noodles are a good base for stir-fries. Substitute: Linguine.

Chicken Soup, Bouillabaisse-Style

Instead of a bevy of high-maintenance seafood, this slow-cooker bouillabaisse recipe boasts boneless, skinless chicken thighs simmered in a traditional saffron broth.

ACTIVE TIME: 30 minutes
SLOW-COOK TIME: 8 hours on Low or 4 hours on High
MAKES: 8 main-dish servings

1	tablespoon olive oil
3	pounds bone-in chicken thighs, skin and fat removed
½	teaspoon salt
¼	teaspoon freshly ground black pepper
1	large bulb fennel (1½ pounds)
½	cup dry white wine
1	onion, chopped
2	garlic cloves, finely chopped
1	can (14½ ounces) chicken broth or 1¾ cups homemade (page 93)
1	can (14½ ounces) diced tomatoes
1	bay leaf
½	teaspoon dried thyme
¼	teaspoon saffron threads, crumbled

crusty French bread (optional)

1. In 12-inch skillet, heat oil over medium-high heat until hot. Sprinkle chicken thighs with salt and pepper. Add chicken to skillet in 2 batches and cook, turning once and adding more oil if necessary, until lightly browned on both sides, 7 to 8 minutes per batch. With tongs, transfer chicken to bowl when browned.

2. Meanwhile, trim stems and tough outer layers from fennel bulb. Cut bulb into quarters, then thinly slice crosswise.

3. After chicken is browned, add wine to skillet and heat to boiling, stirring to loosen any browned bits. Boil 1 minute.

4. In 4¼- to 6-quart slow-cooker bowl, combine fennel, onion, garlic, broth, tomatoes with their juice, bay leaf, thyme, and saffron. Top with chicken, any juices in bowl, and wine mixture from skillet; do not stir. Cover slow cooker and cook on Low 8 hours or on High 4 hours.

5. With tongs, transfer chicken to serving bowls. Discard bay leaf. Skim and discard fat from sauce. Pour sauce over chicken. Serve with bread, if you like.

EACH SERVING: About 175 calories (30 percent calories from fat), 22g protein, 9g carbohydrate, 6g total fat (1g saturated), 3g fiber, 85mg cholesterol, 580mg sodium

Homemade Vegetable Broth

This broth is delicious, nutritious, and great in soups, risottos, and sauces. The optional fennel and parsnip lend a natural sweetness and additional depth of flavor. For an Asian-flavored broth, add minced lemongrass, minced fresh ginger, or chopped fresh cilantro.

ACTIVE TIME: 25 minutes
TOTAL TIME: 2 hours 25 minutes

MAKES: 6 cups

4   large leeks
2 to 4 garlic cloves, not peeled
13   cups water
salt
1   large all-purpose potato, peeled, cut lengthwise in half, and thinly sliced
1   small fennel bulb, trimmed and chopped (optional)
3   parsnips, peeled and thinly sliced (optional)
2   large carrots, peeled and thinly sliced
3   stalks celery with leaves, thinly sliced
4   ounces mushrooms, trimmed and thinly sliced
10   parsley sprigs
4   thyme sprigs
2   bay leaves
1   teaspoon whole black peppercorns, plus additional ground black pepper as needed

1. Cut off roots and trim dark green tops from leeks. Thinly slice leeks and rinse them in large bowl of cold water, swishing to remove sand. Transfer to colander to drain, leaving sand in bottom of bowl.

2. In 6-quart saucepot, combine leeks, garlic, 1 cup water, and pinch salt; heat to boiling. Reduce heat to medium; cover and cook until leeks are tender, about 15 minutes.

3. Add potato, fennel if using, parsnips if using, carrots, celery, mushrooms, parsley and thyme sprigs, bay leaves, peppercorns, and remaining 12 cups water. Heat to boiling; reduce heat and simmer, uncovered, at least 1 hour 30 minutes.

4. Taste and continue cooking if flavor is not concentrated enough. Season with salt and pepper to taste. Strain broth through fine-mesh sieve into containers, pressing on solids with back of wooden spoon to extract liquid; cool. Cover and refrigerate to use within 3 days, or freeze up to 4 months.

EACH CUP: About 20 calories (0 calories from fat), 1g protein, 4g carbohydrate, 0g total fat, 0mg cholesterol, 0g fiber, 9mg sodium ♥ ▤

Homemade Chicken Broth

Nothing beats the rich flavor of homemade chicken broth. It serves as a base for many of our soups and stews. Make large batches and freeze it in sturdy containers for up to four months. Bonus: The cooked chicken can be used in casseroles and salads.

ACTIVE TIME: 30 minutes
TOTAL TIME: 4 hours 40 minutes plus cooling
MAKES: 5½ cups

1	chicken (3 to 3½ pounds), including neck (reserve giblets for another use)
2	carrots, peeled and cut into 2-inch pieces
1	stalk celery, cut into 2-inch pieces
1	onion, unpeeled, cut into quarters
5	parsley sprigs
1	garlic clove, unpeeled
½	teaspoon dried thyme
½	bay leaf
3	quarts water plus more if needed

1. In 6-quart saucepot, combine chicken, chicken neck, carrots, celery, onion, parsley, garlic, thyme, bay leaf, and water. If necessary, add more water to cover broth ingredients; heat to boiling over high heat. With slotted spoon, skim foam from surface. Reduce heat to low; cover and simmer, turning chicken once and skimming foam occasionally, 1 hour.

2. Remove from heat; transfer chicken to large bowl. When chicken is cool enough to handle, remove skin and bones and reserve meat for another use. Return skin and bones to pot and return to boiling over high heat. Skim foam; reduce heat to low and simmer, uncovered, 3 hours.

3. Strain broth through colander into large bowl; discard solids. Strain again though fine-mesh sieve into containers; cool. Cover and refrigerate to use within 3 days, or freeze up to 4 months.

4. Discard fat from surface of chilled broth before use.

EACH CUP: About 35 calories (26 percent calories from fat), 3g protein, 4g carbohydrate, 1g total fat (1g saturated), 0g fiber, 3mg cholesterol, 91mg sodium ♥ ▤

4

Sandwiches, Wraps & Pizzas

Sandwiches, wraps, and even burgers and pizzas are not off-limits in a light and healthy meal plan. You just have to choose both your bread *and* the fillings with care. In this chapter, we provide lots of satisfying low-cal options you can sink your teeth into without guilt.

When it comes to selecting bread, the buzz words are *whole grain*. Look for whole-wheat pitas, tortillas, and burger buns, and multi-grain loaves for sandwiches. Or pick up some readymade whole-wheat pizza dough at your local pizzeria or supermarket. For tips on label-reading, see "How Do You Know It's Whole Grain?" on page 13.

Once you have your bread, it's time to fill it. Our homemade falafel, Tuscan tuna salad, and curried chicken salad are all easy, tasty fillers for pitas. If you're brown-bagging it, pack our turkey and mango wraps or our healthy club sandwiches—we offer both veggie and roast beef options. You can also bypass the bread altogether and prepare our gingery chicken salad; it's made from already cooked rotisserie chicken and served in lettuce cups.

On hectic weeknights or lazy weekends, our chicken quesadillas or turkey fajitas will keep everybody happy. Or, if your family is clamoring for burgers, serve up our turkey burgers with a yogurt and mint sauce or one of our chicken-burger variations. Pair our easy homemade pizza crust with one of four veggie toppings for a light and healthy alternative to grease-laden takeout—your family gets their pizza fix, while you rest easy knowing that they're eating their vegetables, too.

Curried Chicken Pitas (recipe page 98)

Falafel Sandwiches

Serve these small, flat bean patties in pita pockets with lettuce, tomatoes, cucumbers, and tangy plain low-fat yogurt.

ACTIVE TIME: 10 minutes
TOTAL TIME: 20 minutes
MAKES: 4 sandwiches

4   green onions, cut into ½-inch pieces
2   garlic cloves, each cut in half
½   cup packed fresh flat-leaf parsley leaves
2   teaspoons dried mint
1   can (15 to 19 ounces) no-salt-added garbanzo beans, rinsed and drained
½   cup plain dried bread crumbs
1   teaspoon ground coriander
1   teaspoon ground cumin
1   teaspoon baking powder
½   teaspoon salt
¼   teaspoon cayenne (ground red) pepper
¼   teaspoon ground allspice
olive oil nonstick cooking spray
4   (6- to 7-inch) whole-wheat pita breads
sliced romaine lettuce, sliced ripe tomatoes, sliced cucumber, sliced red onion, plain low-fat yogurt

1. In food processor with knife blade attached, finely chop green onions, garlic, parsley, and mint. Add beans, bread crumbs, coriander, cumin, baking powder, salt, cayenne, and allspice, and blend until a coarse puree forms.

2. Shape bean mixture, by scant ½ cups, into eight 3-inch round patties and place on sheet of waxed paper. Coat both sides of patties with cooking spray.

3. Heat nonstick 10-inch skillet over medium heat until hot. Add half of patties and cook until dark golden brown, about 10 minutes, turning once. Transfer patties to paper towels to drain. Repeat with remaining patties.

4. Cut off top third of each pita to form a pocket. Reserve cut-off pieces for another use. Place 2 warm patties in each pita. Serve with choice of accompaniments.

EACH SANDWICH WITHOUT ACCOMPANIMENTS:
About 305 calories (9 percent calories from fat), 13g protein, 58g carbohydrate, 3g total fat (0g saturated), 10g fiber, 0mg cholesterol, 755mg sodium ♥ ♣

Health Club Sandwiches

This carrot, sprout, and bean spread combo will satisfy your palate and ease your conscience.

TOTAL TIME: 25 minutes

MAKES: 4 sandwiches

- 2 tablespoons olive oil
- 2 teaspoons plus 1 tablespoon fresh lemon juice
- 1 teaspoon honey
- 1/8 teaspoon ground black pepper
- 3 carrots, peeled and shredded (1 cup)
- 2 cups alfalfa sprouts
- 1 garlic clove, finely chopped
- 1/2 teaspoon ground cumin
- pinch cayenne (ground red) pepper
- 1 can (15 to 19 ounces) garbanzo beans, rinsed and drained
- 1 tablespoon water
- 12 slices multigrain bread, lightly toasted
- 1 large ripe tomato (12 ounces), thinly sliced
- 1 bunch watercress (4 ounces), tough stems trimmed

1. In medium bowl, stir 1 tablespoon oil, 2 teaspoons lemon juice, honey, and black pepper until mixed. Add carrots and alfalfa sprouts; toss until mixed and evenly coated with dressing.

2. In 2-quart saucepan, heat remaining 1 tablespoon oil over medium heat. Add garlic, cumin, and cayenne and cook until very fragrant, about 1 minute. Stir in beans and remove from heat. Add remaining 1 tablespoon lemon juice and water; mash to a coarse puree.

3. Spread garbanzo-bean mixture on 8 toast slices. Place tomato slices and watercress over 4 garbanzo-topped toast slices. Top remaining 4 garbanzo-topped slices with alfalfa-sprout mixture and place on watercress-topped bread. Cover with 4 remaining toast slices. Cut sandwiches in half.

EACH SANDWICH: About 380 calories (28 percent calories from fat), 14g protein, 57g carbohydrate, 12g total fat (2g saturated), 17g fiber, 0mg cholesterol, 545mg sodium ✅ ✅

Tuscan Tuna Salad Sandwiches

Tuna and cannellini beans are a popular combination in Italy. Tossed with a piquant dressing, it makes a great sandwich filling.

TOTAL TIME: 15 minutes

MAKES: 4 sandwiches

1   can (15 to 19 ounces) low-sodium white kidney beans (cannellini), rinsed and drained
½   cup chopped fresh basil
2   tablespoons capers, drained and chopped
2   tablespoons fresh lemon juice
2   tablespoons olive oil
½   teaspoon salt
¼   teaspoon coarsely ground black pepper
1   can (6 ounces) unsalted tuna packed in water, drained and flaked
1   bunch watercress (4 ounces), tough stems trimmed and sprigs cut in half
4   whole-wheat pita breads
2   ripe medium tomatoes (6 ounces each), thinly sliced

1. In large bowl, mash 1 cup beans. Stir in basil, capers, lemon juice, oil, salt, and pepper until well blended. Add tuna, watercress, and remaining beans; toss to mix.

2. Cut pita breads in half. Spoon tuna mixture onto pita halves; top with tomato slices.

EACH SANDWICH: About 330 calories (26 percent calories from fat), 20g protein, 44g carbohydrate, 10g total fat (1g saturated), 9g fiber, 15mg cholesterol, 724mg sodium ♥ ⓥ

Curried Chicken Pitas

This curry-spiced chicken salad packs extra sweet flavor with the addition of cantaloupe. For photo, see page 94.

TOTAL TIME: 20 minutes

MAKES: 4 sandwiches

¼   cup packed fresh cilantro leaves, finely chopped
¼   cup reduced-fat sour cream
2   tablespoons low-fat mayonnaise
1   tablespoon fresh lime juice
1   teaspoon grated, peeled fresh ginger
¼   teaspoon curry powder
¼   teaspoon ground coriander
⅛   teaspoon salt
2   cups chopped, cooked chicken-breast meat
5   radishes, cut into ¼-inch-thick half-moons
1½ cups chopped cantaloupe (8 ounces)
¼   small red onion, finely chopped
3   tablespoons roasted cashews, chopped
4   pita breads, toasted, each cut into quarters

1. In small bowl, whisk cilantro, sour cream, mayonnaise, lime juice, ginger, curry powder, coriander, and salt until well blended. If making ahead, cover and refrigerate up to 1 day.

2. In bowl, combine chicken, radishes, cantaloupe, and onion. If making ahead, cover and refrigerate up to 1 day. To serve, toss chicken mixture with half of dressing. Sprinkle with cashews. Spoon on top of pita pieces and serve with remaining dressing alongside.

EACH SANDWICH: About 380 calories (21 percent calories from fat), 29g protein, 45g carbohydrate, 9g total fat (3g saturated), 3g fiber, 65mg cholesterol, 535mg sodium ♥ ▤

Gingery Chicken in Lettuce Cups

An Asian-inspired meal with lean chicken and edamame (soybeans) serves up healthy doses of protein, fiber, and heart-boosting phytochemicals—and few calories.

TOTAL TIME: 30 minutes

MAKES: 4 main-dish servings

3	tablespoons reduced-sodium soy sauce
2	teaspoons grated, peeled fresh ginger
1	teaspoon honey
2	teaspoons Asian sesame oil
1¼	pounds chicken tenders, cut into ¼-inch chunks
1	cup frozen shelled edamame (soybeans)
2	medium stalks celery, chopped
12	large Boston lettuce leaves

1. In cup, combine soy sauce, ginger, and honey. Set aside.

2. In 12-inch nonstick skillet, heat sesame oil over medium heat 1 minute. Add chicken chunks and cook 3 minutes, stirring occasionally.

3. Add edamame to chicken in skillet; cook 2 minutes, stirring occasionally. Stir in celery; cook 2 minutes longer. Add soy sauce mixture; cook 1 to 2 minutes or until chicken is cooked through, stirring occasionally to coat chicken with sauce. Makes about 3½ cups.

4. Arrange lettuce leaves on 4 dinner plates. Divide chicken mixture among lettuce leaves, using a generous ¼ cup per leaf. Fold leaves over chicken mixture and eat out of hand.

EACH SERVING: About 260 calories (24 percent calories from fat), 40g protein, 9g carbohydrate, 7g total fat (1g saturated), 3g fiber, 82mg cholesterol, 565mg sodium ⚫

Peking Chicken Roll-Ups

The traditional Chinese recipe for Peking duck is labor-intensive and takes several days to make. Our version, prepared in minutes, is made with grilled boneless chicken thighs and served in flour tortillas with hoisin sauce.

ACTIVE TIME: 25 minutes
TOTAL TIME: 35 minutes

MAKES: 4 main-dish servings

8	(7-inch) low-fat, low-sodium flour tortillas
2	tablespoons honey
2	tablespoons reduced-sodium soy sauce
1	tablespoon grated, peeled fresh ginger
1/8	teaspoon cayenne (ground red) pepper
2	garlic cloves, crushed with garlic press
6	skinless, boneless chicken thighs (about 1 1/4 pounds)
1	teaspoon vegetable oil
1/4	cup hoisin sauce
1/2	English (seedless) cucumber, cut into 2" by 1/4" matchsticks
2	green onions, thinly sliced

1. Prepare outdoor grill for direct grilling over medium-high heat.

2. Stack tortillas and wrap in foil. In small bowl, mix honey, soy sauce, ginger, cayenne, and garlic. Set aside tortillas and honey mixture.

3. Coat chicken with oil and place on hot grill rack over medium-high heat. Grill, turning once, 5 minutes. Brush chicken all over with honey mixture and grill until juices run clear when thickest part of thigh is pierced with tip of knife, 5 to 7 minutes longer, turning over once.

4. While chicken is cooking, place foil-wrapped tortillas on same grill rack and heat until warm, 3 to 5 minutes.

5. Transfer chicken to cutting board and thinly slice. Spread hoisin sauce on one side of each tortilla. Top with chicken, cucumber, and green onions; roll up to serve.

EACH SERVING: About 260 calories (26 percent calories from fat), 35g protein, 65g carbohydrate, 15g total fat (4g saturated), 9g fiber, 93mg cholesterol, 853mg sodium 🌿

Turkey and Mango Roll-Ups

A lime-spiked curried chutney adds zip to this rolled sandwich. If you can't find lavash (an Armenian flatbread), use flour tortillas instead.

TOTAL TIME: 25 minutes plus chilling

MAKES: 4 roll-ups

1	large lime
¼	cup light mayonnaise
3	tablespoons mango chutney, chopped
½	teaspoon curry powder
⅛	teaspoon paprika
1	lavash flatbread (7 ounces)
1	medium cucumber (8 ounces), peeled and thinly sliced
8	ounces thinly sliced smoked turkey breast
1	mango, peeled and finely chopped
6	large green-leaf lettuce leaves

1. From lime, grate ¼ teaspoon peel and squeeze 1 tablespoon juice. In bowl, combine lime peel, lime juice, mayonnaise, chutney, curry powder, and paprika until blended.

2. Unfold lavash; spread evenly with mayonnaise mixture. Arrange cucumber slices over mayonnaise, then top with turkey, mango, and lettuce. From a short side, roll lavash up, jelly-roll fashion.

3. Wrap lavash roll in foil and refrigerate at least 2 hours or up to 4 hours to blend flavors and let bread soften. To serve, trim ends, then cut lavash roll into 4 pieces.

EACH ROLL-UP: About 375 calories (17 percent calories from fat), 18g protein, 54g carbohydrate, 7g total fat (2g saturated), 7g fiber, 29mg cholesterol, 842mg sodium

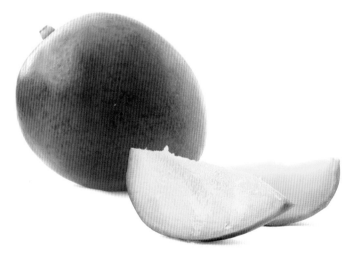

Garden Turkey Sandwiches

Low-fat mayonnaise gets a lift from freshly grated lemon zest. You can also serve this mayo mix as a dip; just add chopped fresh herbs and a pinch of salt.

TOTAL TIME: 10 minutes

MAKES: 4 sandwiches

4	teaspoons grated lemon peel
4	tablespoons low-fat mayonnaise
8	slices whole-grain bread
4	cups loosely packed baby spinach leaves
8	ounces turkey breast, sliced
2	tomatoes, sliced

1. Stir grated lemon peel into mayonnaise; spread on one side of each bread slice.

2. On 4 slices bread, alternately layer equal amounts spinach, turkey, and tomato, starting and ending with spinach. Top with remaining bread slices.

EACH SANDWICH: About 300 calories (21 percent calories from fat), 26g protein, 33g carbohydrate, 7g total fat (2g saturated), 13g fiber, 57mg cholesterol, 320mg sodium ♥ ❤ 🌱

EAT YOUR SPINACH

Popeye had the right idea: Thanks to high levels of beta-carotene, vitamins B_2, B_6, C, and K—plus generous amounts of manganese, folate, and magnesium—spinach is possibly the healthiest vegetable in the world. To avoid the metallic taste of oxalic crystals that form when spinach is cooked, use raw spinach. We replaced lettuce with spinach in these turkey sandwiches. The acids in the lemon mayonnaise temper spinach's bold taste.

Turkey Meatball Pitas

No one need ever know these meatballs are made with turkey instead of beef.

ACTIVE TIME: 20 minutes
TOTAL TIME: 30 minutes
MAKES: 5 sandwiches

1	pound ground turkey
2	slices whole-grain bread, chopped
2	tablespoons grated onion
1	large egg white
1½	teaspoons ground cumin
1	teaspoon salt
3	tablespoons water
5	(6-inch) whole-wheat pita breads
½	large cucumber, peeled and cut into ¾-inch pieces
1	container (8 ounces) plain nonfat yogurt
2	tablespoons chopped fresh cilantro or 1 teaspoon dried mint
4	cups thinly sliced romaine lettuce

1. Preheat oven to 425°F. Coat 15 ½″ by 10 ½″ jelly-roll pan with nonstick cooking spray.

2. In large bowl, with hands, mix turkey, bread, onion, egg white, cumin, ¾ teaspoon salt, and water. Wetting hands for easier shaping, form turkey mixture into 25 meatballs. Place meatballs in prepared jelly-roll pan and bake until cooked through (meatballs will not brown), 12 to 15 minutes.

3. Cut about 1 inch from top of each pita; reserve cut-off pieces for another use. Wrap pitas in foil. After meatballs have baked about 10 minutes, warm pitas in oven until meatballs are done.

4. Meanwhile, in small bowl, mix cucumber, yogurt, cilantro, and remaining ¼ teaspoon salt.

5. To serve, fill pitas with lettuce and meatballs; top with cucumber sauce.

EACH SANDWICH: About 380 calories (26 percent calories from fat), 28g protein, 44g carbohydrate, 11g total fat (3g saturated), 5g fiber, 46mg cholesterol, 909mg sodium ♥ ❂

EAT YOUR ONIONS

They may make you weep at the cutting board, but onions (and their brethren, leeks, shallots, and garlic, known as alliums) contain sulfur compounds that account for their distinctive flavor and aroma—and their nutritional benefits. They can inhibit the formation of blood clots and reduce the body's production of cholesterol. Studies suggest they may also defend against bacteria, fungi, viruses, and parasites.

Roast Beef Waldorf Sandwiches

Horseradish dressing and a crunchy celery-and-apple mixture make rare roast beef taste even better. Soaking the onions in ice water crisps them and tames their bite.

TOTAL TIME: 20 minutes plus standing

MAKES: 4 sandwiches

4	very thin slices red onion
½	Golden Delicious apple, peeled and finely chopped (½ cup)
2	stalks celery, finely chopped
4	tablespoons low-fat mayonnaise
2	tablespoons sour cream
½	teaspoon fresh lemon juice
1	tablespoon bottled white horseradish
8	slices pumpernickel bread, lightly toasted, if desired
8	ounces thinly sliced rare roast beef
1	bunch watercress (4 ounces), tough stems trimmed

1. In small bowl, combine onion with enough *ice water* to cover; let stand 15 minutes. Drain.

2. In separate small bowl, combine apple, celery, 2 tablespoons mayonnaise, 1 tablespoon sour cream, and lemon juice until well blended. In cup, combine remaining 2 tablespoons mayonnaise, remaining 1 tablespoon sour cream, and horseradish until blended.

3. Spread horseradish mixture evenly on 4 bread slices. Layer roast beef, onion, and watercress on top. Spread celery mixture evenly on remaining 4 bread slices and invert onto sandwiches. To serve, cut sandwiches in half.

EACH SANDWICH: About 295 calories (20 percent calories from fat), 22g protein, 40g carbohydrate, 7g total fat (3g saturated), 5g fiber, 31mg cholesterol, 726mg sodium ♥

Steak Sandwiches with Grilled Onions

Marinating the steak with a delicious blend of Asian flavors and grilling it takes this classic sandwich to a new level.

ACTIVE TIME: 15 minutes
TOTAL TIME: 30 minutes plus marinating
MAKES: 4 main-dish servings

¼ cup reduced-sodium soy sauce

¼ cup balsamic vinegar

1 tablespoon brown sugar

1 teaspoon fresh thyme leaves

¼ teaspoon ground black pepper

1 beef flank steak (about 1¼ pounds)

1 (12-inch) metal skewer

1 medium red onion (about 8 ounces), cut into 4 thick slices

8 slices sourdough bread, toasted on grill, if you like

2 ripe medium tomatoes (6 to 8 ounces each), sliced

1 bunch (5 ounces) arugula, trimmed

1. In large zip-tight plastic bag, mix soy sauce, vinegar, brown sugar, thyme, and pepper. Add steak, turning to coat. Seal bag, pressing out excess air. Place bag on plate; let marinate 15 minutes at room temperature or 1 hour in the refrigerator, turning several times.

2. Prepare outdoor grill for covered direct grilling over medium heat.

3. Meanwhile, for easier handling, insert skewer horizontally through onion slices; set aside.

4. Remove steak from marinade; pour marinade into 1-quart saucepan. Heat marinade over high heat to boiling; boil 2 minutes.

5. Place steak and onion slices on hot grill rack over medium heat. Cover grill and cook steak and onions, brushing both with marinade occasionally and turning over once, until onions are browned and tender and meat is medium-rare, 12 to 15 minutes. Transfer steak to cutting board; let stand 10 minutes to allow juices to set for easier slicing. Separate onion into rings.

6. Thinly slice steak diagonally across grain. Arrange onion rings and steak on 4 slices of bread; spoon any meat juices from board over onion and steak. Top with tomatoes, arugula, and remaining slices of bread.

EACH SERVING: About 450 calories (20 percent calories from fat), 40g protein, 51g carbohydrate, 10g total fat (4g saturated), 4g fiber, 84mg cholesterol, 802mg sodium

Barbecue Pork Sandwiches

Good news: These little sandwiches allow you to partake in the barbecue, too. Round out your meal with a big green salad tossed with skinny Buttermilk-Chive Dressing (page 46).

ACTIVE TIME: 10 minutes
TOTAL TIME: 30 minutes

MAKES: 6 main-dish servings

3   tablespoons light molasses
3   tablespoons ketchup
1   tablespoon Worcestershire sauce
1   teaspoon minced, peeled fresh ginger
½   teaspoon grated lemon peel
1   garlic clove, crushed with garlic press
2   whole pork tenderloins (¾ pound each)
12   small, soft dinner rolls

1. Preheat broiler. In medium bowl, combine molasses, ketchup, Worcestershire, ginger, lemon peel, and garlic; add pork, turning to coat.

2. Place pork tenderloins on rack in broiling pan. Spoon any remaining molasses mixture over pork. Place pan in broiler 5 to 7 inches from heat source; broil pork, turning once, until meat is browned on the outside and still slightly pink in the center (internal temperature of tenderloins should be 145°F on meat thermometer), 15 to 20 minutes.

3. To serve, thinly slice pork. Serve on rolls with any juices from broiling pan.

EACH SERVING: About 390 calories (30 percent calories from fat), 32g protein, 35g carbohydrate, 13g total fat (4g saturated), 1g fiber, 70mg cholesterol, 360mg sodium ◉ ♥

Chicken Quesadillas with Avocado Salsa

This tasty Tex-Mex meal calls for lower-fat tortillas and cheese. The splurge: avocado. Though avocados are high in fat, it's mostly the heart-healthy kind; plus, they contain a natural cholesterol reducer.

ACTIVE TIME: 20 minutes
TOTAL TIME: 40 minutes

MAKES: 4 quesadillas

2	teaspoons canola oil
1	green onion, thinly sliced
1	large lime
¼	teaspoon salt
⅛	teaspoon ground black pepper
1	pound skinless, boneless thin-sliced chicken breasts, cut into 1-inch-wide strips
4	burrito-size low-fat flour tortillas
¾	cup (3 ounces) reduced-fat (2%) shredded Mexican cheese blend
½	avocado, peeled, seeded, and cut into ½-inch pieces
¾	cup salsa

1. In nonstick 12-inch skillet, heat oil over medium heat 1 minute. Add green onion and cook about 6 minutes or until tender, stirring occasionally.

2. Meanwhile, from lime, grate 1 teaspoon peel and squeeze 2 tablespoons juice. Evenly season chicken strips on both sides with lime peel, salt, and pepper.

3. Add chicken to green onion in skillet; cook 10 minutes or until chicken is no longer pink inside. Transfer to bowl; stir in lime juice.

4. Evenly divide chicken mixture and cheese on half of each tortilla; fold tortillas over to make 4 quesadillas.

5. In same skillet, cook quesadillas over medium heat, in two batches, 8 minutes per batch or until browned on both sides and heated through. Cut each quesadilla into thirds. Stir avocado into salsa; serve alongside quesadillas.

EACH QUESADILLA: About 400 calories (29 percent calories from fat), 36g protein, 30g carbohydrate, 14g total fat (3g saturated), 10g fiber, 88mg cholesterol, 884mg sodium ♥

Turkey Fajitas

Swapping lean turkey for beef cuts 36 grams of fat, and adding antioxidant-rich sweet peppers boosts heart health. The result: delicioso!

ACTIVE TIME: 25 minutes
TOTAL TIME: 30 minutes
MAKES: 4 main-dish servings

olive oil nonstick cooking spray

2   medium red and/or yellow peppers (4 ounces each), cut into ¼-inch-wide slices

1   medium onion (6 to 8 ounces), cut lengthwise into ¼-inch-wide slices

1   pound turkey-breast cutlets, cut crosswise into ¼-inch-wide strips

3   tablespoons fajita cooking sauce

1   lime

¼   cup reduced-fat sour cream

8   fajita-size flour tortillas (96% fat-free)

1. Spray ridged grill pan with cooking spray; heat over medium-high heat until hot. Spray peppers and onion with cooking spray; place in pan. Cook, tossing often, 12 minutes or until vegetables are tender and grill marks appear.

2. Meanwhile, in bowl, toss turkey strips with cooking sauce; set aside. From lime, grate 1 teaspoon peel. Cut lime into wedges; stir peel into sour cream.

3. Transfer vegetables from grill pan to plate; cover with foil and keep warm.

4. Remove pan from heat; spray with cooking spray. Add turkey and cook over medium-high heat 6 to 7 minutes or until grill marks appear on the outside and turkey is no longer pink inside (cut into turkey to check), turning once. While turkey cooks, wrap tortillas in damp paper towels; microwave on High 1 minute.

5. Top tortillas with turkey and vegetables; fold over. Serve with lime sour cream and lime wedges on the side.

EACH SERVING: About 365 calories (13 percent calories from fat), 33g protein, 44g carbohydrate, 5g total fat (1g saturated), 6g fiber, 82mg cholesterol, 541mg sodium ✔ ✿

Turkey Burgers with Minted Yogurt Sauce

Pita patties, yogurt, feta, and mint add a taste of Greece to this flavorful but slimmed-down (and heart-healthy) summer favorite.

ACTIVE TIME: 20 minutes
TOTAL TIME: 35 minutes

MAKES: 4 burgers

½ cup plus 2 tablespoons plain fat-free yogurt

2 green onions, green and white parts separated and thinly sliced

½ cup packed fresh mint leaves, finely chopped

1 pound ground turkey breast meat

1½ ounces feta cheese, finely crumbled

1½ teaspoons ground coriander

⅛ teaspoon salt

⅛ teaspoon ground black pepper

2 whole-wheat pitas, cut in half

2 tomatoes, thinly sliced

1. Prepare outdoor grill for covered direct grilling over medium heat.

2. In small bowl, combine ½ cup yogurt, white parts of green onions, and half of chopped mint.

3. In large bowl, with hands, combine turkey, feta, coriander, salt, pepper, green parts of green onions, remaining mint, and remaining yogurt. Mix well, then form into 3½-inch round patties each ¾ inch thick.

4. Place turkey patties on hot grill grate; cover and cook 12 to 13 minutes or just until meat loses its pink color throughout, turning once. (Burgers should reach an internal temperature of 165°F.) During last 2 minutes of cooking, add pitas to grill. Cook 2 minutes or until warmed, turning once.

5. Open pitas. Divide burgers, tomato slices, and yogurt sauce among pitas.

EACH BURGER: About 250 calories (16 percent calories from fat), 35g protein, 20g carbohydrate, 5g total fat (2g saturated), 4g fiber, 55mg cholesterol, 412mg sodium ♥

Basic Chicken Burgers

If you're looking for a plain, straightforward burger, here it is. We also have suggestions for jazzing it up, so pick your favorite flavor: teriyaki, barbecue, or herb.

ACTIVE TIME: 20 minutes
TOTAL TIME: 35 minutes

MAKES: 4 burgers

1   pound ground chicken breast
1   medium carrot, peeled and grated (½ cup)
2   green onions, minced
1   garlic clove, crushed with garlic press
4   hamburger buns, split and toasted
sliced cucumber, lettuce leaves, and green onion (optional)

1. Prepare outdoor grill for direct grilling over medium heat.

2. In medium bowl, combine ground chicken, carrot, green onions, and garlic.

3. On waxed paper, shape chicken mixture into four 3 ½-inch round patties (mixture will be very soft and moist).

4. Place patties on hot grill rack over medium heat; if grill has widely spaced grates, place burgers on a perforated grill topper to keep them intact. Grill, turning once, until juices run clear when center of burger is pierced with tip of knife, about 12 minutes. (An instant-read meat thermometer inserted horizontally into center should register 170°F.)

5. Place burgers on toasted buns. Serve with cucumber slices, lettuce leaves, and green onions, if you like.

EACH BURGER: About 275 calories (16 percent calories from fat), 30g protein, 24g carbohydrate, 5g total fat (1g saturated), 2g fiber, 72mg cholesterol, 310mg sodium ♥

TERIYAKI CHICKEN BURGERS: Prepare Basic Burgers as directed, but add *2 tablespoons soy sauce, 1 tablespoon seasoned rice vinegar, 2 teaspoons grated, peeled fresh ginger,* and *2 teaspoons Asian sesame oil* to chicken mixture in step 2. (Ginger will change texture of meat over time; to prevent this, prepare mixture just before grilling.)

EACH TERIYAKI CHICKEN BURGER: About 305 calories (24 percent calories from fat), 31g protein, 26g carbohydrate, 8g total fat (2g saturated), 2g fiber, 72mg cholesterol, 940mg sodium

BARBECUE CHICKEN BURGERS: Prepare Basic Burgers as directed, but add *2 tablespoons chili sauce, 1 tablespoon light (mild) molasses, 2 teaspoons cayenne pepper sauce, 2 teaspoons Worcestershire sauce,* and *¼ teaspoon salt* to chicken mixture in step 2.

EACH BARBECUE CHICKEN BURGER: About 295 calories (15 percent calories from fat), 31g protein, 30g carbohydrate, 5g total fat (1g saturated), 2g fiber, 72mg cholesterol, 715mg sodium

HERB CHICKEN BURGERS: Prepare Basic Burgers as directed, but add *2 tablespoons finely chopped fresh dill, 1 tablespoon dried mint, 1 tablespoon fresh lemon juice, 1 teaspoon ground cumin, ½ teaspoon salt,* and *⅛ teaspoon cayenne (ground red) pepper* to chicken mixture in step 2.

EACH HERB CHICKEN BURGER: About 280 calories (16 percent calories from fat), 31g protein, 25g carbohydrate, 5g total fat (1g saturated), 2g fiber, 72mg cholesterol, 605mg sodium

THE GROUND ROUNDUP

Today's supermarkets offer so many choices in ground meat and poultry. Here's an overview to help you choose.

MEAT	FLAVOR PROFILE	APPROXIMATE NUTRITIONAL VALUES*	COOK-TO-INTERNAL TEMPERATURE
Ground beef, 90% lean	Juicy, rich, bold, robust, hearty	242 calories, 12g fat (5g saturated), 97mg cholesterol	160°F (medium doneness)
Ground lamb	Unique, full flavored, firm texture, aromatic	321 calories, 22g fat (9g saturated), 102mg cholesterol	160°F (medium doneness)
Ground pork	Delicate, mild alternative to beef and poultry	336 calories, 24g fat (9g saturated), 107mg cholesterol	160°F (medium doneness)
Ground chicken	Lean, light texture, tender, subtle flavor	172 calories, 11g fat (3g saturated), 65mg cholesterol	170°F (well-done)
Ground turkey	Moist, delicate flavor, denser texture than chicken	213 calories, 12g fat (3g saturated), 113mg cholesterol	170°F (well-done)

*Per 4-ounce cooked burger. Values vary among brands.

Bulgur Bean Burgers

Why buy expensive veggie burgers in the store when they're so easy to make at home? This version gets its "meaty" texture from a combination of bulgur and black beans. Add an extra helping of grains by serving them up on whole-wheat buns.

ACTIVE TIME: 20 minutes
TOTAL TIME: 30 minutes

MAKES: 4 burgers

1	cup water
¾	teaspoon salt
½	cup bulgur
1	can (15 to 19 ounces) reduced-sodium black beans, rinsed and drained
1	container (6 ounces) plain low-fat yogurt
¼	teaspoon ground allspice
¼	teaspoon ground cinnamon
¼	teaspoon ground cumin
¼	cup packed fresh mint leaves, chopped

nonstick cooking spray

⅛	teaspoon ground black pepper
½	cup grated Kirby (pickling) cucumber (1 small)
4	lettuce leaves
1	ripe tomato, sliced
4	whole-wheat hamburger buns

1. In 1-quart saucepan, heat water and ½ teaspoon salt to boiling over high heat. Stir in bulgur. Reduce heat to low; cover and simmer until water is absorbed, 10 to 12 minutes.

GET YOUR GRAINS: BULGUR

This nutritious staple of the Middle East is a form of whole-wheat kernel that has been parboiled and dried. Bulgur differs from cracked wheat in that it is precooked, so it is quick to prepare and can be served hot or cold. Not only does bulgur contain soluble fiber, it is also a low-fat source of protein, vitamins, and minerals.

2. Meanwhile, in large bowl, with potato masher or fork, mash beans with 2 tablespoons yogurt until almost smooth. Stir in bulgur, allspice, cinnamon, cumin, and half of mint until combined. With lightly floured hands, shape bean mixture into four 3-inch round patties. Coat both sides of each patty lightly with cooking spray.

3. Heat nonstick 12-inch skillet over medium heat until hot. Add burgers and cook until lightly browned and heated through, about 8 minutes, turning once.

4. While burgers are cooking, prepare yogurt sauce: In small bowl, combine remaining yogurt, remaining mint, remaining ¼ teaspoon salt, and pepper. Makes about 1¼ cups.

5. To serve, divide lettuce, tomato slices, and burgers among buns; top with some yogurt sauce. Serve with remaining yogurt sauce.

EACH BURGER: About 295 calories (10 percent calories from fat), 16g protein, 58g carbohydrate, 3g total fat (1g saturated), 13g fiber, 3mg cholesterol, 960mg sodium ◐ ❀

Quick Homemade Pizza Dough

Use this basic dough and method for the four pizza variations that follow—we've included whole-wheat flour for added fiber and flavor. If you're short on time, look to your neighborhood pizza shop. Many of them—and some supermarkets—will sell you raw, raised dough, ready to roll out and top.

TOTAL TIME: 20 minutes

MAKES: enough dough for 1 (15-inch) pizza

1¼ cups whole-wheat flour
1¼ cups all-purpose flour
1 package quick-rise yeast
1 teaspoon salt
1 cup very warm water (120 to 130°F)
2 teaspoons cornmeal

1. Sift together all-purpose and whole-wheat flours. In large bowl, combine 2 cups flour mixture, yeast, and salt. Stir in water until dough is blended and comes away from side of bowl.

2. Turn dough onto floured surface and knead until smooth and elastic, about 8 minutes, working in more flour mixture (about ½ cup) while kneading. Shape dough into a ball; cover with plastic wrap and let rest 10 minutes.

3. Grease 15-inch pizza pan; sprinkle with cornmeal. Pat dough onto bottom of pan, shaping dough into ½-inch-high rim at edge of pan.

Spinach and Feta Pizza

ACTIVE TIME: 20 minutes plus time to make dough
TOTAL TIME: 40 minutes

MAKES: 8 main-dish servings

Quick Homemade Pizza Dough (left)
1 teaspoon olive oil
1 small onion, chopped
1 teaspoon finely chopped garlic
1 package (10 ounces) frozen chopped spinach, thawed and squeezed dry (see Tip)
¼ teaspoon dried dill or mint
1 cup tomato sauce
2 ounces feta cheese, crumbled
12 Kalamata olives

1. Prepare Quick Homemade Pizza Dough. Preheat oven to 450°F.

2. In small skillet, heat oil over medium-high heat; add onion and cook 5 minutes. Stir in garlic, spinach, and dill; heat through.

3. Spread pizza dough with tomato sauce. Top with spinach mixture. Sprinkle with crumbled feta and olives. Bake pizza on bottom rack of oven until crust is browned, 20 to 25 minutes.

EACH SERVING: About 200 calories (20 percent calories from fat), 8g protein, 34g carbohydrate, 5g total fat (1g saturated), 4g fiber, 6mg cholesterol, 650mg sodium

TIP: *To quickly and easily dry frozen spinach, thaw it in the microwave just until the ice crystals melt, about 7 minutes on High, then place the defrosted spinach in a sieve over a bowl or in the sink. Press the spinach with the back of a spoon to drain off most of the excess water.*

Broccoli-Mushroom Pizza

ACTIVE TIME: 20 minutes plus time to make dough
TOTAL TIME: 40 minutes

MAKES: 8 main-dish servings

Quick Homemade Pizza Dough (left)

1 tablespoon light corn-oil spread (56% to 60% fat)

1 package (16 ounces) mushrooms, sliced

1 large garlic clove, crushed with garlic press

1 package (16 ounces) broccoli flowerets

¼ teaspoon salt

½ cup tomato sauce

½ cup packed basil leaves, chopped

1 cup shredded part-skim mozzarella or Monterey Jack cheese

1. Prepare Homemade Pizza Dough.

2. Preheat oven to 450°F.

3. In nonstick 12-inch skillet, melt corn-oil spread over medium-high heat. Add mushrooms and garlic; cook until mushrooms are golden. Meanwhile, in 10-inch skillet, heat *1 inch water* to boiling over high heat. Place steamer basket in skillet; add broccoli. Reduce heat to medium; cover and steam until tender.

4. Remove broccoli; add to mushrooms with salt and toss well to mix.

5. Spread dough with tomato sauce. Spoon broccoli mixture on top. Sprinkle with basil and cheese. Bake 20 to 25 minutes.

EACH SERVING: About 220 calories (16 percent calories from fat), 12g protein, 36g carbohydrate, 4g total fat (2g saturated), 4g fiber, 10mg cholesterol, 542mg sodium

EAT YOUR BROCCOLI

A super source of vitamins C and K (one cup cooked has more than a day's worth of each), broccoli also can help ward off cancer. Sulforaphane, one of its compounds, disarms cancer-causing substances. Try our Broccoli Gratin (page 244), which mashes broccoli with potatoes for a healthy twist on this decadent side dish.

Bistro Pizza

ACTIVE TIME: 20 minutes plus time to make dough
TOTAL TIME: 40 minutes

MAKES: 8 main-dish servings

Quick Homemade Pizza Dough (page 116)
1   pound thin asparagus, trimmed and cut into 2-inch pieces
1   teaspoon olive oil
¼   teaspoon salt
1   medium yellow pepper, cut into thin strips
1   cup part-skim ricotta cheese
2   tablespoons grated Parmesan cheese
¼   teaspoon coarsely ground black pepper

1. Prepare Quick Homemade Pizza Dough. Preheat oven to 450°F.

2. In small bowl, toss asparagus with oil and salt. Top pizza dough with pepper strips and asparagus. Dollop with teaspoons of ricotta; sprinkle with Parmesan and black pepper.

3. Bake pizza on bottom rack of oven until crust is browned, 20 to 25 minutes.

EACH SERVING: About 205 calories (18 percent calories from fat), 10g protein, 33g carbohydrate, 4g total fat (2g saturated), 4g fiber, 11mg cholesterol, 427mg sodium ♥

Garden Pizza

ACTIVE TIME: 20 minutes plus time to make dough
TOTAL TIME: 40 minutes

MAKES: 8 main-dish servings

Quick Homemade Pizza Dough (page 116)
1   tablespoon vegetable oil
1   small zucchini (6 ounces) cut into ¼-inch pieces
1   small yellow straightneck squash (6 ounces), cut into ¼-inch pieces
1   large tomato, seeded and cut into ¼-inch pieces
½   teaspoon dried oregano
¼   teaspoon ground black pepper
¼   teaspoon salt
1   cup (4 ounces) shredded part-skim mozzarella cheese

1. Prepare Quick Homemade Pizza Dough. Preheat oven to 450°F.

2. In 12-inch skillet, heat oil over medium-high heat. Add zucchini and squash and cook until tender. Stir in tomato, oregano, pepper, and salt.

3. Top pizza dough with squash mixture; sprinkle evenly with shredded mozzarella cheese. Bake pizza on bottom rack of oven until crust is golden and crisp, 20 to 25 minutes.

EACH SERVING: About 205 calories (22 percent calories from fat), 9g protein, 32g carbohydrate, 5g total fat (1g saturated), 4g fiber, 0mg cholesterol, 427mg sodium ♥

Grilled Whole-Wheat Veggie Pizza

Everyone's favorite takeout gets a low-cal, high-fiber makeover with a heap of veggies—sweetened by a turn on the grill—a whole-wheat crust, and a sprinkle of cheese.

ACTIVE TIME: 25 minutes
TOTAL TIME: 30 minutes

MAKES: 4 main-dish servings

2	medium portobello mushroom caps, sliced
1	small red onion (4 to 6 ounces), sliced into rounds
1	small yellow summer squash, sliced
1	tablespoon olive oil
¼	teaspoon salt
¼	teaspoon pepper
1	pound whole-wheat pizza dough (see Tip)
2	plum tomatoes, thinly sliced
½	cup (2 ounces) shredded smoked mozzarella
¼	cup packed fresh basil leaves, sliced

1. Preheat grill over medium heat. Brush mushrooms, onion, and squash with oil; sprinkle with salt and pepper.

2. Grill vegetables, covered, 6 minutes or until tender and browned, turning once. Remove from grill and separate onion rings; set aside. Reduce heat on grill to medium-low.

3. Cover large cookie sheet with foil; spray with cooking spray. Stretch dough into 10" by 14" rectangle. Place on cookie sheet.

4. Lift dough and foil; place, dough side down, on grill, gently peeling off foil. Cover; cook 3 minutes or until bottom is crisp. Turn crust over. Quickly top with tomatoes, vegetables, and cheese. Cover; cook 2 minutes longer or until bottom is crisp. Slide onto cutting board; garnish with basil.

EACH SERVING: About 375 calories (26 percent calories from fat), 13g protein, 58g carbohydrate, 10g total fat (2g saturated), 9g fiber, 11mg cholesterol, 695mg sodium

TIP: *You can purchase whole-wheat dough, ready to roll out and bake, at a neighborhood pizza shop and some supermarkets.*

5

Fish & Shellfish

If you're eating light and healthy, fish and shellfish should make regular appearances on your dinner plate. Seafood is low in fat and a rich source of protein, vitamins, and minerals. And oily fish, such as salmon and tuna, are high in omega-3 fatty acids, which can lower blood cholesterol levels. A couple nights a week, try replacing chicken breasts or red meat with salmon, cod, or shrimp—and you and your family will be on your way to a healthier, more varied diet.

If you order fish at restaurants but rarely prepare it at home, let our simple, flavorful recipes lead the way. Keep frozen shrimp in the freezer and you can cook up our shrimp kabobs, a shrimp and veggie risotto, or a handful of tasty stir-fries in a jiffy. If your kids like fish sticks, then they'll love our island-spiced version rolled in panko crumbs and baked in the oven until crisp and ready for dipping in a low-fat lime mayo.

Dinners like our Sicilian-style swordfish with pasta and pan-grilled catfish with salsa can be quickly prepared in a pan, while our Asian-style flounder is wrapped in parchment paper and slow-baked in the oven. Our pan-roasted cod sits on a bed of red cabbage and apples, while our pan-seared scallops top a pile of lemony couscous.

Our recipes use readily available options, but if you can't locate the fish or shellfish called for in a recipe, just ask your fishmonger for the best substitution. Many fish can be easily swapped for other varieties with equally good results.

Caramelized Chili Shrimp (recipe page 128)

Mussels with Tomatoes and White Wine

To enjoy every last drop, serve this saucy dish with crusty bread—or a spoon.

ACTIVE TIME: 20 minutes
TOTAL TIME: 45 minutes
MAKES: 8 first-course or 4 main-dish servings

1	tablespoon olive or vegetable oil
1	small onion, chopped
2	garlic cloves, finely chopped
¼	teaspoon crushed red pepper
1	can (14 to 16 ounces) whole tomatoes
¾	cup dry white wine
4	pounds large mussels, scrubbed and debearded (see Tip)
2	tablespoons chopped fresh parsley

1. In nonreactive 5-quart Dutch oven, heat oil over medium heat. Add onion and cook until tender and golden, 6 to 8 minutes. Add garlic and crushed red pepper and cook 30 seconds longer. Stir in tomatoes with their juice and wine, breaking up tomatoes with side of spoon. Heat to boiling; boil 3 minutes.

2. Add mussels; heat to boiling. Reduce heat; cover and simmer until mussels open, about 5 minutes, transferring mussels to large bowl as they open. Discard any mussels that have not opened after 5 minutes. Pour tomato sauce over mussels and sprinkle with parsley.

EACH FIRST-COURSE SERVING: About 105 calories (25 percent calories from fat), 9g protein, 6g carbohydrate, 3g total fat (1g saturated), 1g fiber, 18mg cholesterol, 277mg sodium ♥

TIP: *Scrub mussels well under cold running water. To debeard, grasp the hairlike beard firmly with your thumb and forefinger and pull it away, or scrape it off with a knife. (Cultivated mussels usually do not have beards.)*

MOULES À LA MARINIÈRE: Prepare Mussels with Tomatoes and White Wine as directed, but substitute *butter* for olive oil and *⅓ cup chopped shallots* for onion. Omit crushed red pepper and tomatoes; use *1 ½ cups dry white wine.*

Crab Boil

A big pot of spiced boiled crabs, a Chesapeake Bay tradition, is a delicious but messy affair. Cover the table with newspaper and have lots of big napkins on hand. Serve with coleslaw and rolls. (If you want to cook crab so you can pick out the meat for use in another recipe, omit the crab boil seasoning and red pepper.)

ACTIVE TIME: 15 minutes
TOTAL TIME: 35 minutes

MAKES: 4 main-dish servings

2	medium onions, coarsely chopped
1	carrot, peeled and coarsely chopped
1	stalk celery, coarsely chopped
1	lemon, sliced
½	cup crab boil seasoning (optional)
1	tablespoon crushed red pepper (optional)
1	tablespoon salt
1	gallon water
1	can (12 ounces) beer
2	dozen live hard-shell blue crabs, rinsed (see Tip)

1. In 12-quart stockpot, combine onions, carrot, celery, lemon, crab boil seasoning and crushed red pepper if using, salt, water, and beer. Heat to boiling over high heat; cook 15 minutes.

2. Using tongs, transfer crabs to stockpot. Cover and heat to boiling; boil 5 minutes (crabs will turn red). With tongs, transfer crabs to colander to drain, then place on warm platter.

3. To eat crab, twist off claws and legs, then crack shell to remove meat. Break off flat pointed apron from underside of crab; remove top shell. Discard feathery gills. With kitchen shears or hands, break body in half down center. With fingers or lobster pick, remove meat.

EACH SERVING: About 150 calories (10 percent calories from fat), 30g protein, 0g carbohydrate, 2g total fat (0g saturated), 0g fiber, 144mg cholesterol, 850mg sodium

TIP: It's best to cook crabs the day they are purchased, but they can be stored up to two days. Place the crabs in a large shallow bowl, then nestle the bowl in a larger bowl of ice. Cover the crabs with a damp kitchen towel. Refrigerate, replacing the ice as needed.

Shrimp Kabobs with Asian BBQ Sauce

Fresh ginger and five-spice powder create a delicious sauce for these succulent shrimp kabobs. Serve on a bed of romaine with extra sauce for dipping.

ACTIVE TIME: 15 minutes
TOTAL TIME: 20 minutes
MAKES: 4 main-dish servings

romaine lettuce leaves

1¼ pounds large shrimp, shelled and deveined, with tail part of shell left on, if you like

4 (10- to 12-inch) wooden skewers

⅓ cup hoisin sauce

3 tablespoons ketchup

1½ teaspoons grated, peeled fresh ginger

¼ teaspoon Chinese five-spice powder

2 tablespoons rice vinegar

2 tablespoons water

1. Soak skewers in hot water at least 20 minutes. Lightly grease grill rack. Prepare outdoor grill for direct grilling over medium heat.

2. Arrange romaine on platter and set aside. Thread shrimp on skewers.

3. In small bowl, stir hoisin sauce, ketchup, ginger, five-spice powder, and 1 tablespoon vinegar to make Asian Barbecue Sauce. Remove ¼ cup barbecue sauce to ramekin; stir in water and remaining 1 tablespoon vinegar and reserve to use as dipping sauce.

4. Brush shrimp with some barbecue sauce from bowl. Place shrimp on hot grill rack over medium heat and cook 2 minutes. Brush with more sauce; turn, brush with remaining sauce, and grill until shrimp turn opaque throughout, 1 to 2 minutes longer.

5. Serve shrimp on skewers over romaine with reserved dipping sauce.

EACH SERVING: About 185 calories (14 percent calories from fat), 25g protein, 13g carbohydrate, 3g total fat (1g saturated), 1g fiber, 175mg cholesterol, 540mg sodium

Shrimp and Asparagus Stir-Fry

Flavored with ginger, soy, and sesame, this entreé is rich in vitamins and minerals (thanks to brown rice and asparagus).

ACTIVE TIME: 15 minutes
TOTAL TIME: 30 minutes

MAKES: 4 main-dish servings

1   cup quick-cooking (10-minute) brown rice

3   teaspoons Asian sesame oil

1½   pounds asparagus, trimmed and cut into 1-inch pieces

1   pound medium shrimp, shelled and deveined

1   tablespoon grated, peeled fresh ginger

2   tablespoons reduced-sodium soy sauce

2   tablespoons fresh lime juice

¼   cup loosely packed fresh basil leaves, thinly sliced

1. Cook rice as label directs.

2. Meanwhile, in nonstick 12-inch skillet, heat 2 teaspoons sesame oil over medium heat 1 minute. Add asparagus and cook 7 to 8 minutes or until asparagus is tender-crisp, stirring occasionally. Add shrimp and ginger; cook 5 to 6 minutes or until shrimp are opaque throughout, stirring occasionally.

3. Stir in soy sauce, lime juice, basil, and remaining 1 teaspoon sesame oil; remove from heat. Serve over rice.

EACH SERVING: About 265 calories (24 percent calories from fat), 29g protein, 22g carbohydrate, 7g total fat (1g saturated), 2g fiber, 172mg cholesterol, 455mg sodium

FROZEN SHRIMP TO THE RESCUE

Shrimp, with just fewer than 2 grams of fat in a 4-ounce serving, should be a savvy dieter's go-to seafood. Although fresh shrimp can be expensive, frozen shrimp, available at wholesale food clubs and larger supermarkets, is a bargain. Because it is flash-frozen for easy transport, the flavor and texture are preserved. Keep some on hand in the freezer and it will be a snap to whip up low-fat stir-fries, pastas, and main-dish salads. The shrimp is sold individually frozen in bags or in a block. To defrost, put the individually frozen shrimp in a colander and place under cold running water until thawed. For block-frozen shrimp, place under cold running water and pull off the amount of shrimp you need as they thaw; return the remaining block of shrimp to the freezer immediately.

Spring Vegetable Risotto with Shrimp

Made in the microwave, this creamy dish—full of fiber, protein, and rich Parmesan flavor—is as healthy as it is easy.

ACTIVE TIME: 10 minutes
TOTAL TIME: 35 minutes

MAKES: 10 cups or 6 main-dish servings

1	carton (32 ounces) chicken broth (4 cups)
1¼	cups water
½	cup dry white wine
8	ounces asparagus, cut into 1-inch pieces
1	tablespoon olive oil
1	small onion (4 to 6 ounces), finely chopped
1	carrot, peeled and finely chopped
2	cups Arborio or Carnaroli rice (short-grain Italian rice)
1	pound large shrimp, shelled and deveined
1	cup frozen peas
2	tablespoons fresh lemon juice
1	tablespoon chopped fresh parsley or basil leaves
¼	teaspoon salt
¼	teaspoon ground black pepper

1. In 2-quart saucepan, heat broth, water, and wine to boiling over high heat. When boiling, add asparagus and cook 2 minutes. With slotted spoon, remove asparagus to small bowl; set aside.

2. Meanwhile, in microwave-safe 4-quart bowl or casserole, combine oil, onion, and carrot. Cook, uncovered, in microwave on High 3 minutes or until vegetables begin to soften. Add rice and stir to coat with oil; cook, uncovered, on High 1 minute.

3. Stir hot broth mixture into rice mixture. Cover bowl with vented plastic wrap, and cook in microwave on Medium 15 minutes or until most of liquid is absorbed and rice is tender but still firm, stirring halfway through cooking.

4. Add shrimp, frozen peas, and cooked asparagus; cover and cook in microwave on High 3 to 4 minutes longer or just until shrimp lose their pink color throughout. Do not overcook; mixture will look loose and soupy but will soon thicken to the proper creamy consistency.

5. Stir in lemon juice, parsley, salt, and pepper.

EACH SERVING: About 425 calories (9 percent calories from fat), 24g protein, 67g carbohydrate, 4g total fat (1g saturated), 3g fiber, 115mg cholesterol, 545mg sodium

Caramelized Chile Shrimp

Thanks to a trio of insta-ingredients—preshelled shrimp, thin vermicelli, and bagged broccoli—this streamlined seafood stir-fry is ideal on time-is-tight nights. For photo, see page 120.

ACTIVE TIME: 15 minutes
TOTAL TIME: 25 minutes

MAKES: 4 main-dish servings

6	ounces rice stick noodles (rice vermicelli; see page 89)
1	pound broccoli florets
1	green onion, finely chopped
¼	teaspoon salt
3	tablespoons sugar
1	tablespoon water
1	tablespoon vegetable oil
3	garlic cloves, very thinly sliced
¼	teaspoon crushed red pepper
1	tablespoon reduced-sodium Asian fish sauce (see Tip, page 88)
1	pound jumbo shrimp, shelled and deveined
¼	cup packed fresh cilantro leaves
¼	teaspoon ground black pepper

1. In heavy 12-inch skillet, heat *1 inch water* to boiling over high heat. Add noodles and cook 1 to 2 minutes or until just tender. With tongs, transfer noodles to fine-mesh sieve. Rinse under cold water and drain.

2. When water in skillet returns to boiling, add broccoli. Cook 3 minutes or until tender-crisp; drain and transfer to large bowl. Toss with green onion and salt. Wipe skillet dry.

3. In same skillet, cook sugar and water over medium-high (stirring just until sugar dissolves), 3 to 4 minutes or until mixture turns dark amber. Stir in oil, garlic, and red pepper. Cook 10 seconds, then stir in fish sauce and shrimp.

4. Cook 2 to 3 minutes or until shrimp just turn opaque throughout, stirring frequently. Remove from heat, and stir in cilantro and black pepper.

5. Evenly divide noodles and broccoli among four dinner plates. Spoon shrimp with chile sauce on top of noodles.

EACH SERVING: About 340 calories (13 percent calories from fat), 22g protein, 53g carbohydrate, 5g total fat (1g saturated), 4g fiber, 168mg cholesterol, 600mg sodium

Pan-Seared Scallops with Lemon Couscous

Lemony couscous and peppery arugula create a flavorful bed for these succulent scallops.

ACTIVE TIME: 20 minutes
TOTAL TIME: 45 minutes
MAKES: 6 main-dish servings

1	large red pepper
1	onion
12	ounces medium mushrooms
1	pound sea scallops
4	teaspoons olive oil or vegetable oil
1	lemon
1½	cups water
1	cup couscous (Moroccan pasta)
¾	teaspoon salt
1	package (8 ounces) frozen sugar snap peas
2	tablespoons soy sauce
2	bunches arugula (8 ounces) stems trimmed

1. Thinly slice red pepper and onion. Cut each mushroom into quarters. Rinse scallops under cold running water to remove sand from crevices. Pat scallops dry with paper towels.

2. In nonstick 12-inch skillet over medium-high heat, heat 2 teaspoons oil and cook red pepper and onion until golden brown. Remove mixture to plate.

3. In same skillet, heat 1 teaspoon oil; cook mushrooms until golden brown. Remove mushrooms to plate with red-pepper mixture.

4. Meanwhile, from lemon, grate ½ teaspoon peel and squeeze 1½ teaspoons juice. In 2-quart saucepan over high heat, heat lemon juice and water to boiling. Stir in couscous and salt. Cover saucepan and remove from heat. Let stand 5 minutes; stir in lemon peel. Keep warm.

5. Prepare frozen sugar snap peas as label directs; drain.

6. In same skillet over medium-high heat, heat remaining 1 teaspoon oil and cook scallops until opaque throughout, stirring occasionally, 3 to 4 minutes. Return vegetable mixture to skillet with scallops; stir in soy sauce. Cook mixture over medium-high heat until heated through; stir in snap peas.

7. Arrange arugula on plates. Top with couscous and scallop mixture.

EACH SERVING: About 265 calories (14 percent calories from fat), 20g protein, 36g carbohydrate, 4g total fat (1g saturated), 12g fiber, 25mg cholesterol, 770mg sodium ☻

Grilled Fish Tacos

Coated with a bold, Baja-style rub of cayenne and oregano and then char-crusted on the grill, the tilapia in these taqueria-worthy tacos tastes anything but fishy. A from-scratch salsa with corn and avocado adds to the meal's authenticity.

ACTIVE TIME: 15 minutes
TOTAL TIME: 20 minutes
MAKES: 4 main-dish servings

1	large lemon
2½	teaspoon vegetable oil
½	teaspoon plus pinch salt
2	ears corn, husked
1	avocado, cut in half and pitted
3	garlic cloves, crushed with press
½	teaspoon dried oregano
¼	teaspoon cayenne (ground red) pepper
1	pound skinless tilapia fillets (see Tip)
12	corn tortillas
1	large ripe tomato, finely chopped

fresh cilantro leaves and lime wedges,
    for serving

1. Prepare outdoor grill for direct grilling over medium-high heat. From lemon, grate 2 teaspoons peel and squeeze 2 tablespoons juice.

2. Use ½ teaspoon oil and pinch salt to rub all over corn and cut sides of avocado; set aside on a plate. On another plate, combine garlic, oregano, cayenne, lemon peel, ¼ teaspoon salt, and remaining 2 teaspoons oil. Place fish on mixture and rub all over to coat.

3. Place fish, corn, and avocado, cut sides down, on hot grill grate. Cook fish 3 to 4 minutes or until opaque throughout, turning over once; cook vegetables 5 minutes or until charred, turning occasionally.

4. Transfer fish, corn, and avocado to cutting board. Let cool while warming tortillas: Place tortillas on grill in single layer and cook 1 minute, turning once. Stack on large sheet of foil and wrap tightly.

5. Cut kernels from corncobs. Peel and finely chop avocado. Break fish into large chunks. In large bowl, mix together tomato, corn, avocado, lemon juice, and remaining ¼ teaspoon salt. Divide fish and tomato mixture among tortillas and serve with cilantro and lime wedges.

EACH SERVING: About 420 calories (28 percent calories from fat), 31g protein, 49g carbohydrate, 13g total fat (2g saturated), 9g fiber, 52mg cholesterol, 425mg sodium ⬤ ♥ ✿

TIP: *Flounder, catfish, or any mild white fish would be a good substitute for the tilapia. Grill fish fillets only 8 to 10 minutes per inch of thickness.*

Greek-Style Tilapia

This healthy Mediterranean fish dish is ready in 30 minutes.

ACTIVE TIME: 20 minutes
TOTAL TIME: 30 minutes

MAKES: 4 main-dish servings

2	lemons
1½	pounds tilapia fillets
1	tablespoon fresh oregano leaves, chopped, plus sprigs for garnish
¼	teaspoon salt
¼	teaspoon ground black pepper
1	pint grape tomatoes, cut lengthwise in half
8	ounces orzo

1. Preheat oven to 400°F. From lemons, grate ½ teaspoon peel and squeeze ¼ cup juice.

2. In 13″ by 9″ glass or ceramic baking dish, arrange tilapia fillets. Evenly sprinkle fillets with lemon juice and peel, chopped oregano, salt, and pepper. Add tomatoes to baking dish around tilapia; cover with foil and roast 16 to 18 minutes or until tilapia is opaque throughout and tomatoes are tender.

3. Meanwhile, heat covered 4-quart saucepan of salted *water* to boiling over high heat. Add orzo and cook as label directs. Drain well.

4. Serve tilapia, tomatoes, and orzo with juices from baking dish.

EACH SERVING: About 395 calories (14 percent calories from fat), 36g protein, 50g carbohydrate, 6g total fat (0g saturated), 2g fiber, 0mg cholesterol, 310mg sodium ♥ ♥

Catfish with Chipotle Salsa over Polenta

Polenta, the Italian cousin of Southern grits, is made from finely ground yellow cornmeal. We make this side dish with 1 percent milk and chicken broth to keep it low in fat.

ACTIVE TIME: 30 minutes
TOTAL TIME: 50 minutes
MAKES: 4 main-dish servings

4	large plum tomatoes (about 1 pound), each cut lengthwise in half
1	small red onion, cut crosswise into ½-inch-thick rings
	nonstick cooking spray
4	catfish fillets (about 6 ounces each)
¾	teaspoon chipotle chile powder
¾	teaspoon salt
2	cups low-fat (1%) milk
1	can (14 to 14½ ounces) reduced-sodium chicken broth (1¾ cups)
1	cup water
¾	cup instant polenta
1	cup fresh corn kernels (from 2 ears corn) or 1 cup frozen (thawed) corn kernels
2	teaspoons fresh lime juice

1. Preheat large ridged grill pan over medium-high heat. On sheet of waxed paper, place tomato halves and onion slices. Spray vegetables on both sides with nonstick cooking spray. Place tomatoes and onion on grill pan and cook 10 minutes or until lightly browned and softened, turning over once. Transfer vegetables to cutting board.

2. While tomatoes and onion are cooking, place catfish fillets on same waxed paper. Sprinkle with ½ teaspoon chipotle chile powder and ¼ teaspoon salt to season both sides, then spray both sides with nonstick cooking spray.

3. Place catfish on grill pan over medium-high heat; cook 7 to 8 minutes or just until it turns opaque throughout, turning over once.

4. While catfish is cooking, prepare polenta: In 3-quart saucepan, combine milk, broth, water, and ¼ teaspoon salt; cover and heat to boiling over high heat. Remove cover; slowly whisk in polenta and cook until mixture begins to thicken, stirring constantly. Reduce heat to low; cover saucepan and simmer 5 minutes, stirring occasionally. Stir in corn. Remove saucepan from heat.

5. Coarsely chop grilled tomatoes and onion; transfer, with any juices, to medium bowl. Stir in lime juice and remaining ¼ teaspoon each chipotle chile powder and salt. Makes about 1¾ cups salsa.

6. To serve, divide polenta among four dinner plates; top with grilled catfish and tomato-chipotle salsa.

EACH SERVING: About 410 calories (26 percent calories from fat), 32g protein, 43g carbohydrate, 12g total fat (3g saturated), 3g fiber, 90mg cholesterol, 870mg sodium

Island-Spiced Fish Sticks

Turn cod fillets into spicy fish sticks, using thyme, allspice, a jalapeño chile pepper, and a coating of panko bread crumbs. Bake them in the oven for a low-fat finish.

ACTIVE TIME: 20 minutes
TOTAL TIME: 30 minutes plus chilling
MAKES: 4 main-dish servings

nonstick olive oil cooking spray

2   limes
2   green onions, light and dark green parts only
¼   cup packed fresh parsley leaves
½   jalapeño chile, seeds removed
1   teaspoon fresh thyme leaves
¼   teaspoon ground allspice
½   teaspoon plus ⅛ teaspoon salt
1   large egg white
1   pound skinless cod fillet
¾   cup panko (Japanese-style bread crumbs)
2   tablespoons light mayonnaise
2   tablespoons reduced-fat sour cream
1   bag (5 to 6 ounces) baby spinach

1. Lightly coat cookie sheet with nonstick cooking spray. From 1 lime, grate 1 teaspoon peel and squeeze 2 teaspoons juice. In small bowl, place juice and ½ teaspoon peel. Finely chop 1 tablespoon green onion and add to bowl with lime juice; set aside. Cut remaining green onions into large pieces.

2. In food processor with knife blade attached, place parsley, jalapeño, thyme, allspice, green onion pieces, ½ teaspoon salt, and remaining ½ teaspoon lime peel. Pulse until finely chopped.

3. In medium bowl, lightly beat egg white; set aside. Remove and discard any bones from cod and cut into 2-inch chunks. Place in food processor with green onion mixture; pulse just until cod is coarsely chopped. Transfer cod mixture and 2 tablespoons panko to bowl with egg white; stir until well combined.

4. On large sheet of waxed paper, place remaining panko. With measuring cup, scoop out heaping ¼ cup cod mixture (mixture will be soft); shape by hand into 3″ by 1½″ stick (about 1 inch thick), then place in panko, patting gently to cover all sides. Place fish stick on prepared cookie sheet. Repeat, forming 8 fish sticks in all. Cover loosely; refrigerate at least 30 minutes or up to 1 day.

5. Meanwhile, preheat oven to 450°F. Into bowl with lime juice mixture, stir mayonnaise, sour cream, and remaining ⅛ teaspoon salt until well blended. If not using right away, cover and refrigerate up to 1 day. Makes about ⅓ cup dipping sauce.

6. Lightly spray fish with cooking spray; bake 10 to 13 minutes or until opaque throughout. Cut remaining lime into wedges. Arrange spinach on plates; top with fish. Serve with sauce and lime wedges on the side.

EACH SERVING: About 190 calories (24 percent calories from fat), 24g protein, 12g carbohydrate, 5g total fat (1g saturated), 5g fiber, 54mg cholesterol, 585mg sodium 🌿 🍽

Snapper Livornese

Vibrant with olives, capers, and basil, this preparation works beautifully with any lean white fish.

ACTIVE TIME: 10 minutes
TOTAL TIME: 30 minutes

MAKES: 4 main-dish servings

1	tablespoon olive oil
1	garlic clove, finely chopped
1	can (14½ ounces) diced tomatoes
⅛	teaspoon crushed red pepper
4	red snapper or flounder fillets (6 ounces each)
⅛	teaspoon salt
½	cup fresh basil leaves, thinly sliced
¼	cup Kalamata or Gaeta olives, pitted and coarsely chopped
2	teaspoons capers, drained

1. In nonstick 12-inch skillet, heat oil over medium heat until hot. Add garlic and cook 1 minute, stirring. Stir in tomatoes with their juice and crushed red pepper; heat to boiling over medium-high heat. Reduce heat to low and simmer, uncovered, 8 to 10 minutes or until mixture thickens slightly.

2. Meanwhile, with tweezers, remove any bones from snapper fillets.

3. Place fillets, skin side down, in tomato mixture in skillet; sprinkle with salt. Cover and cook 8 to 10 minutes or just until fish turns opaque throughout.

4. With wide slotted spatula, transfer snapper to warm platter. Stir basil, olives, and capers into tomato mixture; spoon over snapper.

EACH SERVING: About 250 calories (29 percent calories from fat), 36g protein, 6g carbohydrate, 8g total fat (1g saturated), 1g fiber, 63mg cholesterol, 571mg sodium

THE DRILL ON OIL

Wondering which oil to use tonight? Olive oil is still a winner. It has big flavor, which means you can use less for more taste with fewer calories. And since olive oil is predominantly monounsaturated fat, it's heart-healthy as well. When you're looking for more neutral-tasting oil at a reasonable price, canola oil is a standout. Not only is it rich in monounsaturated fat, it contains the plant version of an omega-3 fatty acid. Specialty oils—like grape seed, sesame, and walnut—are healthful but expensive, so use them in small quantities for an epicurean touch.

Pan-Roasted Cod on Cabbage and Apples

Light and easy to prepare, this fish dinner showcases the cool-weather flavors of tart apple and caraway-scented sautéed cabbage.

ACTIVE TIME: 12 minutes
TOTAL TIME: 20 minutes

MAKES: 4 main-dish servings

2	tablespoons butter or margarine
1	small head red cabbage (1¼ pounds), cored and thinly sliced
1	pound (2 to 3 medium) Granny Smith or Gala apples, cored and cut into ½-inch chunks
2	tablespoons water
1	tablespoon cider vinegar
½	teaspoon caraway seeds
½	teaspoon salt
¼	teaspoon coarsely ground black pepper
4	cod or scrod fillets (6 ounces each)

1. In deep nonstick 12-inch skillet, melt butter over medium-high heat. Stir in cabbage, apples, water, vinegar, caraway seeds, and ¼ teaspoon salt. Reduce heat to medium; cover skillet and cook cabbage mixture 8 minutes or until cabbage begins to wilt, stirring occasionally.

2. Top cabbage mixture with cod, folding thin tail end under for even cooking. Sprinkle cod with remaining ¼ teaspoon salt and pepper. Cover skillet and cook about 10 minutes or until cod turns opaque throughout.

EACH SERVING: About 290 calories (25 percent calories from fat), 32g protein, 25g carbohydrate, 8g total fat (1g saturated), 5g fiber, 73mg cholesterol, 470mg sodium ● ♥ ●

Roasted Halibut with Fennel and Potatoes

Popular brands of anise-flavored liqueur include Pernod and Ricard. A jigger of these spirits subtly enhances the natural licorice flavor found in fennel.

ACTIVE TIME: 15 minutes
TOTAL TIME: 1 hour

MAKES: 4 main-dish servings

1	large leek
1	pound Yukon Gold potatoes, unpeeled and thinly sliced
1	medium bulb fennel, cored and thinly sliced, or 4 stalks celery, thinly sliced
1	tablespoon plus 1 teaspoon extra-virgin olive oil
¾	teaspoon salt
⅜	teaspoon ground black pepper
4	pieces skinless halibut fillet (6 ounces each)
2	tablespoons anise-flavored liqueur or white wine
1	teaspoon fennel seeds
1	lemon, thinly sliced
	fennel fronds (optional)

1. Cut off roots and trim dark-green top from leek. Discard any tough outer leaves. Thinly slice leek. Rinse leek thoroughly in bowl of cold water; swish to remove any sand. With hands, transfer leek to colander, leaving sand in bottom of bowl. Drain well.

2. Preheat oven to 425°F. Spray 13" by 9" glass baking dish with nonstick cooking spray. To baking dish, add leek, potatoes, fennel, 1 tablespoon oil, ½ teaspoon salt, and ¼ teaspoon pepper; toss to coat, then spread evenly. Roast vegetables 35 minutes or until tender, stirring once halfway through roasting.

3. Remove baking dish from oven. Place halibut on vegetables; drizzle with liqueur and remaining 1 teaspoon oil. Sprinkle with fennel seeds, ¼ teaspoon salt, and ⅛ teaspoon pepper. Place lemon slices on halibut; return dish to oven and roast 10 to 12 minutes or just until halibut turns opaque in center. To serve, sprinkle with fennel fronds, if using.

EACH SERVING: About 365 calories (22 percent calories from fat), 39g protein, 33g carbohydrate, 9g total fat (1g saturated), 6g fiber, 54mg cholesterol, 570mg sodium ❂

Asian-Style Flounder Baked in Parchment

Baking in parchment packets is a simple nonfat way to seal in the juices and flavor of delicate fish. You may substitute aluminum foil for the parchment paper.

TOTAL TIME: 25 minutes

MAKES: 4 main-dish servings

2	large green onions
2	tablespoons soy sauce
2	tablespoons seasoned rice vinegar
4	flounder fillets (6 ounces each)
4	sheets cooking parchment or foil (12" by 16" each, folded in half to 12" by 8")
2	teaspoons grated, peeled fresh ginger

1. Preheat oven to 425°F. Cut green onion tops into 2-inch by 1/4-inch strips; reserve for garnish. Thinly slice white part of green onions.

2. In cup, combine soy sauce and vinegar.

3. Place 1 flounder fillet on one side of each opened parchment sheet. Sprinkle with ginger and sliced green onions; drizzle with soy mixture. Fold parchment over fish; beginning at a corner where parchment is folded, make 1/2-inch-wide folds, overlapping previous folds, until packet is completely sealed. Packet will resemble half circle. Place packets in jelly-roll pan. Bake 8 minutes (packets will puff up and brown).

4. To serve, cut packets open and garnish fish with reserved green-onion strips.

EACH SERVING: About 170 calories (11 percent calories from fat), 33g protein, 3g carbohydrate, 2g total fat (0g saturated), 0g fiber, 82mg cholesterol, 802mg sodium ☺

Pasta with Tuna Puttanesca

We've used tuna instead of anchovies in this tasty no-cook twist on traditional puttanesca sauce. For best flavor use extra-virgin olive oil.

ACTIVE TIME: 5 minutes
TOTAL TIME: 15 minutes

MAKES: 6 main-dish servings

1	package (16 ounces) fusilli or corkscrew pasta
3	tablespoons capers, drained and chopped
3	tablespoons minced shallot
2	tablespoons red wine vinegar
1	tablespoon olive oil
1/2	teaspoon grated lemon peel
1/2	teaspoon salt
1/4	teaspoon coarsely ground black pepper
1	can (6 ounces) light tuna in olive oil
2	medium bunches watercress, tough stems removed
1/2	cup loosely packed fresh basil leaves, chopped

1. In large saucepot, cook pasta as label directs.

2. Meanwhile, in a large bowl, with fork, stir capers, shallot, vinegar, oil, lemon peel, salt, and pepper until well mixed. Add undrained tuna and watercress; toss well.

3. When pasta has reached desired doneness, remove *1/2 cup pasta cooking water*. Drain pasta and return to saucepot. Add tuna mixture, reserved cooking water, and basil; toss well.

EACH SERVING: About 375 calories (19 percent calories from fat), 17g protein, 58g carbohydrate, 8g total fat (1g saturated), 3g fiber, 4mg cholesterol, 540mg sodium ☺

Tuna au Poivre with Lemon-Caper Lentils

Lean tuna replaces fattier beef loin steak in this favorite—and a surprise side of lentils, in place of the expected calorie-laden French fries, adds an earthy boost of fiber.

ACTIVE TIME: 10 minutes
TOTAL TIME: 35 minutes

MAKES: 4 main-dish servings

2⅔ cups water
1⅓ cups green lentils
1 teaspoon salt
4 tuna steaks, 1 inch thick (6 ounces each)
4 teaspoons cracked black peppercorns
1 tablespoon olive oil
1 medium shallot, finely chopped
1 cup reduced-sodium chicken broth
1 tablespoon capers, chopped
1 tablespoon fresh lemon juice

1. In 2-quart saucepan, combine water, lentils, and ½ teaspoon salt; heat to boiling over high heat. Reduce heat to low; cover and simmer 20 to 25 minutes or until lentils are tender. Drain lentils and return to pan; cover to keep warm.

2. Meanwhile, evenly season tuna, on both sides, with remaining ½ teaspoon salt and all pepper, pressing in pepper. In 12-inch cast-iron skillet, heat oil over medium-high heat until hot. Add tuna and cook 5 to 8 minutes for medium or until desired doneness, turning over once. Transfer to plate; cover to keep warm.

3. To same skillet, add shallot and cook 1 minute, stirring. Add broth and capers; heat to boiling. Boil 3 minutes or until liquid is reduced by half. Add lentils; heat through. Remove from heat; stir in lemon juice. Serve tuna over lentils.

EACH SERVING: About 445 calories (12 percent calories from fat), 58g protein, 40g carbohydrate, 6g total fat (1g saturated), 20g fiber, 76mg cholesterol, 830mg sodium ☻

Salt-Baked Fish

Baking a whole fish in a crust of kosher salt seals in the juices and guarantees exquisitely moist—and surprisingly unsalty—fish.

ACTIVE TIME: 5 minutes
TOTAL TIME: 30 minutes

MAKES: 2 main-dish servings

4   cups kosher salt
1   whole red snapper, striped bass, or porgy (1½ to 2 pounds), cleaned and scaled
1   lemon
3   sprigs rosemary or thyme

1. Preheat oven to 450°F. Line 13″ by 9″ baking pan with foil; spread 2 cups salt in bottom of pan.

2. Rinse snapper inside and out with cold running water; pat dry with paper towels. From 1 lemon, cut 3 slices. Cut remaining lemon into wedges and set aside.

3. Place lemon slices and rosemary in cavity of fish. Place fish on bed of salt; cover with remaining 2 cups salt. Bake until fish is just opaque throughout when knife is inserted at backbone, about 30 minutes.

4. To serve, tap salt crust to release from top of fish; discard salt. Slide cake server under front section of top fillet and lift off fillet; transfer to platter. Slide server under backbone and lift it away from bottom fillet; discard. Slide server between bottom fillet and skin and transfer fillet to platter. Serve with reserved lemon wedges.

EACH SERVING: About 190 calories (14 percent calories from fat), 37g protein, 6g carbohydrate, 3g total fat (1g saturated), 0g fiber, 66mg cholesterol, 800mg sodium ●

Steamed Scrod Fillets

These fresh fillets are steamed on a bed of bok choy and carrots with a drizzle of a ginger-soy mixture for added flavor.

ACTIVE TIME: 15 minutes
TOTAL TIME: 25 minutes

MAKES: 4 main-dish servings

3   tablespoons reduced-sodium soy sauce
2   tablespoons seasoned rice vinegar
1   tablespoon finely chopped, peeled fresh ginger
1   garlic clove, crushed with garlic press
1   pound bok choy, coarsely chopped
1¾ cups peeled, shredded carrots
4   scrod fillets (6 ounces each)
3   green onions, sliced

1. In small bowl, with fork, mix soy sauce, vinegar, ginger, and garlic.

2. In 12-inch skillet, toss bok choy and carrots. Fold thin ends of scrod fillets under to create even thickness; place on top of vegetables. Add soy-sauce mixture and sprinkle with green onions; cover and heat to boiling over high heat. Reduce heat to medium; cook until scrod is just opaque throughout, about 10 minutes.

EACH SERVING: About 200 calories (9 percent calories from fat), 34g protein, 12g carbohydrate, 2g total fat (0g saturated), 3g fiber, 73mg cholesterol, 820mg sodium ●

Miso-Glazed Salmon

For a satisfying low-fat dinner, we spread a sweet and savory sauce on salmon fillets and broil them to make a rich glaze. Serve with a side of aromatic jasmine or basmati rice, or a salad of edamame and sliced radishes.

ACTIVE TIME: 10 minutes
TOTAL TIME: 20 minutes
MAKES: 4 main-dish servings

¼	cup white miso (see Tip)
5	teaspoons sugar
4	teaspoons seasoned rice vinegar
1	tablespoon water
1	tablespoon minced, peeled fresh ginger
4	salmon fillets, 1 inch thick (5 ounces each)
1	green onion, thinly sliced diagonally

1. Preheat broiler. Lightly spray rack in broiling pan with nonstick cooking spray.

2. In small bowl, mix miso, sugar, vinegar, water, and ginger; set aside.

3. Place salmon fillets on rack in broiling pan. Place pan in broiler at closest position to heat source; broil salmon 5 minutes. Remove pan from broiler and spread half of miso mixture on salmon; broil 1 minute longer.

4. Remove pan from broiler; turn salmon over and top with remaining miso mixture. Broil salmon until miso mixture is bubbly and salmon is opaque throughout, 3 to 4 minutes longer. Sprinkle with green onion before serving.

EACH SERVING: About 260 calories (24 percent calories from fat), 35g protein, 13g carbohydrate, 7g total fat (1g saturated), 0g fiber, 86mg cholesterol, 870mg sodium 🔵

TIP: *Miso—a paste made of fermented soybeans—comes in a variety of flavors, colors, and textures that fall into three basic categories: red, which has a strong flavor; golden, which is mild; and white, which is mellow and slightly sweet. Miso can be purchased in health-food stores and Asian markets.*

Mustard-Dill Salmon with Herbed Potatoes

A light and creamy sauce adds piquant flavor to succulent salmon. After you make the sauce, sauté snow peas in a nonstick skillet with a teaspoon of vegetable oil for a healthy side dish.

ACTIVE TIME: 20 minutes
TOTAL TIME: 30 minutes

MAKES: 4 main-dish servings

12	ounces small red potatoes, cut into 1-inch chunks
12	ounces small white potatoes, cut into 1-inch chunks
1½	teaspoons salt
3	tablespoons chopped fresh dill
½	teaspoon coarsely ground black pepper
4	pieces salmon fillet (6 ounces each)
2	tablespoons light mayonnaise
1	tablespoon white wine vinegar
2	teaspoons Dijon mustard
¾	teaspoon sugar

1. In a 3-quart saucepan, heat potatoes, 1 teaspoon salt, and enough *water* to cover to boiling over high heat. Reduce heat to low; cover and simmer until potatoes are fork-tender, about 15 minutes. Drain potatoes and toss with 1 tablespoon dill, ¼ teaspoon salt, and ¼ teaspoon pepper; keep the potatoes warm.

2. Meanwhile, preheat boiler. Grease rack in broiling pan. Place salmon on rack; sprinkle with ⅛ teaspoon salt and ⅛ teaspoon pepper. Place broiling pan at closest position to heat source. Broil until salmon is just opaque throughout, 8 to 10 minutes.

3. While salmon is broiling, prepare sauce: In small bowl, mix mayonnaise, vinegar, mustard, sugar, remaining 2 tablespoons dill, ⅛ teaspoon salt, and ⅛ teaspoon pepper.

4. Serve salmon with sauce and potatoes.

EACH SERVING: About 335 calories (19 percent calories from fat), 37g protein, 31g carbohydrate, 7g total fat (1g saturated), 2g fiber, 86mg cholesterol, 655mg sodium

GET YOUR OMEGA-3s

Despite a reputation for clogging arteries and packing on unwanted pounds, all fats are not villainous. Indeed, one type of polyunsaturated fat, omega-3, is thought to combat heart disease. Omega-3s help inhibit the formation of blood clots and reduce the incidence of heartbeat abnormalities. You'll find omega-3s in fish—and the oilier the fish, the more omega-3 it contains. So, be sure to include oily fish like salmon, bluefin tuna, mackerel, and sardines in your diet once a week.

Soba Noodles with Shrimp, Snow Peas, and Carrots

Soba (thin Japanese noodles made from buckwheat flour) cook quickly, and the shrimp, peas, and carrots cook in the same water as the noodles. Then just toss with a delicious peanut sauce that takes a couple of minutes to put together and dinner is served.

ACTIVE TIME: 15 minutes
TOTAL TIME: 20 minutes
MAKES: 4 main-dish servings

¼	cup creamy natural peanut butter
2	teaspoons grated, peeled fresh ginger
2	tablespoons reduced-sodium soy sauce
1	tablespoon distilled white vinegar
1	teaspoon Asian sesame oil
½	teaspoon hot pepper sauce
1	teaspoon salt
1	package (8 ounces) whole-wheat soba noodles
½	bag (10 ounces) shredded or matchstick carrots (1½ cups)
1	pound large shrimp, shelled and deveined, with tail part left on, if you like
4	ounces snow peas, strings removed
½	cup loosely packed fresh cilantro leaves, chopped, plus additional sprigs for garnish

1. In small bowl, place peanut butter, ginger, soy sauce, vinegar, sesame oil, and hot pepper sauce. Set aside.

2. Heat covered 5- to 6-quart saucepot of *water* and salt to boiling over high heat. Add noodles and cook 4 minutes. Add carrots and cook 1 minute. Add shrimp and snow peas and cook 2 minutes more. Reserve *½ cup noodle cooking water*. Drain noodles, shrimp, and vegetables into large colander, then transfer to large bowl.

3. With wire whisk, beat peanut-butter mixture until well blended. Add peanut sauce and chopped cilantro to noodle mixture in bowl and toss until evenly coated.

4. To serve, spoon into four large bowls; garnish each serving with a cilantro sprig.

EACH SERVING: About 430 calories (25 percent calories from fat), 33g protein, 53g carbohydrate, 12g total fat (2g saturated), 6g fiber, 140mg cholesterol, 960mg sodium ✔ ✿

Seafood Fra Diavolo

A tempting mix of squid, mussels, and shrimp in a robust tomato sauce. Simply add garlic bread and a green salad, and dinner is ready.

ACTIVE TIME: 25 minutes
TOTAL TIME: 1 hour

MAKES: 6 main-dish servings

8	ounces cleaned squid
1	tablespoon olive oil
1	large garlic clove, finely chopped
¼	teaspoon crushed red pepper
1	can (28 ounces) plum tomatoes
½	teaspoon salt
1	dozen mussels, scrubbed and debearded (see Tip, page 122)
8	ounces medium shrimp, shelled and deveined
1	package (16 ounces) linguine or spaghetti
¼	cup chopped fresh parsley leaves

1. Rinse squid and pat dry with paper towels. Slice squid bodies crosswise into ¼-inch rings. Cut tentacles into several pieces if they are large.

2. In nonreactive 4-quart saucepan, heat oil over medium heat. Add garlic and crushed red pepper; cook just until fragrant, about 30 seconds. Stir in tomatoes with their juice and salt, breaking up tomatoes with side of spoon. Heat to boiling over high heat. Add squid and return to boiling. Reduce heat; cover and simmer 30 minutes, then simmer uncovered 15 minutes longer.

3. Increase heat to high. Add mussels; cover and cook 3 minutes. Stir in shrimp; cover and cook until mussels open and shrimp are just opaque throughout, about 2 minutes longer. Discard any mussels that have not opened after 5 minutes.

4. Meanwhile, cook pasta as label directs. Drain. In warm serving bowl, toss pasta with seafood mixture and parsley.

EACH SERVING: About 410 calories (11 percent calories from fat), 25g protein, 65g carbohydrate, 5g total fat (1g saturated), 3g fiber, 140mg cholesterol, 588mg sodium

Sicilian-Style Swordfish with Pasta

Chunks of grilled fish are tossed with pasta in a light vinaigrette made with fresh mint and tomato. If you don't have fresh mint, substitute fresh basil or parsley.

ACTIVE TIME: 15 minutes
TOTAL TIME: 25 minutes plus standing
MAKES: 6 main-dish servings

3 ripe medium tomatoes (6 to 8 ounces each), cut into ½-inch chunks (about 2½ cups)
¼ cup chopped fresh mint
1 tablespoon red wine vinegar
1 small garlic clove, minced
3 tablespoons olive oil
¾ teaspoon salt
½ teaspoon coarsely ground black pepper
1 teaspoon freshly grated orange peel
1 swordfish steak, 1 inch thick (about 1 pound)
1 package (16 ounces) penne or bow-tie pasta

1. In large bowl, combine tomatoes, mint, vinegar, garlic, 2 tablespoons oil, ½ teaspoon salt, and ¼ teaspoon pepper. Cover and let stand at room temperature 30 minutes.

2. Prepare outdoor grill for direct grilling over medium heat.

3. In cup, combine grated orange peel and remaining 1 tablespoon oil, ¼ teaspoon salt, and ¼ teaspoon pepper. Brush mixture on both sides of swordfish.

4. Place swordfish on hot grill rack over medium heat. Grill until just opaque throughout, 8 to 10 minutes, turning over once. Transfer to cutting board and cut into 1-inch pieces.

5. Meanwhile, cook pasta as label directs. Drain.

6. Add swordfish and pasta to tomato mixture; toss to combine.

EACH SERVING: About 440 calories (23 percent calories from fat), 24g protein, 61g carbohydrate, 11g total fat (2g saturated), 4g fiber, 26mg cholesterol, 430mg sodium ♥

Chicken, Turkey & Duck

On busy weeknights or when unexpected company drops in for dinner, poultry is the solution many of us turn to again and again—and with good reason. It's simple to prepare in a multitude of satisfying ways, whether you quickly stir-fry, pan-fry or grill it, or stick it in the oven to slowly braise in its own juices or roast until it's succulent and golden brown. Better still, it's a lean and healthy option, especially if you prepare white meat or remove the skin from dark meat before serving (see "The Skinny on Poultry," page 174).

In this chapter, we offer a selection of our favorite go-to recipes, beginning with a bevy of skillet dishes paired with flavorful sauces you can whip up in the same pan, just the thing when you need to get dinner on the table in 30 minutes or less. Our pear and tarragon turkey cutlets—and a duck recipe featuring a tart cherry sauce—are equally speedy to prepare, but perfect for special nights when you want to cook to impress.

Then it's onto the stir-fries, from a zesty tangerine chicken tossed with broccoli flowerets and carrots to an Asian chicken-noodle option featuring buckwheat soba noodles. If grilling is your quick-cooking method of choice, then our poultry recipes paired with three different fruity salsas are sure to inspire you.

But if you prefer to spend a little time upfront, and then let the oven do its magic, you'll welcome our recipes for roasted birds, baked "fried" chicken, and even a (turkey) shepherd's pie.

Tangerine Chicken Stir-Fry (recipe page 162)

Chicken Breasts with a Trio of Quick Sauces

Simply sauté boneless chicken breasts, then take your pick from six easy sauces.

ACTIVE TIME: 2 minutes plus making sauce
COOK: 10 minutes plus making sauce

MAKES: 4 main-dish servings

4   medium skinless, boneless chicken breast halves (1¼ pounds)

sauce of your choice (see below)

1. In nonstick 12-inch skillet, heat oil over medium heat until hot. Add chicken and cook until chicken is golden brown and loses its pink color throughout, 5 to 6 minutes per side. Transfer chicken to platter; keep warm.

2. Prepare sauce and serve.

CHINESE GINGER SAUCE: After removing chicken from skillet, reduce heat to medium and add *1 teaspoon vegetable oil* to the skillet. Add *1 red pepper, thinly sliced,* and cook until tender-crisp. Add *½ cup water, 2 tablespoons soy sauce, 2 tablespoons seasoned rice vinegar,* and *1 tablespoon grated, peeled fresh ginger.* Heat to boiling; boil 1 minute. Spoon over chicken and sprinkle with *2 green onions, chopped.*

EACH SERVING WITH CHICKEN: About 195 calories (18 percent calories from fat), 34g protein, 4g carbohydrate, 4g total fat (1g saturated), 1g fiber, 82mg cholesterol, 757mg sodium

CREAMY MUSHROOM SAUCE: After removing chicken, add *1 teaspoon vegetable oil* to skillet. Add *10 ounces mushrooms, trimmed and sliced, 1 onion, thinly sliced,* and *¾ teaspoon salt.* Cook, stirring, until vegetables are golden brown and tender. Reduce heat to low; stir in *½ cup light sour cream* and *¼ cup water;* heat through (do not boil). Spoon over chicken.

EACH SERVING WITH CHICKEN: About 260 calories (28 percent calories from fat), 37g protein, 9g carbohydrate, 8g total fat (3g saturated), 1g fiber, 92mg cholesterol, 548mg sodium

PROVENÇAL SAUCE: After removing chicken from skillet, reduce heat to medium and add *1 teaspoon olive or vegetable oil* to skillet. Add *1 onion, chopped,* and cook, stirring, until tender. Stir in *1 can (14½ ounces) Italian-style stewed tomatoes, ½ cup pitted ripe olives, each cut in half, 1 tablespoon drained capers,* and *¼ cup water.* Cook, stirring, until heated through, about 1 minute. Spoon over chicken.

EACH SERVING WITH CHICKEN: About 255 calories (25 percent calories from fat), 35g protein, 11g carbohydrate, 7g total fat (1g saturated), 3g fiber, 82mg cholesterol, 785mg sodium

Green-Chile Skillet Chicken

This Tex-Mex specialty relies on canned green chiles for its heat—choose mild, medium, or hot chiles, depending on your preference.

ACTIVE TIME: 10 minutes
TOTAL TIME: 20 minutes
MAKES: 4 main-dish servings

4	medium skinless, boneless chicken breast halves (1¼ pounds)
¼	teaspoon salt
⅛	teaspoon ground black pepper
1	tablespoon olive oil
1	can (4 to 4½ ounces) diced green chiles, drained
1	cup grape tomatoes, each cut in half
¾	cup reduced-sodium chicken broth
½	teaspoon ground cumin
1	garlic clove, crushed with garlic press
2	tablespoons chopped fresh cilantro

1. With meat mallet, pound chicken breast halves to even ½-inch thickness (or place chicken between two sheets of plastic wrap or waxed paper and pound with rolling pin). Sprinkle with salt and pepper.

2. In nonstick 12-inch skillet, heat oil over medium heat until hot. Add chicken breasts and cook, turning once, until chicken is browned on both sides and loses its pink color throughout, 6 to 7 minutes. Transfer chicken breasts to platter; cover loosely with foil to keep warm.

3. To skillet, add chiles, tomatoes, broth, cumin, garlic, and juices from platter; cook, stirring occasionally, until sauce is slightly reduced, about 3 minutes. Stir in cilantro. To serve, spoon sauce over chicken.

EACH SERVING: About 205 calories (22 percent calories from fat), 33g protein, 4g carbohydrate, 5g total fat (1g saturated), 0g fiber, 82mg cholesterol, 445mg sodium 💛 ❤️

Chicken Sauté
with Artichokes

This easy chicken and artichoke sauté will make you think of spring. Happily, you can make it anytime with the convenience of frozen artichoke hearts. Lemon juice, mint, and crumbled feta cheese add color and bright flavor.

ACTIVE TIME: 15 minutes
TOTAL TIME: 30 minutes

MAKES: 4 main-dish servings

2	medium skinless, boneless chicken breast halves (1½ pounds)
¼	teaspoon salt
⅛	teaspoon ground black pepper
4	teaspoons olive oil
1	package (8 to 10 ounces) frozen artichoke hearts, thawed
¾	cup canned or homemade chicken broth (page 93)
¼	cup loosely packed fresh mint leaves, chopped, plus additional for garnish
1	tablespoon fresh lemon juice
¼	cup crumbled feta cheese

1. With meat mallet or bottom of skillet, pound chicken breast halves (placed between 2 sheets plastic wrap) to an even ½-inch thickness; sprinkle with salt and pepper on both sides.

2. In 12-inch skillet, heat 2 teaspoons oil over medium heat. Add chicken and cook 12 to 14 minutes or until chicken is browned on both sides and loses its pink color throughout, turning over once. Transfer chicken to shallow serving bowl; cover with foil to keep warm.

3. To same skillet, add remaining 2 teaspoons oil and heat over medium heat until hot. Add artichokes and cook 3 minutes or until browned, stirring occasionally. Stir in broth and heat to boiling over medium-high; boil 2 to 3 minutes or until liquid is reduced by half. Remove skillet from heat; stir in mint and lemon juice.

4. To serve, spoon artichoke sauce over chicken; top with feta. Garnish with additional chopped mint leaves.

EACH SERVING: About 285 calories (25 percent calories from fat), 43g protein, 7g carbohydrate, 9g total fat (3g saturated), 3g fiber, 107mg cholesterol, 515mg sodium ●

Apple-Dijon Chicken

The maple syrup in this autumn-inspired dish enhances the flavor of the apples and provides a sweet counterpoint to the zesty Dijon mustard. For best results, look for 100 percent pure maple syrup, not "maple-flavored" syrup, which is a mixture of corn syrup and a very small amount of real maple syrup or extract.

ACTIVE TIME: 15 minutes
TOTAL TIME: 30 minutes

MAKES: 4 main-dish servings

4	medium skinless, boneless chicken breast halves (1¼ pounds)
½	teaspoon salt
⅛	teaspoon freshly ground black pepper
1	tablespoon olive oil
2	Golden Delicious apples, each cored and cut crosswise into 6 rings
1	small red onion, sliced
¾	cup reduced-sodium chicken broth
2	tablespoons maple syrup
1	tablespoon Dijon mustard with seeds
⅓	cup half-and-half
1	teaspoon cornstarch

1. With meat mallet or bottom of skillet, pound chicken breast halves (placed between two sheets plastic wrap) to even ½-inch thickness; sprinkle with ¼ teaspoon salt and pepper.

2. In nonstick 12-inch skillet, heat oil over medium heat until hot. Add chicken breasts and cook, turning once, until chicken is browned on both sides and loses its pink color throughout, 6 to 7 minutes. Transfer chicken breasts to platter; cover loosely with foil to keep warm. Do not wash skillet.

3. Meanwhile, in microwave-safe pie plate, combine apples and onion. Cover with waxed paper and microwave on High, stirring once, until tender, 3 to 4 minutes.

4. Add apple mixture to skillet and cook over medium heat until browned, about 2 minutes. Add broth, maple syrup, mustard, and remaining ¼ teaspoon salt. Cook until broth mixture is slightly reduced, about 2 minutes.

5. In small bowl, blend half-and-half and cornstarch until smooth; stir into apple mixture with juices from platter. Cook until sauce is slightly thickened, about 1 minute. To serve, spoon sauce over chicken.

EACH SERVING: About 295 calories (24 percent calories from fat), 34g protein, 21g carbohydrate, 8g total fat (2g saturated), 2g fiber, 90mg cholesterol, 500mg sodium ◉

Basil-Orange Chicken with Couscous

Marinating the chicken in orange and basil gives it a bright, fresh flavor. Served over whole-wheat couscous with steamed sugar snap peas, this light dish is perfect for warmer weather. For photo, see page 5.

ACTIVE TIME: 20 minutes
TOTAL TIME: 30 minutes

MAKES: 4 main-dish servings

2	large navel oranges
3	lemons
½	cup packed fresh basil leaves, chopped
2	tablespoons olive oil
⅜	teaspoon salt
⅜	teaspoon ground black pepper
4	medium skinless, boneless chicken breast halves (1½ pounds)
½	teaspoon sugar
1	cup whole-wheat couscous
1	package (8 ounces) stringless sugar snap peas

1. From 1 orange, grate 1½ teaspoons peel and squeeze 4 tablespoons juice. From 2 lemons, grate 1½ teaspoons peel and squeeze ⅓ cup juice. Cut remaining orange and lemon into slices and set aside.

2. In medium bowl, combine 1 teaspoon of each peel and 1 tablespoon orange juice with half of basil, 1 tablespoon olive oil, ¼ teaspoon salt, and ¼ teaspoon pepper.

3. Place chicken breast between two sheets plastic wrap and, with flat side of meat mallet, pound to an even ½-inch thickness. Add chicken to citrus mixture, turning to coat; set aside.

4. In small pitcher or bowl, combine sugar, remaining ⅛ teaspoon salt, remaining ⅛ teaspoon pepper, citrus peels, citrus juices, basil, and oil; set aside. (Dish can be made to this point up to 8 hours ahead. Cover chicken and citrus sauce and refrigerate.)

5. Preheat large ridged grill pan or prepare outdoor grill for direct grilling over medium-high heat. Meanwhile, prepare couscous as label directs. In 4-quart saucepan filled with *½ inch water,* place a vegetable steamer. Heat to boiling over high.

6. Add chicken to hot grill pan or grate; cook 4 minutes. Turn chicken over and cook 3 to 4 minutes longer or until no longer pink in center. Grill reserved citrus slices as well.

7. While chicken is cooking on second side, add snap peas to steamer; cook 2 to 3 minutes or until tender-crisp. Fluff couscous and spoon onto large platter; top with chicken and snap peas. Drizzle sauce over all. Garnish with grilled citrus slices.

EACH SERVING: About 400 calories (20 percent calories from fat), 46g protein, 33g carbohydrate, 9g total fat (1g saturated), 6g fiber, 99mg cholesterol, 365mg sodium ♡ ♥ ⊛ ⌷

Chicken Bolognese

This delicious twist on a beloved pasta dish trims the calories and fat without sacrificing the richly satisfying flavor.

ACTIVE TIME: 25 minutes
TOTAL TIME: 40 minutes

MAKES: 6 main-dish servings

12	ounces linguine or fettuccine
4	teaspoons olive oil
1	pound ground chicken breast
½	teaspoon salt
2	carrots, peeled and chopped
2	stalks celery, chopped
1	large onion (12 ounces), chopped
1	garlic clove, crushed with press
1	can (28 ounces) crushed tomatoes
¼	teaspoon ground black pepper
½	cup reduced-fat (2%) milk
⅓	cup freshly grated Parmesan cheese
¼	cup loosely packed fresh parsley leaves, chopped

1. In large saucepot, cook pasta as label directs.

2. Meanwhile, in 12-inch nonstick skillet, heat 2 teaspoons oil over medium heat 1 minute. Add ground chicken to skillet; sprinkle with ¼ teaspoon salt. Cook chicken 8 to 9 minutes, or until it is no longer pink, stirring occasionally. Transfer chicken along with any juices to bowl.

3. To same skillet, add remaining 2 teaspoons oil with carrots, celery, onion, and garlic; cook 10 to 12 minutes or until vegetables are lightly browned and tender, stirring occasionally. Stir in tomatoes with their juice, remaining ¼ teaspoon salt, and pepper; heat to boiling. Reduce heat to medium-low and simmer, uncovered, 10 minutes, stirring occasionally. Stir in cooked chicken and milk; heat through.

4. Reserve *¼ cup pasta cooking water*. Drain pasta and return to saucepot; stir in sauce from skillet, Parmesan, parsley, and reserved cooking water, and toss to coat.

EACH SERVING: About 410 calories (13 percent calories from fat), 29g protein, 59g carbohydrate, 6g total fat (2g saturated), 5g fiber, 49mg cholesterol, 800mg sodium ♥

Crispy Duck Breasts with Tart Cherry Sauce

This streamlined classic recipe is also great made with pork. You can substitute two 6-ounce, ¾-inch-thick boneless pork loin chops for the duck. In step 2, season the chops and cook them in 1 teaspoon vegetable oil over medium heat for about 8 minutes, turning them once. Then proceed as directed.

ACTIVE TIME: 25 minutes
TOTAL TIME: 30 minutes

MAKES: 4 main-dish servings

1	package (6 ounces) white-and-wild rice blend (optional)
4	small duck breast halves (6 ounces each; see Tip)
½	teaspoon salt
½	teaspoon ground black pepper
⅔	cup port wine
2	cans (14½ ounces each) tart cherries in water, well drained
¼	cup sugar

steamed green beans (optional)

1. If desired, prepare rice blend as label directs. Keep warm.

2. Meanwhile, pat duck breasts dry with paper towels. Make several ¼-inch-deep diagonal slashes in duck skin. Place breasts, skin side down, in nonstick 10-inch skillet; sprinkle with salt and pepper. Cook over medium heat until skin is deep brown, about 12 minutes; turn breasts and cook 3 minutes longer for medium. Transfer breasts, skin side down, to cutting board; let stand 5 minutes for easier slicing. Discard fat from skillet but do not wash.

3. Meanwhile, add port to skillet; heat to boiling over medium heat. Boil until reduced by half, about 5 minutes. Add cherries and sugar and simmer, stirring occasionally, until most of liquid has evaporated, 3 to 4 minutes.

4. To serve, slice breasts crosswise. Transfer slices, skin side up, to four dinner plates. Spoon cherry sauce over duck. Serve with rice and green beans, if you like.

EACH SERVING: About 320 calories (28 percent calories from fat), 23g protein, 36g carbohydrate, 10g total fat (3g saturated), 1g fiber, 120mg cholesterol, 380mg sodium ☻ ♥

TIP: *If you can only find the larger duck breasts, which weigh in at 12 to 13 ounces each, buy two and cook them on medium-low 20 minutes, skin side down; turn them over and continue cooking 4 minutes longer. Slice to serve, as in step 4, and divide among four dinner plates.*

Turkey Cutlets with Pears and Tarragon

This good-for-you recipe contains lean proteins (turkey) and green veggies (spinach). The best pears for this recipe are Anjou and Bosc, which are juicy and keep their shape when cooked.

ACTIVE TIME: 15 minutes
TOTAL TIME: 25 minutes

MAKES: 4 main-dish servings

1	tablespoon olive oil
4	turkey breast cutlets (about 1 pound)
¼	teaspoon salt
⅛	teaspoon ground black pepper
2	large firm, ripe pears, peeled, cored, and cut into ½-inch-thick wedges (see Tip)
1	cup chicken broth
¼	cup dried tart cherries or cranberries
2	tablespoons Dijon mustard with seeds
½	teaspoon dried tarragon
1	bag (9 ounces) ready-to-microwave-in-bag spinach

1. In 12-inch skillet, heat oil over high heat until hot. Sprinkle turkey breast cutlets with salt and pepper. Add cutlets to skillet and cook, turning once, until turkey is golden brown on both sides and has just lost pink color throughout, 3 to 4 minutes. Transfer cutlets to plate; keep warm.

2. To same skillet, add pears. Reduce heat to medium-high and cook pears, turning occasionally, until browned, about 3 minutes. Add broth, cherries, Dijon mustard, and tarragon to skillet. Increase heat to high and cook, stirring occasionally, until sauce thickens slightly and pears are tender, 4 to 5 minutes.

3. Meanwhile, in microwave oven, cook spinach in bag as label directs.

4. Return cutlets to skillet; heat through, spooning pear sauce over cutlets.

5. To serve, spoon spinach onto four dinner plates. Top with turkey, pears, and sauce.

EACH SERVING: About 255 calories (21 percent calories from fat), 31g protein, 20g carbohydrate, 6g total fat (1g saturated), 8g fiber, 71mg cholesterol, 565mg sodium 🟢 🌱

TIP: *Peel and cut the pears just before you are ready to use them; like cut apples, they discolor. If you want to prep them in advance, place them in a bowl of cold water to which you've added 1 teaspoon lemon juice. Drain and pat dry before using.*

Tangerine Chicken Stir-Fry

Toss stir-fried chicken and mixed vegetables with a citrus-infused sauce for a quick and delicious meal. For photo, see page 150.

ACTIVE TIME: 20 minutes
TOTAL TIME: 30 minutes
MAKES: 4 main-dish servings

3	tangerines
¼	cup dry sherry
1	tablespoon grated, peeled fresh ginger
1	teaspoon Asian sesame oil
1	teaspoon plus 1 tablespoon cornstarch
2	tablespoons reduced-sodium soy sauce
1½	pounds skinless, boneless chicken breast halves, cut into ½-inch-wide strips
1	cup quick-cooking (10 minute) brown rice
4	teaspoons vegetable oil
1	bag (12 ounces) broccoli florets
2	carrots, peeled and thinly sliced diagonally
3	green onions, cut into 1-inch pieces
⅓	cup water

1. From 1 tangerine, with vegetable peeler, remove peel in strips. Using small knife, remove and discard any white pith from peel; set peel aside. Into 1-cup liquid measuring cup, squeeze ½ cup juice from tangerines. Stir in sherry, ginger, sesame oil, and 1 teaspoon cornstarch; set juice mixture aside.

2. In medium bowl, combine soy sauce and remaining 1 tablespoon cornstarch. Add chicken and toss to coat; set chicken mixture aside.

3. Cook rice as label directs. Meanwhile, in 12-inch skillet, heat 2 teaspoons vegetable oil over medium-high until hot. Add peel and cook 1 minute or until lightly browned. With tongs or slotted spoon, transfer peel to large bowl.

4. To same skillet, add broccoli, carrots, and green onions; stir to coat with oil. Add water; cover and cook 4 minutes, stirring once. Uncover and cook 1 minute longer or until vegetables are tender-crisp, stirring frequently (stir-frying). Transfer vegetables to bowl with peel.

5. To same skillet, add remaining 2 teaspoons vegetable oil; reduce heat to medium. Add chicken mixture and cook 6 to 7 minutes or until chicken is golden and loses its pink color throughout, stirring frequently. Transfer chicken to bowl with cooked vegetables.

6. Add juice mixture to skillet and heat to boiling over medium-high heat; boil 1 minute, stirring until browned bits are loosened. Return chicken and vegetables to skillet and cook 1 minute to heat through, stirring. To serve, spoon brown rice into four shallow dinner bowls; top with chicken and vegetables.

EACH SERVING: About 390 calories (21 percent calories from fat), 45g protein, 32g carbohydrate, 9g total fat (1g saturated), 5g fiber, 99mg cholesterol, 420mg sodium ♥ ❤ ✤

Thai-Style Coconut Chicken

Unsweetened coconut milk, a staple in Thai cuisine readily available at the supermarket, is a great ingredient to have handy if you're looking for rich-tasting, long-simmering flavor but are pressed for time. If you can't find jasmine rice, substitute basmati or Texmati, which is a cross between American long-grain rice and basmati.

ACTIVE TIME: 20 minutes
TOTAL TIME: 30 minutes

MAKES: 4 main-dish servings

1	cup jasmine rice or long-grain white rice
1	can (14 ounces) light coconut milk (not cream of coconut)
1	cup canned or homemade chicken broth (page 93)
1	tablespoon cornstarch
4	thin slices peeled fresh ginger
2	strips (3" by ½") fresh lime peel
1	pound skinless, boneless chicken breasts, cut into ½-inch-wide strips
6	ounces snow peas (2 cups), strings removed
1	tablespoon reduced-sodium Asian fish sauce (see Tip, page 88)
¼	cup loosely packed fresh cilantro leaves, chopped
lime wedges	

1. Prepare rice as label directs.

2. Meanwhile, in 12-inch nonstick skillet, stir coconut milk, broth, cornstarch, ginger, and lime peel; heat to boiling over medium-high heat, stirring frequently. Boil 1 minute.

3. Add chicken and snow peas to skillet; cover and cook until chicken loses its pink color throughout, 4 to 5 minutes. Remove skillet from heat; stir in fish sauce and cilantro. Serve with rice and lime wedges.

EACH SERVING: About 405 calories (17 percent calories from fat), 31g protein, 43g carbohydrate, 11g total (6g saturated), 2g fiber, 66mg cholesterol, 465mg sodium ●

Red-Cooked Chicken, Slow-Cooker Style

Traditional Chinese "red cooked" chicken involves slowly cooking it in a soy sauce–based liquid, which gives the dish a deep red color. Here the slow cooker makes it ready when you are.

ACTIVE TIME: 20 minutes
SLOW-COOK TIME: 8 hours on Low or 4 hours on High
MAKES: 4 main-dish servings

½	cup dry sherry
⅓	cup reduced-sodium soy sauce
¼	cup packed brown sugar
2	tablespoons grated, peeled fresh ginger
1	teaspoon Chinese five-spice powder
3	garlic cloves, crushed with garlic press
1	bunch green onions, white parts cut into 2-inch pieces and green parts chopped
3	pounds bone-in chicken thighs, skin and fat removed
1	bag (16 ounces) fresh vegetables for stir-fry (i.e. snow peas, carrots, broccoli, pepper)

1. In 5- to 6-quart slow cooker, combine sherry, soy sauce, sugar, ginger, five-spice powder, garlic, and white parts of green onions. (Keep remaining chopped green parts refrigerated until serving time.) Add chicken thighs and toss to coat with sherry mixture. Cover slow cooker and cook as manufacturer directs, 8 hours on Low or 4 hours on High.

2. Just before serving, place vegetables in microwave-safe medium bowl and cook in microwave as label directs.

3. With tongs, transfer chicken thighs to deep platter. Stir vegetables into sauce in slow cooker. Spoon vegetable mixture around chicken. Sprinkle with reserved green onions.

EACH SERVING: About 410 calories (21 percent calories from fat), 41g protein, 24g carbohydrate, 8g total fat (2g saturated), 2g fiber, 161mg cholesterol, 930mg sodium 🝙

CHICKEN-BREAST SAVVY

The demand for chicken breasts has increased with consumers' growing commitment to cut back on fat (see "The Skinny on Poultry," page 174). Now companies market several variations. Skinless, boneless breast halves may be labeled exactly that, or they may be called *skinless, boneless split breasts* or *portions*. If the label doesn't indicate that the breast is cut into two pieces, it could be whole—the clues to look for are the terms *halves, split,* or *portions*.

Poultry companies also package tenderloins (the narrow pieces of chicken from the underside of breasts). These could be labeled *tenders* or *fillets*—either way, they are boneless, very tender, and perfect for chicken fingers, stir-fries, and salads. Thin-sliced chicken breast cutlets are breast halves cut horizontally for quicker cooking. They're great in place of pounded chicken breasts, or instead of veal for a lower-fat take on veal scaloppine.

Chicken-Noodle Stir-Fry

Dark, slender soba noodles are a specialty of Japan. We love their nutty flavor combined with stir-fried strips of chicken breasts, bok choy, and red pepper.

ACTIVE TIME: 15 minutes
TOTAL TIME: 30 minutes

MAKES: 4 main-dish servings

1   package (about 8 ounces) soba noodles (see page 89)
2   tablespoons vegetable oil
1   pound boneless, skinless chicken breasts, cut lengthwise into ½-inch-wide strips
2   tablespoons reduced-sodium soy sauce
3   green onions, thinly sliced
1   large red pepper, cut lengthwise into ¼-inch-wide strips
1   medium head bok choy (about 1½ pounds), cut crosswise into ½-inch-wide ribbons
1   cup low-sodium chicken broth
2   garlic cloves, crushed with garlic press
1   tablespoon grated, peeled fresh ginger
1   tablespoon seasoned rice vinegar
2   teaspoons cornstarch
1   teaspoon sugar

1. Cook soba noodles as label directs. Drain noodles; rinse under cold running water and drain again. Set aside.

2. Meanwhile, in nonstick 12-inch skillet, heat 1 tablespoon oil over medium-high heat until hot. Add chicken and 1 tablespoon soy sauce, and cook until chicken loses its pink color throughout, about 5 minutes, stirring often (stir-frying). Transfer chicken to plate.

3. Add remaining 1 tablespoon oil to skillet; add green onions and red pepper, and cook 3 minutes, stirring often (stir-frying). Add bok choy and cook until vegetables are tender-crisp, about 3 minutes longer.

4. Meanwhile, in 2-cup glass measuring cup, whisk together broth, garlic, ginger, vinegar, cornstarch, sugar, and remaining 1 tablespoon soy sauce.

5. Add noodles and sauce mixture to bok-choy mixture and heat to boiling; cook 1 minute, stirring to coat noodles. Add chicken and toss just until heated through.

EACH SERVING: About 440 calories (23 percent calories from fat), 34g protein, 54g carbohydrate, 11g total fat (1g saturated), 7g fiber, 73mg cholesterol, 684mg sodium ♥ ☻

Grilled Chicken Bruschetta

Add grilled chicken breasts to this popular appetizer, and you have a lean dinner, rich in fiber and vitamin C, that's good for your heart—and your taste buds.

ACTIVE TIME: 20 minutes
TOTAL TIME: 25 minutes

MAKES: 4 main-dish servings

3	garlic cloves, peeled
3	teaspoons extra-virgin olive oil
3/8	teaspoon salt
3/8	teaspoon ground black pepper
4	skinless, boneless chicken breast halves (6 ounces each)
1 3/4	pounds tomatoes, chopped
1	small shallot, finely chopped
1/4	cup packed fresh basil leaves, finely chopped
2	tablespoons red wine vinegar
1	loaf round crusty whole-wheat bread (8 ounces), sliced

1. Preheat outdoor grill over medium heat. Crush 2 garlic cloves with press.

2. In 9-inch pie plate, mix crushed garlic, 1 teaspoon oil, and 1/4 teaspoon each salt and pepper, then rub all over chicken.

3. In large bowl, combine tomatoes, shallot, basil, vinegar, 1 teaspoon oil, and 1/8 teaspoon each salt and pepper. Let stand.

4. Grill chicken, covered, 10 to 13 minutes or until juices run clear when thickest part of chicken is pierced, turning once. Transfer to cutting board. Let rest 10 minutes; slice.

5. Brush bread with remaining 1 teaspoon oil. Grill 1 minute, turning once. Cut remaining clove garlic in half. Rub cut sides all over bread. Divide bread and chicken among serving plates; top with tomato mixture.

EACH SERVING: About 365 calories (17 percent calories from fat), 45g protein, 31g carbohydrate, 7g total fat (1g saturated), 5g fiber, 99mg cholesterol, 325mg sodium ♥ ♥ ✦

Coffee-Spice Chicken and Fruit-Basil Salsa

A jerk-style seasoning of Jamaican allspice and java gives this Caribbean chicken its caffeinated kick. Balancing the heat: a cooling summer salsa of just-picked nectarines and juicy watermelon.

ACTIVE TIME: 30 minutes
TOTAL TIME: 40 minutes

MAKES: 8 main-dish servings

3	cups seedless watermelon cubes, cut into ½-inch chunks (from 4-pound piece of watermelon)
1	large ripe nectarine, pitted and cut into ½-inch chunks
3	tablespoons finely chopped red onion
1	tablespoon fresh lemon juice
2	tablespoons instant coffee
1	tablespoon grated, peeled fresh ginger
1	tablespoon olive oil
1¼	teaspoons ground allspice
¾	teaspoon salt
8	skinless, boneless chicken breast halves (3 pounds)
½	cup packed fresh basil leaves, coarsely chopped

1. In medium bowl, combine watermelon, nectarine, red onion, and lemon juice. Cover and refrigerate while preparing chicken. Makes about 4 cups salsa.

2. Prepare outdoor grill for covered direct grilling over medium heat.

3. In large bowl, with spoon or fingers, press coffee to pulverize. Add ginger, oil, allspice, and ½ teaspoon salt; stir to combine. Add chicken and toss to evenly coat with spice mixture (you may need to pat spice mixture onto chicken with fingers).

4. Place chicken breasts on hot grill rack. Cover and cook 8 to 10 minutes or until juices run clear when thickest part of chicken is pierced with tip of knife, turning once. Transfer chicken to cutting board and let rest 5 minutes. Meanwhile, stir basil and remaining ¼ teaspoon salt into salsa. Slice chicken crosswise and serve with salsa on the side.

EACH SERVING: About 235 calories (15 percent calories from fat), 40g protein, 8g carbohydrate, 4g total fat (1g saturated), 1g fiber, 99mg cholesterol, 310mg sodium ♥

Lemon-Oregano Chicken

This fresh-flavored chicken dish is perfect for outdoor grilling on one of those surprisingly warm days in early spring. For even cooking, it's a good idea to pound chicken breasts to a uniform thickness with a meat mallet.

ACTIVE TIME: 15 minutes
TOTAL TIME: 30 minutes

MAKES: 4 main-dish servings

3	medium zucchini (8 ounces each)
2	tablespoons olive oil
½	teaspoon salt
½	cup loosely packed fresh mint leaves, chopped
4	medium skinless, boneless chicken breast halves (1½ pounds)
3	lemons
1	tablespoon chopped fresh oregano
½	teaspoon coarsely ground black pepper

1. Prepare outdoor grill for covered direct grilling over medium heat.

2. With mandoline or sharp knife, slice zucchini very thinly lengthwise. In large bowl, toss zucchini with 1 tablespoon oil, ¼ teaspoon salt, and half of mint.

3. Place chicken breast between two sheets plastic wrap and, with meat mallet, pound to uniform ¼-inch thickness. From 2 lemons, grate 1 tablespoon peel and squeeze 2 tablespoons juice. Cut remaining lemon into 4 wedges; set aside. In medium bowl, combine lemon peel and juice with oregano, pepper, and remaining 1 tablespoon oil and ¼ teaspoon salt. Add chicken to bowl and toss until evenly coated.

4. Place zucchini slices, in batches, on hot grill rack over medium heat and cook until grill marks appear and zucchini is tender, 2 to 4 minutes, turning over once. Remove zucchini from grill; place on large platter and sprinkle with remaining mint.

5. Place chicken on hot grill rack. Cover grill and cook chicken until juices run clear when chicken is pierced with tip of knife, 6 to 8 minutes, turning over once. Transfer chicken to platter with zucchini; serve with lemon wedges.

EACH SERVING: About 280 calories (29 percent calories from fat), 42g protein, 8g carbohydrate, 9g total fat (2g saturated), 3g fiber, 99mg cholesterol, 390mg sodium 💚 ❤️

Prosciutto Turkey Cutlets with Melon

When buying turkey cutlets for this recipe, make sure not to get ones that are very thinly sliced for scaloppine.

ACTIVE TIME: 20 minutes
TOTAL TIME: 30 minutes

MAKES: 4 servings

2   limes
1½ cups chopped, peeled cantaloupe
1½ cups chopped, peeled honeydew melon
1   small Kirby cucumber, shredded (½ cup)
1   jalapeño chile, seeded and finely chopped
¼   cup loosely packed fresh basil leaves, chopped
¼   teaspoon salt
4   turkey breast cutlets (1 pound total)
¼   teaspoon coarsely ground black pepper
4   ounces thinly sliced prosciutto

1. Grease grill rack. Prepare outdoor grill for direct grilling over medium heat.

2. From 1 lime, grate 1 teaspoon peel and squeeze 2 tablespoons juice. Cut remaining lime into 4 wedges and set aside. In bowl, combine lime juice, cantaloupe, melon, cucumber, jalapeño, basil, and salt. Makes about 3 cups salsa.

3. Sprinkle turkey cutlets with lime peel and pepper. Wrap turkey cutlets with prosciutto, pressing prosciutto firmly onto turkey.

4. Place turkey on hot grill rack over medium heat and cook until turkey loses its pink color throughout, 5 to 7 minutes, turning over once. Transfer turkey to plate; serve with salsa and lime wedges.

EACH SERVING TURKEY: About 185 calories (20 percent calories from fat), 35g protein, 0g carbohydrate, 4g total fat (1g saturated), 0g fiber, 86mg cholesterol, 815mg sodium ●

EACH ¼ CUP SALSA: About 10 calories (0 calories from fat), 0g protein, 3g carbohydrate, 0g total fat, 0g fiber, 0mg cholesterol, 50mg sodium ● ♥

Roasted Tandoori-Style Chicken Breasts

Plain yogurt tenderizes the chicken, while the exotic spices add lots of flavor.

ACTIVE TIME: 10 minutes
TOTAL TIME: 40 minutes plus marinating
MAKES: 6 main-dish servings

2   limes
1   container (8 ounces) plain low-fat yogurt
½   small onion, chopped
1   tablespoon minced, peeled fresh ginger
1   tablespoon paprika
1   teaspoon ground cumin
1   teaspoon ground coriander
¾   teaspoon salt
¼   teaspoon cayenne (ground red) pepper
pinch ground cloves
6   medium bone-in chicken breast halves (3 pounds), skin removed

1. From 1 lime, squeeze 2 tablespoons juice. Cut remaining lime into 6 wedges; set aside for garnish. In blender, puree lime juice, yogurt, onion, ginger, paprika, cumin, coriander, salt, cayenne, and cloves until smooth. Place chicken and yogurt marinade in medium bowl or in zip-tight plastic bag, turning to coat chicken. Cover bowl or seal bag and refrigerate chicken 30 minutes to marinate.

2. Preheat oven to 450°F. Arrange chicken on rack in medium roasting pan (14″ by 10″). Spoon half of marinade over chicken; discard remaining marinade.

3. Roast chicken until juices run clear when thickest part of chicken is pierced with tip of knife, about 30 minutes.

4. Transfer chicken to warm platter; garnish with lime wedges to serve.

EACH SERVING: About 200 calories (14 percent calories from fat), 36g protein, 5g carbohydrate, 3g total fat (1g saturated), 0g fiber, 88mg cholesterol, 415mg sodium ♥ ▤

Chicken Thighs Provençal

The quintessentially Provençal combination of thyme, basil, fennel, and orange makes sensational chicken.

ACTIVE TIME: 30 minutes
TOTAL TIME: 1 hour 45 minutes
MAKES: 8 main-dish servings

2   pounds skinless, boneless chicken thighs, fat removed and each cut into quarters
¾   teaspoon salt
3   teaspoons olive oil
2   red peppers, cut into ¼-inch-wide strips
1   yellow pepper, cut into ¼-inch-wide strips
1   jumbo onion (1 pound), thinly sliced
3   cloves garlic, crushed with garlic press
1   can (28 ounces) plum tomatoes
¼   teaspoon dried thyme
¼   teaspoon fennel seeds, crushed
3   strips (3" by 1" each) orange peel
½   cup loosely packed fresh basil leaves, chopped

1. Sprinkle chicken with ½ teaspoon salt. In nonreactive 5-quart Dutch oven, heat 1 teaspoon oil over medium-high heat until very hot. Add half of chicken and cook until golden brown, about 5 minutes per side. With tongs, transfer chicken pieces to bowl as they are browned. Repeat with 1 teaspoon oil and remaining chicken pieces.

2. Reduce heat to medium. To drippings in Dutch oven, add remaining 1 teaspoon oil, red and yellow peppers, onion, and remaining ¼ teaspoon salt. Cook, stirring frequently, until vegetables are tender and lightly browned, about 20 minutes. Add garlic; cook 1 minute longer.

3. Return chicken to Dutch oven. Add tomatoes with their juice, thyme, fennel seeds, and orange peel; heat to boiling, breaking up tomatoes with side of spoon. Reduce heat; cover and simmer until chicken loses its pink color throughout, about 15 minutes. Transfer to serving bowl and sprinkle with basil to serve.

EACH SERVING: About 215 calories (29 percent calories from fat), 24g protein, 12g carbohydrate, 7g total fat (1g saturated), 3g fiber, 94mg cholesterol, 480mg sodium ♥ 🍲

EAT YOUR PEPPERS

Bell peppers come in a rainbow of rich colors, and, while there's no such thing as an unhealthy choice, some are nutrition standouts. Red peppers pack the most powerful antioxidant punch, but yellow and orange peppers are close behind, say researchers from Louisiana State University. Yellow peppers are also the vitamin C champs: Just one delivers 340 milligrams of the vitamin—more C than you'd get in three 8-ounce glasses of orange juice. Green peppers, which haven't matured to their final color, also haven't developed their full array of nutrients. Still, eating one will ensure that you meet your 60-milligram vitamin C quota for the day.

Honey-Mustard Chicken and Potatoes

Everything for this meal cooks in the oven at the same time. If you'd like to add something green, steamed fresh green beans make a delicious accompaniment.

ACTIVE TIME: 10 minutes
TOTAL TIME: 1 hour 35 minutes
MAKES: 4 main-dish servings

1½ pounds small red potatoes, each cut into quarters
1 jumbo onion (1 pound), cut into 8 wedges
6 teaspoons olive oil
¾ teaspoon salt
¼ teaspoon coarsely ground black pepper
4 medium chicken breast halves, skin removed
2 tablespoons honey mustard

1. Preheat oven to 450°F. In small roasting pan (13" by 9"), toss potatoes and onion with 4 teaspoons oil, salt, and pepper. Place pan on middle rack and roast 25 minutes.

2. Meanwhile, place chicken breast halves in separate small roasting pan (13" by 9"); coat chicken with 1 teaspoon oil. In cup, mix remaining 1 teaspoon oil with honey mustard; set aside.

3. After potatoes and onions have baked 25 minutes, remove pan from oven and carefully turn pieces with metal spatula. Return to oven, placing pan on lower oven rack. Place chicken on upper rack.

4. After chicken has baked 10 minutes, remove from oven and brush with honey mustard mixture. Continue baking chicken, along with potatoes and onions, 12 to 15 minutes longer, until juices run clear when thickest part of chicken is pierced with a knife and potatoes and onions are golden and tender. Serve hot.

EACH SERVING: About 380 calories (24 percent calories from fat), 31g protein, 44g carbohydrate, 10g total fat (1g saturated), 3g fiber, 66mg cholesterol, 630mg sodium

THE SKINNY ON POULTRY

The breast is the most tender part of the bird—and also the leanest. Consider everyone's favorite, chicken: A three-and-a-half-ounce portion of breast meat without skin has about 4 grams of fat. The same amount of skinless dark meat has about 10 grams of fat.

And, whether you're eating chicken, turkey, duck, or Cornish hen, keep in mind that removing poultry skin slashes the amount of fat almost in half. You may prefer, however, to cook poultry with the skin on to keep the moisture in. Then simply remove the skin before eating. The fat reduction is practically the same, but the cooked bird will be juicier and more flavorful.

Rosemary Roast Turkey Breast

When a whole turkey is too much, use just the breast. It will make white-meat fans very happy.

ACTIVE TIME: 20 minutes
TOTAL TIME: 2 hours 35 minutes
MAKES: 10 main-dish servings

1   bone-in turkey breast (6 to 7 pounds)
1½ teaspoons dried rosemary, crumbled
1   teaspoon salt
¾   teaspoon coarsely ground black pepper
1   cup canned or homemade chicken broth
     (page 93)

1. Preheat oven to 350°F. Rinse turkey breast with cold running water and drain well; pat dry with paper towels. In cup, combine rosemary, salt, and pepper. Rub rosemary mixture on both inside and outside of turkey breast.

2. Place turkey, skin side up, on rack in small roasting pan (13″ by 9″). Cover turkey with loose tent of foil. Roast turkey 1 hour 30 minutes. Remove foil; roast, occasionally basting with pan drippings, 45 to 60 minutes longer. Start checking for doneness during last 30 minutes of cooking. Turkey breast is done when temperature on meat thermometer inserted into thickest part of breast (not touching bone) reaches 170°F and juices run clear when thickest part of breast is pierced with tip of knife.

3. Transfer turkey to warm platter. Let stand 15 minutes to set juices for easier carving.

4. Meanwhile, pour broth into drippings in hot roasting pan; heat to boiling, stirring until browned bits are loosened from bottom of pan. Strain mixture through sieve into 1-quart saucepan; let stand 1 minute. Skim and discard fat. Heat over medium heat until hot; serve with turkey. Remove skin before eating.

EACH SERVING WITHOUT SKIN OR PAN JUICES: About 250 calories (23 percent calories from fat), 55g protein, 0g carbohydrate, 2g total fat (0g saturated), 0g fiber, 152mg cholesterol, 428mg sodium

Healthy Makeover
Fried Chicken

The crunchy coating is what seals in the juices, giving traditional Southern fried chicken its finger-licking flavor. Too bad it also absorbs so much fat. By stripping the bird of its skin, baking instead of frying, and ditching the batter for panko crumbs, our crispy cheat carves off 240 calories and 22 grams of fat per serving.

ACTIVE TIME: 10 minutes
TOTAL TIME: 45 minutes plus marinating
MAKES: 4 main-dish servings

1½ cups buttermilk
½   teaspoon cayenne (ground red) pepper
¾   teaspoon salt
1   (3 pound) cut-up chicken (8 pieces), skin removed from all pieces except wings
1½ cups panko (Japanese-style) bread crumbs
1   teaspoon grated fresh lemon peel

1. In large zip-tight plastic bag, place buttermilk, cayenne, and salt; add chicken pieces, turning to coat. Seal bag, pressing out excess air. Refrigerate chicken at least 1 hour or preferably overnight, turning bag over once.

2. Preheat oven to 425°F. Spray 15½″ by 10½″ jelly-roll pan with nonstick spray. In large bowl, combine panko and lemon peel.

3. Remove chicken from marinade, shaking off excess. Discard marinade. Add chicken pieces, a few at a time, to panko mixture, turning to coat. Place chicken in prepared pan.

4. Bake 30 to 35 minutes or until coating is crisp and juices run clear when thickest part of chicken is pierced with tip of knife. For browner coating, after chicken is cooked, turn oven to broil. Broil chicken 5 to 6 inches from source of heat 1 to 2 minutes or until golden brown.

EACH SERVING: About 305 calories (27 percent calories from fat), 36g protein, 16g carbohydrate, 9g total fat (3g saturated), 1g fiber, 101mg cholesterol, 370mg sodium ♥

Crispy Chicken Tenders with BBQ Sauce

Chinese five-spice powder, a robust blend of cinnamon, cloves, fennel seed, star anise, and Szechuan peppercorns, is a handy helper when you want to keep the number of ingredients to a minimum. It is available in Asian markets and most supermarkets.

TOTAL TIME: 30 minutes

MAKES: 4 main-dish servings

¾   cup panko (Japanese-style bread crumbs)
2   tablespoons sesame seeds
1   large egg white
1   teaspoon Chinese five-spice powder
½   teaspoon salt
1   pound chicken breast tenders
1   tablespoon olive oil
1   small onion, chopped
½   cup ketchup
1   tablespoon brown sugar
1½ teaspoons cider vinegar
1½ teaspoons Worcestershire sauce

1. Preheat oven to 475°F. In 10-inch skillet, toast bread crumbs and sesame seeds over high heat, stirring frequently, until golden, about 5 minutes. Transfer crumb mixture to plate. Do not wash skillet.

2. In medium bowl, with wire whisk or fork, mix egg white, ½ teaspoon five-spice powder, and salt until foamy. Dip chicken tenders in egg-white mixture, then in crumb mixture to coat. Place tenders on cookie sheet. Bake tenders, without turning, until they lose their pink color throughout, 13 to 15 minutes.

3. Meanwhile, in same skillet, heat oil over medium heat until hot. Add onion and cook until soft and lightly browned, 8 to 10 minutes. Remove skillet from heat; stir in ketchup, brown sugar, vinegar, Worcestershire, and remaining ½ teaspoon five-spice powder. Pour sauce into small bowl and serve with tenders.

EACH SERVING: About 280 calories (23 percent calories from fat), 30g protein, 23g carbohydrate, 8g total fat (1g saturated), 1g fiber, 66mg cholesterol, 775mg sodium

Turkey Shepherd's Pie

Here's a good way to use up those Thanksgiving leftovers: a turkey-meat filling topped with leftover mashed potatoes. Although the canned chicken broth called for here works well, the dish is even better if you use the turkey carcass to make a flavorful homemade turkey broth.

ACTIVE TIME: 30 minutes
TOTAL TIME: 1 hour

MAKES: 4 main-dish servings

1	tablespoon olive oil
2	carrots, peeled and finely chopped
1	onion, finely chopped
1	celery stalk, finely chopped
2	cups mashed potatoes
¾	cup milk
2	tablespoons all-purpose flour
1	cup canned or homemade chicken broth (page 93) or turkey broth
8	ounces cooked turkey meat, cut into bite-size pieces (2 cups)
1	cup frozen peas
¼	teaspoon salt
⅛	teaspoon coarsely ground black pepper

pinch dried thyme

1. In 5- to 6-quart Dutch oven, heat oil over medium heat. Add carrots, onion, and celery; cook until vegetables are tender and lightly browned, about 15 minutes.

2. Meanwhile, in small bowl, stir mashed potatoes with ¼ cup milk until combined.

3. Preheat oven to 450°F. In cup, with fork, mix flour with broth and remaining ½ cup milk until blended. Pour broth mixture into Dutch oven with vegetables. Cook over high heat, stirring often, until mixture boils and thickens slightly. Boil 1 minute. Reduce heat to medium; add turkey, frozen peas, salt, pepper, and thyme; heat through.

4. Place four 1½-cup ramekins or soufflé dishes on 15½" by 10½" jelly-roll pan for easier handling. Spoon warm turkey mixture into ramekins; top with potato mixture. Bake until hot, bubbly, and potatoes are lightly browned, 30 minutes.

EACH SERVING: About 320 calories (28 percent calories from fat), 25g protein, 33g carbohydrate, 10g total fat (3g saturated), 3g fiber, 54mg cholesterol, 615mg sodium

Chicken and Apple Meat Loaves

Easy to prepare chicken meat loaves spiced with fennel seeds, parsley, and brushed with an apple jelly and mustard sauce make for a scrumptious and calorie-saving main dish.

ACTIVE TIME: 25 minutes
TOTAL TIME: 1 hour

MAKES: 4 main-dish servings

1	slice whole wheat bread
¼	cup low-fat (1%) milk
4	medium Golden Delicious apples
1	pound ground dark-meat chicken
½	cup finely chopped onion
¼	cup packed fresh flat-leaf parsley leaves, finely chopped
1	large egg, lightly beaten
1½	teaspoons fennel seeds
½	teaspoon salt
½	teaspoon ground black pepper
1	tablespoon vegetable oil
¼	cup apple jelly
1	tablespoon Dijon mustard with seeds

Green beans for serving (optional)

1. Preheat oven to 450°F. In food processor with knife blade attached, pulse bread into fine crumbs. Transfer to large bowl and stir in milk; let crumbs soak. Meanwhile, grate half of 1 apple on large holes of box grater. Cut remaining apple half and remaining 3 apples into wedges, removing and discarding cores; set aside.

2. To bowl with crumbs, add chicken, onion, parsley, egg, grated apple, ½ teaspoon fennel seeds, salt, and pepper. With hands, mix until well combined. Divide mixture into 4 equal pieces. On 18" by 12" jelly-roll pan, form each piece into 4 ½" by 2 ½" loaf, spacing loaves 3 inches apart.

3. In large bowl, toss apples, oil, and remaining 1 teaspoon fennel seeds until well combined; scatter in even layer around meat loaves. Roast 10 minutes.

4. Meanwhile, stir together apple jelly and mustard until well blended. Brush or spoon thick layer of mixture onto meat loaves. Roast 10 minutes or until tops are browned and temperature on meat thermometer inserted into center of meat loaves reaches 165°F. Transfer apples and meat loaves to serving plates. Serve with green beans, if you like.

EACH SERVING: About 380 calories (26 percent calories from fat), 27g protein, 44g carbohydrate, 11g total fat (2g saturated), 6g fiber, 145mg cholesterol, 515mg sodium

Beef, Pork, Veal & Lamb

If you're trying to cut back on red meat to lower your intake of saturated fat and cholesterol, you're not alone. The good news: You don't have to eliminate beef, pork, or even veal and lamb from your diet altogether (unless your doctor prescribes it). Simply focus on lean cuts of meat, like flank steak and pork tenderloin, and explore low-fat cooking methods, from grilling to roasting. We've provided lots of flavorful recipes—many rounded out with wholesome veggies and grains—so fire up your grill or preheat that oven. It's time to enjoy a little meat.

If you love steak and chops, our steak- and pepper-filled fajitas, flank steak sandwiches, rosemary lamb chops, and Brazilian-style pork chops allow you to indulge. See also "The Skinny on Grilled Meat" (page 185) for other lean cuts you can sink your teeth into. Or heat up a skillet and stir-fry slices of lean beef or pork with mixed vegetables; our orange-flavored pork and asparagus stir-fry is a winner.

We also offer low-maintenance slow-cooking roasts that make it easy for you to get a hot, home-cooked meal on the dinner table. Try our sweet and savory pork, which gets its sweetness from prunes and its salt from olives and capers, or our simple soy-honey roast tenderloin—just toss some sweet potatoes into the pot and you have a meal.

Pasta with meat sauce is a classic combination. We provide recipes for a whole-wheat penne with a zesty beef and picadillo sauce and even a lighter take on classic beef stroganoff.

Soy-Honey Pork with Sweet Potatoes (recipe page 199)

Pastrami-Spiced Flank Steak Sandwiches

Pastrami, a popular New York City deli item, probably came to us via the Romanians, who prepared many of their meats by rubbing them with aromatic spices and then smoking them. Although our pastrami isn't smoked, it is similarly coated with spices. Serve it on sliced rye with a side of coleslaw, deli style.

ACTIVE TIME: 15 minutes
TOTAL TIME: 30 minutes plus marinating
MAKES: 6 main-dish servings

1	tablespoon coriander seeds
1	tablespoon paprika
1	tablespoon cracked black pepper
2	teaspoons ground ginger
1½	teaspoons salt
1	teaspoon sugar
½	teaspoon crushed red pepper
3	garlic cloves, crushed with garlic press
1	beef flank steak (about 1½ pounds), well trimmed
12	slices rye bread

deli-style mustard

1. In mortar with pestle or in zip-tight plastic bag with rolling pin, crush coriander seeds. In cup, mix coriander, paprika, black pepper, ginger, salt, sugar, and crushed red pepper.

2. Rub garlic on both sides of steak, then pat with spice mixture. Place steak in large zip-tight plastic bag; seal bag, pressing out excess air. Place bag on plate; refrigerate at least 2 hours or up to 24 hours.

3. Prepare outdoor grill for direct grilling over medium heat.

4. Remove steak from bag. Place steak on hot grill rack over medium heat and grill, turning once, 13 to 15 minutes for medium-rare or until desired doneness.

5. Place bread slices on grill rack over medium heat and toast, without turning, just until grill marks appear on underside of bread.

6. Transfer steak to cutting board and let stand 10 minutes to allow juices to set for easier slicing. Thinly slice steak across the grain and serve mounded on grilled rye bread with mustard alongside.

EACH SERVING: About 380 calories (28 percent calories from fat), 33g protein, 35g carbohydrate, 12g total fat (4g saturated), 3g fiber, 47mg cholesterol, 1,015mg sodium

TIP: *Crushing whole spices in a mortar with a pestle releases their flavorful oils, which makes the steak even tastier.*

Steak and Pepper Fajitas

Arrange the meat and condiments in pretty dishes and let each person make his own.

ACTIVE TIME: 10 minutes
TOTAL TIME: 30 minutes
MAKES: 4 main-dish servings

1	beef top round steak, 1 inch thick (¾ pound), well trimmed
1	jar (8 ounces) medium-hot chunky salsa
1	tablespoon light corn-oil spread (56% to 60% fat)
1	red onion, thinly sliced
1	green pepper, thinly sliced
1	red pepper, thinly sliced
2	tablespoons chopped fresh cilantro leaves
8	(6-inch) low-fat flour tortillas, warmed as label directs
1	container (8 ounces) fat-free sour cream
8	ounces fat-free sharp Cheddar cheese, shredded (2 cups)

chile peppers, lime wedges, and cilantro sprigs for garnish

1. Preheat broiler. Place steak on rack in broiling pan; spread ¼ cup salsa on top. Place pan in broiler at closest position to source of heat; broil steak 8 minutes. Turn steak over and spread ¼ cup salsa on top; broil 8 minutes longer for medium-rare or until desired doneness.

2. Meanwhile, in nonstick 12-inch skillet, melt corn-oil spread over medium heat. Add red onion, green pepper, and red pepper; cook until vegetables are tender-crisp. Stir in chopped cilantro. Spoon mixture into serving bowl.

3. Slice steak crosswise into thin slices. Serve steak with pepper mixture, tortillas, sour cream, shredded cheese, and remaining salsa. Garnish with chile peppers, lime wedges, and cilantro.

EACH SERVING: About 450 calories (14 percent calories from fat), 45g protein, 55g carbohydrate, 7g total fat (1g saturated), 6g fiber, 51mg cholesterol, 1,060mg sodium

---

THE SKINNY ON GRILLED MEAT

Grilling lends mouthwatering flavor to even the leanest cuts of meat. Try these options the next time you fire up your grill.

+ **BEEF:** Look for round or loin (eye or top round, tenderloin, or flank steak).
+ **PORK:** Choose loin or leg (tenderloin, loin, or sirloin chops).
+ **LAMB:** The leanest cuts are loin chops, boneless leg shank halves, or leg and shoulder cubes for kabobs.
+ **VEAL:** Get cutlets from leg or loin chops.

All of these cuts are 185 calories or less and have just 3 to 9 grams of fat per trimmed, cooked 3-ounce serving. When selecting meat, *rib* is the clue to high fat; so is *ground*—except if specifically labeled *90 percent lean* or higher. If you're craving burgers, preparing turkey or chicken patties is a smart, low-fat alternative. See "The Ground Roundup," page 113, for details.

Steak and Oven Fries

While the potatoes are in the oven, you can pan-fry the steak, make the red-wine-and-shallot sauce, and even whip up a salad and dressing. This dish pairs nicely with a simple salad such as romaine tossed with a vinaigrette.

ACTIVE TIME: 15 minutes
TOTAL TIME: 40 minutes

MAKES: 4 main-dish servings

Oven Fries (page 260)
1   beef flank steak (1 pound)
¼   teaspoon coarsely ground black pepper
2   teaspoons olive oil
1   large shallot, finely chopped
½   cup dry red wine
½   cup canned or homemade chicken broth (page 93)
2   tablespoons chopped fresh parsley

1. Prepare Oven Fries.

2. Meanwhile, pat steak dry with paper towels; sprinkle with pepper on both sides. Heat non-stick 12-inch skillet over medium heat until hot. Add steak and cook 7 minutes per side, turning over once, for medium-rare, or until desired doneness. Transfer steak to cutting board; keep warm.

3. To drippings in skillet, add olive oil; heat over medium heat. Add shallot and cook, stirring occasionally, until golden, about 2 minutes. Increase heat to medium-high. Add wine and broth; heat to boiling. Cook 3 to 4 minutes. Stir in parsley.

4. To serve, holding knife blade almost parallel to cutting surface, slice steak crosswise into thin slices. Spoon red-wine sauce over steak slices and serve with Oven Fries.

EACH SERVING WITH OVEN FRIES: About 390 calories (25 percent calories from fat), 31g protein, 40g carbohydrate, 11g total fat (4g saturated), 4g fiber, 46mg cholesterol, 455mg sodium ♥

COOKING WITH WINE

Wine adds fat-free flavor and body to quick pan sauces, stews, and poached fruit desserts. Because the success of any dish is determined by the quality of its ingredients, it is important to cook with good wine. Avoid the cooking wines sold in supermarkets; they're high in salt and low in flavor. Instead, consider using the leftovers from a bottle of wine served the night before or some of the wine you'll serve with the dish.

Beef Eye Round au Jus

Roast some herbed new potatoes while you prepare the beef. And for the tenderest results, do not roast this cut to more than medium-rare.

ACTIVE TIME: 30 minutes
TOTAL TIME: 1 hour 40 minutes
MAKES: 12 main-dish servings

1½   teaspoons salt
½   teaspoon dried thyme
¼   teaspoon ground black pepper
1   beef eye round roast (4 ½ pounds), trimmed
2   tablespoons olive oil
1   bag (16 ounces) carrots, peeled and cut into 2" by ¼" matchstick strips
1   pound leeks (3 medium), white and light green parts only, cut into 2" by ¼" matchstick strips
4   garlic cloves, thinly sliced
1¼   cups dry red wine
½   cup water
1   bay leaf

1. Preheat oven to 450°F. In small bowl, combine salt, thyme, and pepper; use to rub on roast. In 12-inch skillet, heat oil over medium-high heat until very hot. Add beef and cook until browned on all sides, about 10 minutes. Transfer beef to nonreactive medium roasting pan (14" by 10").

2. Add carrots, leeks, and garlic to skillet and cook, stirring occasionally, until carrots are tender, about 7 minutes. Arrange vegetable mixture around beef.

3. Roast beef 25 minutes. Add wine, water, and bay leaf to roasting pan. Turn oven control to 325°F and roast until meat thermometer inserted in center of roast reaches 140°F, about 45 minutes longer. Internal temperature of meat will rise to 145°F (medium) upon standing. Or roast until desired doneness. Remove and discard bay leaf.

4. When roast is done, transfer to warm large platter and let stand 15 minutes to set juices for easier slicing. To serve, cut roast into thin slices and serve with vegetables.

EACH SERVING: About 230 calories (28 percent calories from fat), 33g protein, 6g carbohydrate, 8g total fat (2g saturated), 1g fiber, 76mg cholesterol, 358mg sodium ♥

Stir-Fried Steak and Vegetables

This healthy-in-a-hurry recipe contains whole grains (brown rice), yellow-orange veggies (red pepper and carrots), protein-rich beef (top round steak), and green veggies (broccoli and snow peas).

TOTAL TIME: 25 minutes

MAKES: 4 main-dish servings

1	beef top round steak (1 pound)
⅓	cup reduced-sodium soy sauce
2	large garlic cloves, crushed with garlic press
1	onion
1	red pepper
2	teaspoons vegetable oil
1	package (8 ounces) sliced cremini mushrooms
2	cups broccoli florets
2	carrots, thinly sliced
3	ounces snow peas, trimmed and cut in thirds
2	tablespoons grated, peeled fresh ginger
¾	cup water
1	pouch (8½ ounces) precooked brown rice, heated as label directs

1. With knife blade held in slanted position, almost parallel to cutting surface, cut steak crosswise into ⅛-inch-thick slices (see Tip). In medium bowl, toss steak slices with 1 tablespoon soy sauce and 1 crushed garlic clove. Let stand 5 minutes.

2. Meanwhile, cut onion in half, then cut crosswise into thin slices. Cut red pepper into ¼-inch-thick slices. Set aside.

3. In deep nonstick 12-inch skillet, heat 1 teaspoon oil over medium heat until very hot but not smoking. Add half of beef and stir frequently (stir-fry) just until beef is no longer pink, 30 to 45 seconds. Transfer beef to plate. Without adding additional oil to skillet, repeat with remaining beef.

4. In same skillet, heat remaining 1 teaspoon oil until hot. Add mushrooms and onion; cover and cook, stirring occasionally, until mushrooms are browned, 3 to 4 minutes.

5. Add broccoli, carrots, snow peas, red pepper, ginger, water, and remaining soy sauce and garlic to skillet. Stir-fry until vegetables are tender-crisp, 5 to 6 minutes. Remove skillet from heat; stir in beef with its juices. Serve over rice.

EACH SERVING: About 380 calories (28 percent calories from fat), 34g protein, 34g carbohydrate, 12g total fat (4g saturated), 7g fiber, 68mg cholesterol, 790mg sodium ⊘ ❤

TIP: *To cut raw beef into thin, even slices for stir-fries, first freeze the beef for about fifteen minutes until it is firm. Then be sure to choose a sharp knife for slicing. By the time you finish cutting it, the meat will have lost its chill, and you can proceed with the recipe as directed.*

Beef and Barley
with Mushrooms

This is a hearty dinner of sautéed beef tossed
with a rich barley-and-mushroom pilaf.
Because top round steak is a very lean cut,
it must be thinly sliced across the grain—
otherwise it may be tough.

ACTIVE TIME: 30 minutes
TOTAL TIME: 1 hour 10 minutes
MAKES: 6 main-dish servings

3	cups boiling water
1	package (½ ounce) dried porcini mushrooms
1	beef top round steak, ¾ inch thick (about 1½ pounds)
1	teaspoon olive oil
1	tablespoon soy sauce
1	package (8 ounces) sliced white mushrooms
2	carrots, peeled, cut lengthwise in half, then crosswise into ¼-inch-thick slices
1	onion, finely chopped
½	teaspoon salt
¼	teaspoon ground black pepper
¼	teaspoon dried thyme
1½	cups pearl barley
1	can (14½ ounces) chicken broth or 1¾ cups homemade (page 93)
½	cup loosely packed fresh parsley leaves

1. Into medium bowl, pour boiling water over porcini; let stand 10 minutes.

2. Meanwhile, cut steak lengthwise in half. With knife blade held in slanted position, almost parallel to cutting surface, slice each half of steak crosswise into ⅛-inch-thick slices (see Tip, page 188).

3. In deep nonstick 12-inch skillet, heat oil over medium heat until hot. Add half of steak slices and cook until they just lose their pink color, about 2 minutes, stirring constantly. Transfer steak to medium bowl; repeat with remaining steak. Toss steak slices with soy sauce; set aside.

4. To same skillet, add mushrooms, carrots, onion, salt, pepper, and thyme; cook over medium-high heat until vegetables are tender-crisp, about 12 minutes, stirring occasionally.

5. While vegetables are cooking, with slotted spoon, remove porcini from soaking water, reserving liquid. Rinse porcini to remove any sand; coarsely chop. Strain soaking water through sieve lined with paper towel into medium bowl.

6. Add barley, broth, porcini, and mushroom soaking water to vegetables in skillet; heat mixture to boiling over medium-high heat. Reduce heat to medium-low; cover and simmer until barley and vegetables are tender and most of the liquid has evaporated, 35 to 40 minutes, stirring occasionally. Stir in steak mixture and parsley; heat through.

EACH SERVING: About 320 calories (20 percent calories from fat), 47g carbohydrate, 20g protein, 7g total fat (2g saturated), 10g fiber, 34mg cholesterol, 695mg sodium 🍲 🍱

Meatballs in Spicy Tomato Sauce

Dishes like meatballs and meat loaf are perfect vehicles for injecting whole-grain healthiness into the menu without anyone in your family being any the wiser! Here, cracked wheat is added to the meatball mix. Enjoy this over your favorite pasta shape (choose one that's whole grain, if possible) or rice (brown rice is a good pick to up the fiber content).

ACTIVE TIME: 35 minutes
TOTAL TIME: 55 minutes

MAKES: 6 main-dish servings

½	cup coarse cracked wheat
2 ¾	cups cold water
1	onion
1	pound lean (90%) ground beef, preferably sirloin
¼	cup lightly packed fresh mint leaves, chopped, plus an additional ¼ cup, torn
1	large egg, lightly beaten
1	teaspoon ground cumin
1	teaspoon salt
½	teaspoon ground black pepper
1	tablespoon olive oil
2	large garlic cloves, minced
¼	teaspoon ground cinnamon
⅛ to ¼	teaspoon cayenne (ground red) pepper
1	can (28 ounces) plum tomatoes
⅓	cup golden raisins
3	tablespoons crumbled feta cheese

1. Place cracked wheat in medium bowl; bring 2 cups water to a boil and pour over wheat. Cover bowl with plastic wrap and let stand 30 minutes. Pour into a large sieve and drain.

2. Meanwhile, preheat oven to 400°F. Line 15½″ by 10½″ jelly-roll pan with foil and spray with nonstick cooking spray. On large holes of box grater, grate enough onion to make ¼ cup. Chop remaining onion and set aside.

3. In large bowl, combine cracked wheat, grated onion, ground beef, chopped mint, egg, ½ teaspoon cumin, ½ teaspoon salt, ¼ teaspoon black pepper, and ¼ cup cold water until well blended, but not overmixed.

4. Shape ground beef mixture by heaping tablespoonfuls into 24 meatballs. Place 1 inch apart on prepared pan. Bake until cooked through, about 20 minutes.

5. Meanwhile, in large nonstick skillet over medium heat, heat oil until hot. Add reserved chopped onion and cook until tender and starting to brown, about 8 minutes, stirring often. Stir in garlic, cinnamon, cayenne, remaining ½ teaspoon cumin, ½ teaspoon salt, and ¼ teaspoon black pepper; cook until fragrant, about 30 seconds. Add tomatoes with their juice, raisins, and remaining ½ cup water; bring to boiling over high heat, breaking up tomatoes with side of spoon. Reduce heat, cover, and simmer, stirring occasionally, until sauce thickens, about 20 minutes.

6. Add meatballs and simmer until meatballs are hot, about 5 minutes. Sprinkle with feta and torn mint leaves.

EACH SERVING: 250 calories (29 percent calories from fat), 20g protein, 24g carbohydrate, 8g total fat (3g saturated), 4g fiber, 80mg cholesterol, 776mg sodium

Bulgur and Beef Stuffed Peppers

This recipe is so delicious, we've doubled it so you'll have an extra casserole on hand. To freeze it, wrap casserole completely in foil, crimping edges to seal well.

ACTIVE TIME: 40 minutes
TOTAL TIME: 1 hour 15 minutes
MAKES: 2 casseroles, 4 main-dish servings each

8	large red, yellow, orange, and/or green peppers, with stems, if possible
2	cans (14½ ounces each) low-sodium chicken broth or 3½ cups homemade (page 93)
1½	cups bulgur
1	tablespoon olive oil
1	onion, chopped
3	garlic cloves, crushed with garlic press
1	pound lean (90%) ground beef
1	package (10 ounces) frozen chopped spinach, thawed and squeezed dry
½	cup loosely packed fresh dill, chopped
2	cans (28 ounces each) crushed tomatoes
4	ounces feta cheese, crumbled (1 cup)
¼	teaspoon salt
¼	teaspoon coarsely ground black pepper

1. Cut ¾-inch-thick slices from top of each pepper; reserve tops, including stems. Remove seeds and ribs, and cut thin slice from bottom so each pepper will stand upright.

2. Arrange 4 peppers and tops (separately) on a microwave-safe plate. Cook, uncovered, in microwave on High 4 minutes. With tongs, transfer tops to paper towel. Microwave peppers 4 to 5 minutes longer, until just tender. Invert peppers onto double thickness of paper towels to drain. Repeat with remaining peppers and tops.

3. In microwave-safe large bowl, combine broth and bulgur. Microwave, uncovered, on High 12 to 15 minutes, until bulgur is tender but still slightly chewy and most of broth is absorbed.

4. Meanwhile, in deep 12-inch skillet, heat oil over medium heat until hot. Add onion and garlic, and cook until onion begins to turn golden, about 5 minutes, stirring frequently. Remove ¼ cup onion mixture and reserve. Add beef to remaining onion in skillet and cook until beef is no longer pink, 6 to 8 minutes, breaking up beef with spoon. Remove skillet from heat.

5. Into beef in skillet, stir bulgur, spinach, dill, 1 cup crushed tomatoes, and ¾ cup feta. Fill peppers with bulgur mixture, using 1 generous cup for each; sprinkle with remaining ¼ cup feta. Replace pepper tops.

6. Preheat oven to 350°F. Wipe skillet clean.

7. In same skillet, combine remaining tomatoes, reserved onion mixture, salt, and pepper; heat to boiling over medium-high heat, stirring occasionally. Divide tomato sauce evenly between two 2-quart shallow casseroles or 8-inch square glass baking dishes. Place 4 peppers in each dish. Cover one dish with foil and bake until peppers are hot, about 35 minutes. Wrap second dish well for freezing. To reheat, first defrost casserole in refrigerator for 24 hours. To reheat, bake, loosely covered with foil, in 350°F oven 1 hour; uncover and heat 45 minutes longer.

EACH SERVING: About 380 calories (28 percent calories from fat), 24g protein, 49g carbohydrate, 12g total fat (5g saturated), 13g fiber, 52mg cholesterol, 616mg sodium 🟡 🧺

Thai Noodles with Beef and Basil

Why spring for takeout when you can toss together a healthier noodle stir-fry for a fraction of the cost?

ACTIVE TIME: 20 minutes
TOTAL TIME: 25 minutes

MAKES: 4 main-dish servings

1   package (7 to 8 ounces) rice stick noodles (see page 89)

1   tablespoon vegetable oil

4   garlic cloves, thinly sliced

3-inch piece fresh ginger, peeled, cut into thin slivers

1   onion, thinly sliced

12 ounces lean (90%) ground beef

½   cup canned or homemade chicken broth (page 93)

3   tablespoons Asian fish sauce (see Tip, page 88)

1   teaspoon sugar

¾   teaspoon crushed red pepper

¼   cup chopped fresh cilantro

¼   cup sliced fresh basil

1   small cucumber, cut lengthwise in half and thinly sliced crosswise

½   cup bean sprouts, rinsed and drained

¼   cup unsalted peanuts, chopped

1   lime, cut into wedges

1. In large bowl, soak rice stick noodles in enough *hot water* to cover for 15 minutes. (Do not soak longer or noodles may become too soft.) Drain well.

2. Meanwhile, heat oil in 12-inch skillet over medium heat. Add garlic, ginger, and onion; cook, stirring occasionally, until golden, 8 to 10 minutes. Stir in beef; cook, stirring and breaking up beef with spoon, until meat is no longer pink, about 5 minutes. Stir in broth, fish sauce, sugar, and crushed red pepper; simmer, uncovered, until thickened slightly, about 5 minutes.

3. Add drained noodles, cilantro, and basil to beef mixture; cook, stirring, until heated through. Divide noodle mixture among four bowls; top each with cucumber, bean sprouts, and peanuts. Serve with lime wedges.

EACH SERVING: About 450 calories (28 percent calories from fat), 25g protein, 60g carbohydrate, 14g total fat (3g saturated), 4g fiber, 40mg cholesterol, 720mg sodium

Lean Beef Stroganoff

This comfort food favorite typically contains a lot of calories and fat. Here we offer a skinnier version that gets its creaminess from nonfat sour cream.

ACTIVE TIME: 20 minutes
TOTAL TIME: 30 minutes

MAKES: 6 main-dish servings

1	boneless beef top sirloin steak, ¾ inch thick (1 pound), well trimmed

olive-oil nonstick cooking spray

3	teaspoons olive oil
1	pound mushrooms, trimmed and thickly sliced
1	onion, chopped
1	teaspoon cornstarch
1	cup beef broth
½	cup chili sauce
2	tablespoons spicy brown mustard
2	tablespoons plus ¼ cup water
2	bags (6 ounces each) radishes, halved if large
12	ounces sugar snap peas or snow peas, strings removed
½	teaspoon salt
1	package (12 ounces) extra-wide curly noodles, cooked as label directs
6	tablespoons nonfat sour cream
2	tablespoons chopped fresh parsley leaves

1. Holding knife blade almost parallel to cutting surface, slice steak crosswise into very thin slices (see Tip, page 188).

2. Spray nonstick 12-inch skillet lightly with olive-oil nonstick cooking spray. Heat skillet over medium heat. Add half of meat and cook, stirring quickly and constantly, until meat loses its pink color, about 2 minutes. Transfer to bowl. Without using more nonstick spray, repeat with remaining meat.

3. In same skillet, heat 2 teaspoons olive oil over medium heat. Add mushrooms and onion and cook, stirring, until tender. In cup, mix cornstarch and beef broth; stir into mushroom mixture with chili sauce and mustard. Cook, stirring, until mixture boils and thickens slightly. Return beef to skillet; heat through.

4. Meanwhile, in nonstick 10-inch skillet, heat remaining 1 teaspoon olive oil and 2 tablespoons water over medium heat until hot. Add sugar snap peas and cook until tender-crisp, 5 to 7 minutes. Transfer to bowl. In same skillet, pour remaining ¼ cup water and cook radishes over medium-high heat, until tender-crisp, 5 to 7 minutes. Add sugar snap peas and salt to radishes; heat through.

5. Spoon noodles onto six dinner plates. Spoon beef mixture over noodles; top each serving with 1 tablespoon sour cream and sprinkle with parsley. Serve with sugar snap peas and radishes.

EACH SERVING: About 430 calories (19 percent calories from fat), 30g protein, 58g carbohydrate, 9g total fat (2g saturated), 5g fiber, 90mg cholesterol, 740mg sodium ✓ ✦

Penne Rigate with Picadillo Sauce

Here pasta gets a Spanish twist, with a meat sauce similar to the filling you might find in empanadas.

ACTIVE TIME: 10 minutes
TOTAL TIME: 25 minutes

MAKES: 6 main-dish servings

1	package (16 ounces) whole-wheat penne rigate, bow ties (farfalle), or radiatore
2	teaspoons olive oil
1	small onion (4 to 6 ounces), finely chopped
2	garlic cloves, crushed with garlic press
¼	teaspoon ground cinnamon
⅛ to ¼	teaspoon cayenne (ground red) pepper
¾	pound lean (90%) ground beef
½	teaspoon salt, plus additional for seasoning
1	can (14¼ ounces) tomatoes in puree, preferably reduced sodium
½	cup dark seedless raisins
¼	cup salad olives or chopped pimiento-stuffed olives, drained

chopped fresh parsley for garnish

1. In large saucepot, cook pasta as label directs.

2. Meanwhile, in nonstick 12-inch skillet, heat oil over medium heat until hot. Add onion and cook, stirring frequently, until tender, about 5 minutes. Stir in garlic, cinnamon, and cayenne; cook 30 seconds. Add beef and salt and cook, stirring frequently, until beef begins to brown, about 8 minutes. Spoon off any excess fat as necessary. Stir in tomatoes with their puree, raisins, and olives, breaking up tomatoes with side of spoon, and cook until sauce thickens slightly, about 5 minutes longer.

3. When pasta has reached desired doneness, remove *1 cup pasta cooking water;* set aside. Drain pasta and return to saucepot. Add beef mixture and reserved cooking water; toss well to coat pasta. Season with salt to taste. Garnish with parsley to serve.

EACH SERVING: About 450 calories (24 percent calories from fat), 22g protein, 67g carbohydrate, 12g total fat (3g saturated), 9g fiber, 37mg cholesterol, 175mg sodium (if using reduced-sodium tomatoes) ● ❤ ⓥ

WHITE VERSUS WHOLE-WHEAT PASTA

Whole-wheat and multigrain pastas pack a nutritious punch. Enriched brands of whole-wheat pasta have more thiamin, riboflavin, and folic acid than regular pasta and contain five times the amount of fiber. And the nutty taste of the whole wheat makes it a great choice for fall and winter cooking.

Some brands have a strong grainy taste and a chewy texture, so experiment until you find one that suits your palate. Note: Unless the label says *100 percent whole wheat*, the product is actually a whole-wheat blend, which still provides a higher fiber content than regular pasta.

Whole-wheat and multigrain pastas have a shorter shelf life than semolina pasta; use them within six months of purchase.

Pork Roast with Salsa Verde

Tomatillos are the main ingredient in salsa verde (green sauce). They bring a bright hint of lemon to this slow-cooker dish.

ACTIVE TIME: 10 minutes
SLOW-COOK TIME: 8 hours on Low or 5 hours on High
MAKES: 8 main-dish servings

1	large bunch cilantro
3	garlic cloves, sliced
2	pounds small red potatoes (about 8), cut into quarters
1	bone-in pork-shoulder roast (about 3 pounds), well trimmed
1	jar (16 to 18 ounces) salsa verde

1. From bunch of cilantro, remove and set aside 15 large sprigs. Remove enough leaves from remaining cilantro to equal ½ cup, loosely packed. Refrigerate leaves for garnish.

2. In 4½- to 6-quart slow-cooker pot, combine cilantro sprigs, garlic, and potatoes. Place pork on top of potato mixture. Pour salsa over and around pork. Cover slow cooker with lid and cook as manufacturer directs on Low 8 to 10 hours or on High 5 to 5½ hours.

3. Transfer pork to cutting board and slice. Transfer pork and potatoes to warm deep platter. Skim and discard fat and cilantro from cooking liquid. Spoon cooking liquid over pork and potatoes. Sprinkle reserved cilantro over pork.

EACH SERVING: About 300 calories (27 percent calories from fat), 25g protein, 27g carbohydrate, 9g total fat (3g saturated), 2g fiber, 79mg cholesterol, 295mg sodium ♥ 🍽

Sweet and Savory Pork

Salty olives and capers interplay with sweet prunes to create a mouthwatering sauce.

ACTIVE TIME: 15 minutes
TOTAL TIME: 25 minutes
MAKES: 4 main-dish servings

1	pork tenderloin (1 pound), cut crosswise into 1-inch-thick slices, patted dry
2	tablespoons brown sugar
3	garlic cloves, crushed with garlic press
¾	teaspoon salt
¼	teaspoon ground black pepper
2	teaspoons olive oil
½	cup dry white wine
2	tablespoons red wine vinegar
1	teaspoon cornstarch
¼	teaspoon dried oregano
½	cup pitted prunes, coarsely chopped
¼	cup pitted green olives, coarsely chopped
2	tablespoons capers, drained

1. On waxed paper, combine brown sugar, garlic, salt, and pepper; use to coat pork.

2. In nonstick 12-inch skillet, heat oil over medium heat until hot. Add pork and cook until slices are lightly browned and lose their pink color throughout, about 3 minutes per side. Transfer pork to plate.

3. In cup, blend wine, vinegar, cornstarch, and oregano. Stir cornstarch mixture into skillet. Heat to boiling, stirring. Return pork to skillet. Add prunes, olives, and capers; heat through.

EACH SERVING: About 270 calories (23 percent calories from fat), 25g protein, 22g carbohydrate, 7g total fat (2g saturated), 2g fiber, 74mg cholesterol, 892mg sodium ⊘

Soy-Honey Pork with Sweet Potatoes

Honey-soy glaze unites sweet potatoes and pork tenderloin for a very tasty meal. Let the hot oven do the work for you and enjoy your hassle-free dinner in only 40 minutes. For photo, see page 182.

ACTIVE TIME: 15 minutes
TOTAL TIME: 40 minutes

MAKES: 4 main-dish servings

¼	cup reduced-sodium soy sauce
2	tablespoons hoisin sauce
2	tablespoons honey
1	tablespoon rice vinegar
1	teaspoon grated, peeled fresh ginger
2	garlic cloves, crushed with press
1	whole pork tenderloin (1¼ pounds)
1½	pounds sweet potatoes
1	tablespoon vegetable oil
¼	teaspoon salt
⅛	teaspoon ground black pepper
2	green onions, cut into slivers

1. Preheat oven to 475°F. In small bowl, whisk soy sauce, hoisin, honey, vinegar, ginger, and half of garlic until well blended. Pour into gallon-size zip-tight plastic bag. Add pork; seal bag and turn until pork is well coated. Set aside.

2. Meanwhile, peel sweet potatoes. Cut each into ½-inch-thick rounds. In large bowl, combine oil and remaining garlic. Add sweet potatoes, salt, and pepper. Toss until well coated.

3. Transfer pork from marinade to center of 18″ by 12″ jelly-roll pan, shaking off any excess marinade into bag. Tuck tapered ends under pork to ensure even cooking. Arrange sweet potato rounds in single layer on pan around pork. Roast 10 minutes.

4. Meanwhile, transfer marinade to 2-quart saucepan. Heat to boiling over medium-high heat. Boil 3 minutes or until thickened and syrupy. Transfer half of marinade to small serving bowl; set aside. Turn sweet potatoes and pork over. Brush remaining marinade on pork. Roast 10 to 15 minutes longer or until temperature on meat thermometer inserted into thickest part of pork registers 155°F and sweet potatoes are browned. Cover pork loosely with foil and let stand 5 minutes.

5. Cut pork into ½-inch-thick slices.

6. Transfer pork and sweet potatoes to large platter. Garnish with green onions and serve with reserved marinade.

EACH SERVING: About 430 calories (19 percent total fat), 44g protein, 45g carbohydrate, 9g total fat (2g saturated), 4g fiber, 103mg cholesterol, 875mg sodium

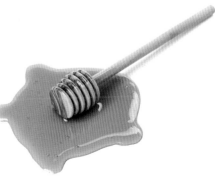

Pork Tenderloin with Roasted Grapes

If you've never had roasted grapes, try this recipe. They are absolutely delicious and a perfect match for the pork.

ACTIVE TIME: 15 minutes
TOTAL TIME: 30 minutes

MAKES: 4 main-dish servings

1	teaspoon fennel seeds, crushed
½	teaspoon salt
½	teaspoon coarsely ground black pepper
1	pork tenderloin (1 pound)
2	teaspoons extra-virgin olive oil
3	cups seedless red and green grapes (about 1 pound)
½	cup canned or homemade chicken broth (page 93)

1. Preheat oven to 475°F. In cup, with fork, stir fennel seeds, salt, and pepper. Rub mixture all over pork.

2. In 12-inch skillet with oven-safe handle, heat oil over medium-high heat until very hot. Add pork and cook 5 minutes, turning to brown all sides of tenderloin.

3. Add grapes and broth to skillet; heat to boiling. Cover and place in oven. Roast until meat thermometer inserted in center of roast reaches 150°F, 15 to 18 minutes. Internal temperature of meat will rise to 160°F upon standing. Transfer pork to warm platter.

4. Meanwhile, heat grape mixture to boiling over high heat; boil until liquid has thickened slightly, about 1 minute. Slice pork; serve with grapes and pan juices.

EACH SERVING: About 245 calories (26 percent calories from fat), 25g protein, 22g carbohydrate, 7g total fat (2g saturated), 2g fiber, 74mg cholesterol, 475mg sodium ♥ ❤

Pork Steak with Plum Glaze

For this recipe, we butterfly pork tenderloin, then pound it for quick, even cooking. A meat mallet is a handy tool for this job, but a small heavy skillet or a rolling pin will work, too.

ACTIVE TIME: 25 minutes
TOTAL TIME: 30 minutes
MAKES: 4 main-dish servings

1	pork tenderloin (1 pound), trimmed
1	teaspoon salt
¼	teaspoon coarsely ground black pepper
½	cup plum jam or preserves
1	tablespoon brown sugar
1	tablespoon grated, peeled fresh ginger
1	tablespoon fresh lemon juice
½	teaspoon ground cinnamon or Chinese five-spice powder
2	garlic cloves, crushed with garlic press
4	large plums (1 pound), each cut in half and pitted

cooked white rice (optional)

1. Prepare grill for covered direct grilling over medium heat, or preheat ridged grill pan over medium heat until very hot.

2. Holding knife blade parallel to cutting surface and against long side of tenderloin, cut pork lengthwise almost in half, being careful not to cut all the way through. Open tenderloin like a book and spread flat. With meat mallet, pound pork to even ¼-inch thickness (or place pork between two sheets of plastic wrap and pound with rolling pin). Cut tenderloin crosswise into 4 steaks; season with salt and pepper.

3. In small bowl, with fork, mix jam, sugar, ginger, lemon juice, cinnamon, and garlic. Brush one side of each pork steak and cut side of each plum half with plum glaze.

4. Place steaks and plums, glaze side down, on grill over medium heat. Cover and cook 3 minutes. Brush steaks and plums with remaining glaze; turn steaks and plums and grill until steaks are browned on both sides and just lose their pink color throughout and plums are tender, about 3 minutes longer. Serve with rice, if desired.

EACH SERVING: About 310 calories (15 percent calories from fat), 25g protein, 42g carbohydrate, 5g total fat (1g saturated), 2g fiber, 66mg cholesterol, 524mg sodium ♥

Hoisin Pork Tenderloin with Grilled Pineapple

When choosing a pineapple, pick one that is slightly soft with a deep, sweet fragrance. Pineapples are harvested ripe and will not get any sweeter with time.

ACTIVE TIME: 10 minutes
TOTAL TIME: 30 minutes
MAKES: 4 main-dish servings

¼	cup hoisin sauce
1	tablespoon honey
1	tablespoon grated, peeled fresh ginger
1	teaspoon Asian sesame oil
1	pork tenderloin (1¼ pounds), trimmed
½	medium pineapple
2	tablespoons brown sugar

1. Prepare outdoor grill for covered direct grilling over medium heat. In small bowl, combine hoisin sauce, honey, ginger, and sesame oil.

2. Place pork on hot grill rack over medium heat. Cover grill and cook pork until an instant-read meat thermometer inserted in thickest part of tenderloin registers 155°F, 18 to 20 minutes, turning occasionally. Pork will be browned on the outside and still slightly pink in the center.

3. Meanwhile, with serrated knife, cut pineapple half into 4 wedges. Rub cut sides of pineapple with brown sugar.

4. Grill pineapple on rack with pork until browned on both sides, about 5 minutes, turning over once. While pineapple is grilling, brush pork with hoisin-honey glaze and turn frequently.

5. Transfer pork to cutting board; let stand 5 minutes to allow juices to set for easier slicing. Transfer pineapple to platter. Thinly slice pork and serve with pineapple wedges.

EACH SERVING: About 275 calories (20 percent calories from fat), 31g protein, 23g carbohydrate, 6g total fat (2g saturated), 2g fiber, 92mg cholesterol, 245mg sodium ♥ ♥

Pork, Cabbage, and Apple Sauté

A splash of cider vinegar adds tang to this hearty skillet supper of pan-browned pork chops, shredded cabbage, sliced apples, red potatoes, and caramelized onions.

ACTIVE TIME: 15 minutes
TOTAL TIME: 55 minutes

MAKES: 4 main-dish servings

1 teaspoon olive oil

4 bone-in pork loin chops, ¾ inch thick (about 6 ounces each), trimmed

¾ teaspoon salt

¼ teaspoon ground black pepper

1 large onion (12 ounces), thinly sliced

1 bag (16 ounces) shredded cabbage mix for coleslaw

2 large Golden Delicious or Gala apples (8 ounces each), cored and cut into ½-inch-thick slices

12 ounces red potatoes, cut into 1-inch pieces

¾ cup apple cider

¼ teaspoon dried thyme

1 tablespoon cider vinegar

1. In nonstick 12-inch skillet, heat oil over medium heat until hot. Add pork chops; sprinkle with ¼ teaspoon salt and ⅛ teaspoon pepper. Cook chops until golden on the outside and still slightly pink inside, about 4 minutes per side. Transfer chops to a plate; keep warm.

2. Add onion to skillet, and cook over medium heat, covered, stirring occasionally, until tender and golden, 8 to 10 minutes. Gradually stir in the cabbage mix and cook until wilted, about 5 minutes. Add apples, potatoes, apple cider, thyme, and remaining ½ teaspoon salt and ⅛ teaspoon pepper; heat to boiling. Reduce heat to medium-low, and simmer, covered, until potatoes are tender, about 15 minutes.

3. Stir in vinegar. Tuck chops into cabbage mixture and heat through.

EACH SERVING: About 380 calories (26 percent calories from fat), 26g protein, 46g carbohydrate, 11g total fat (3g saturated), 8g fiber, 69mg cholesterol, 535mg sodium

Brazilian Pork Chops

An excellent example of Brazilian-influenced cuisine, this spicy dish, with a hint of citrus, is accompanied by black beans.

ACTIVE TIME: 15 minutes
TOTAL TIME: 30 minutes

MAKES: 4 main-dish servings

4	boneless pork loin chops, ¾ inch thick (5 ounces each), trimmed
½	teaspoon ground cumin
½	teaspoon ground coriander
¼	teaspoon dried thyme
⅛	teaspoon ground allspice
½	teaspoon salt
1	teaspoon olive oil
1	onion, chopped
3	garlic cloves, crushed with garlic press
1	can (15 to 19 ounces) black beans, rinsed and drained
½	cup canned or homemade chicken broth (page 93)
1	tablespoon fresh lime juice
¼	teaspoon coarsely ground black pepper
¼	cup packed fresh cilantro leaves, chopped

fresh orange wedges (optional)

1. Pat pork chops dry with paper towels. In cup, mix cumin, coriander, thyme, allspice, and ¼ teaspoon salt. Rub both sides of pork chops with spice mixture.

2. Heat nonstick 12-inch skillet over medium heat until hot. Add pork chops and cook until lightly browned outside and still slightly pink inside, about 4 minutes per side. Transfer pork to platter; keep warm.

3. In same skillet, heat oil over medium heat. Add onion and cook, stirring frequently, until golden, about 5 minutes. Add the garlic and cook, stirring, 1 minute longer. Add beans, broth, lime juice, pepper, and remaining ¼ teaspoon salt; heat through.

4. To serve, spoon bean mixture over pork; sprinkle with cilantro. Serve with orange wedges, if you like.

EACH SERVING: About 340 calories (29 percent calories from fat), 42g protein, 25g carbohydrate, 11g total fat (3g saturated), 10g fiber, 76mg cholesterol, 760mg sodium

Orange Pork and Asparagus Stir-Fry

Slices of lean pork tenderloin are quickly cooked with fresh asparagus and juicy orange pieces. For photo, see page 8.

ACTIVE TIME: 20 minutes
TOTAL TIME: 25 minutes
MAKES: 4 main-dish servings

2	navel oranges
1	teaspoon olive oil
1	pork tenderloin (about ¾ pound), trimmed and thinly sliced diagonally
¾	teaspoon salt
¼	teaspoon ground black pepper
1½	pounds thin asparagus, trimmed and each stalk cut crosswise in half
1	garlic clove, crushed with garlic press
¼	cup water

1. From 1 orange, grate 1 teaspoon peel and squeeze ¼ cup juice. Remove peel and white pith from remaining orange. Cut orange into ¼-inch-thick slices; cut each slice into quarters.

2. In nonstick 12-inch skillet, heat ½ teaspoon oil over medium heat until hot. Add half the pork, and sprinkle with ¼ teaspoon salt and ⅛ teaspoon pepper; cook, stirring frequently (stir-frying), until pork just loses its pink color, 2 minutes. Transfer pork to plate. Repeat with remaining pork, again using ½ teaspoon oil, ¼ teaspoon salt, and remaining ⅛ teaspoon pepper. Transfer pork to same plate.

3. To the same skillet, add asparagus, garlic, grated orange peel, remaining ¼ teaspoon salt, and water; cover and cook, stirring occasionally, until asparagus is tender-crisp, about 3 minutes. Return pork to skillet. Add reserved orange juice and orange pieces; heat through, stirring often.

EACH SERVING: About 165 calories (22 percent calories from fat), 24g protein, 8g carbohydrate, 4g total fat (1g saturated), 2g fiber, 50mg cholesterol, 495mg sodium

EAT YOUR ASPARAGUS

Fresh asparagus is a springtime treat not to be missed. It's a great source of folic acid, which protects against heart disease and birth defects, so women of child-bearing years should add it to their menu. Enjoy it with rich salmon, or steam up a handful (it takes less than 10 minutes), sprinkle lightly with salt or a little grated Parmesan cheese, and enjoy. At 3 calories a spear, you can afford to eat a whole bunch.

Sesame Pork Stir-Fry

So gingery good—and this one-dish meal is only 375 calories per serving.

ACTIVE TIME: 20 minutes
TOTAL TIME: 40 minutes
MAKES: 4 main-dish servings

Aromatic Brown Rice (page 250)

1   cup loosely packed watercress leaves, coarsely chopped

1   pork tenderloin (12 ounces), trimmed and thinly sliced

2   tablespoons soy sauce

1   tablespoon minced, peeled fresh ginger

1   teaspoon Asian sesame oil

1   garlic clove, crushed with garlic press

¾   cup canned or homemade chicken broth (page 93)

1¼ teaspoons cornstarch

2   teaspoons olive oil

3   carrots, peeled and cut into 2" by ¼" matchstick strips

1   red pepper, cut into ¼-inch-wide strips

1   tablespoon water

1   medium zucchini (about 8 ounces), cut into 2" by ¼" matchstick strips

1. Prepare Aromatic Brown Rice. Stir in watercress and keep warm.

2. Meanwhile, in medium bowl, toss pork, soy sauce, ginger, sesame oil, and garlic. In cup, mix broth and cornstarch; set aside.

3. In nonstick 12-inch skillet, heat 1 teaspoon olive oil over medium heat until hot. Add carrots and red pepper; cook, stirring frequently (stir-frying), until lightly browned, about 5 minutes. Add water and stir-fry until vegetables are tender-crisp, 3 to 5 minutes longer. Transfer to bowl.

4. In same skillet, heat remaining 1 teaspoon olive oil. Add zucchini; stir-fry until tender-crisp, about 3 minutes. Transfer zucchini to bowl with other vegetables.

5. To same skillet, add pork mixture and stir-fry until pork just loses its pink color. Stir cornstarch mixture; add to pork. Stir in vegetables; heat to boiling. Boil until sauce thickens, 1 minute. Serve stir-fry with watercress rice.

EACH SERVING: About 375 calories (24 percent calories from fat), 23g protein, 48g carbohydrate, 10g total fat (2g saturated), 3g fiber, 56mg cholesterol, 975mg sodium

Osso Buco with Gremolata

This aromatic recipe from northern Italy is a wonderful choice for company. A risotto is the traditional accompaniment, or for a lower-calorie meal, pair the veal with broccoli rabe tossed with a little balsamic vinegar.

ACTIVE TIME: 40 minutes
TOTAL TIME: 2 hours 40 minutes
MAKES: 4 main-dish servings

4   meaty veal shank cross cuts (osso buco), each about 2 inches thick (1 pound total)
½   teaspoon salt
¼   teaspoon ground black pepper
1   tablespoon olive oil
2   onions, chopped
3   carrots, peeled and chopped
2   stalks celery, chopped
4   garlic cloves, finely chopped
1   can (14½ to 16 ounces) tomatoes in puree
1   cup dry white wine
1   cup canned or homemade chicken broth (see page 93)
1   bay leaf
2   tablespoons chopped fresh parsley
½   teaspoon freshly grated lemon peel

1. Preheat oven to 350°F. Sprinkle shanks with salt and pepper. In nonreactive 5-quart Dutch oven, heat oil over medium-high heat until very hot. Add shanks and cook until browned on both sides, about 10 minutes, transferring shanks to plate as they are browned.

2. Add onions to Dutch oven and cook over medium heat, stirring occasionally, until slightly browned, about 5 minutes. Add carrots, celery, and three-fourths of garlic and cook 2 minutes longer.

3. Return veal to Dutch oven. Stir in tomatoes with their puree, wine, broth, and bay leaf; heat to boiling over high heat. Cover and place in oven. Bake until veal is tender when pierced with fork, about 2 hours.

4. Meanwhile, prepare gremolata: In small bowl, mix parsley, lemon peel, and remaining garlic. Cover and refrigerate until ready to serve.

5. Transfer veal to platter. Heat sauce in Dutch oven to boiling over high heat; boil until it has reduced to 4 cups, about 10 minutes. Pour sauce over veal and sprinkle with gremolata.

EACH SERVING: About 375 calories (17 percent calories from fat), 53g protein, 20g carbohydrate, 8g total fat (2g saturated), 4g fiber, 183mg cholesterol, 874mg sodium

Glazed Rosemary Lamb Chops

These rosemary-scented lamb chops are broiled with an apple-jelly and balsamic-vinegar glaze. Keep this glaze in mind for pork, too.

ACTIVE TIME: 10 minutes
TOTAL TIME: 20 minutes

MAKES: 4 main-dish servings

8	lamb loin chops, 1 inch thick (4 ounces each)
1	large garlic clove, cut in half
2	teaspoons chopped fresh rosemary or ½ teaspoon dried rosemary, crumbled
¼	teaspoon salt
¼	teaspoon coarsely ground black pepper
¼	cup apple jelly
1	tablespoon balsamic vinegar

1. Preheat broiler as manufacturer directs. Rub both sides of each lamb chop with garlic. Sprinkle lamb with rosemary, salt, and pepper. In cup, combine apple jelly and balsamic vinegar.

2. Place chops on rack in broiling pan. With pan at closest position to source of heat; broil chops 4 minutes. Brush chops with half of apple-jelly mixture; broil 1 minute. Turn chops and broil 4 minutes longer. Brush chops with remaining jelly mixture and broil 1 minute longer for medium-rare or until desired doneness.

3. Transfer lamb to warm platter. Skim and discard fat from drippings in pan. Serve chops with pan juices or drizzle lamb with additional balsamic vinegar.

EACH SERVING: About 240 calories (30 percent calories from fat), 26g protein, 14g carbohydrate, 8g total fat (3g saturated), 0g fiber, 82mg cholesterol, 223mg sodium 💚 🖤

Lamb Kabobs and Salad Slaw

This is a delicious meal in one.

ACTIVE TIME: 40 minutes
TOTAL TIME: 50 minutes
MAKES: 4 main-dish servings

1	pound boneless leg of lamb, from shank
⅓	cup chili sauce
2	tablespoons teriyaki sauce
¼	head red cabbage
1	head romaine lettuce
1	bunch green onions
1	large navel orange
¼	cup orange juice
2	tablespoons low-fat mayonnaise
1	tablespoon cider vinegar
1	teaspoon prepared mustard
¼	teaspoon cracked black pepper
⅛	teaspoon salt
4	(12-inch) metal skewers

1. Trim all fat from lamb. Cut lamb into 12 chunks. In medium bowl, mix lamb, chili sauce, and teriyaki sauce until lamb is coated; set aside.

2. Thinly slice cabbage; discard any tough ribs. Cut romaine crosswise into ¼-inch-thick ribbons. Cut green onions into 2-inch pieces. Cut orange in half; cut each half into 3 wedges; cut each wedge crosswise in half.

3. In large bowl, stir orange juice, mayonnaise, vinegar, mustard, pepper, and salt until blended. Add cabbage and lettuce; toss salad slaw until dressing is evenly distributed.

4. Prepare outdoor grill for direct grilling over medium heat.

5. On skewers, alternately thread lamb chunks, green-onion pieces, and orange pieces. Place skewers on hot grill rack over medium heat. Cook lamb 10 to 12 minutes for medium-rare or until desired doneness, turning once.

6. Transfer skewers to platter. Serve kabobs with salad slaw and orange wedges.

EACH SERVING: About 265 calories (30 percent calories from fat), 28g protein, 20g carbohydrate, 9g total fat (3g saturated), 7g fiber, 74mg cholesterol, 810mg sodium 🌿

EAT YOUR CITRUS

Looking for some vitamin C? Head to the citrus section of your supermarket! Go beyond the traditional oranges and try diminutive clementines, garnet-fleshed blood oranges, giant yellow and pink grapefruit, and bite-size kumquats—all are rich in vitamin C. On average, a single piece of citrus fruit also contains 3 grams of fiber and only about 50 calories. While a glass of fresh-squeezed OJ is pretty sweet in the morning, you'll miss out on that good fiber if you drink your citrus instead of eating it.

Meatless
Mains

Looking to incorporate more grains and greens into your family's diet? We have the perfect solution: Go vegetarian a couple nights a week. Here, we provide so many tasty options, your kids will be looking forward to Meatless Mondays in no time.

Start with familiar favorites. Serve our hearty black bean burgers with a side of oven-fried potatoes (page 260) or our crunchy carrot coleslaw (page 61). Or simmer a big pot of our spicy vegetarian chili made special with white beans and tomatillos. Hankering for pizza? Our broccoli and ricotta version, featuring a crust made from precooked rounds of polenta, is fresh and healthy.

If vegetables for dinner sound boring, try stuffing them for a fun new twist. Our artichokes filled with couscous make a complete meal. Or bake our gingery napa cabbage and bulgur casserole for a hot, satisfying dish on a cold night.

And, of course, we have not forgotten the noodles. Our ratatouille rigatoni, sprinkled with just a little Parmesan cheese, has the power to entice even the most adamant eggplant detractors. Other options include our family-style lasagna (it's brimming with healthy veggies) or mac and cheese, which features whole-grain pasta and tomato slices for a more wholesome take on everybody's go-to comfort food.

Rataouille Rigatoni (recipe page 231)

Vegetarian Souvlaki

No one will miss the meat in these yummy pita sandwiches. Make the filling by cutting up your favorite veggie burgers.

ACTIVE TIME: 20 minutes
TOTAL TIME: 25 minutes

MAKES: 4 sandwiches

1   tablespoon olive oil
1   large onion, cut in half and thinly sliced
4   frozen vegetarian soy burgers (10- to 12-ounce package), cut into 1-inch pieces
¼   teaspoon ground black pepper
½   teaspoon salt
1   container (8 ounces) plain nonfat yogurt
1   English (seedless) cucumber (8 ounces), cut into ¼-inch dice
1   teaspoon dried mint
1   small garlic clove, crushed with garlic press
4   (6- to 7-inch) pita breads, warmed
1   ripe medium tomato (6 ounces), cut into ½-inch dice
1   ounce feta cheese, crumbled (¼ cup)

1. In nonstick 12-inch skillet, heat oil over medium heat until hot. Add onion and cook until tender and golden, 12 to 15 minutes, stirring occasionally. Add burger pieces, pepper, and ¼ teaspoon salt, and cook until heated through, about 5 minutes.

2. Meanwhile, in medium bowl, stir yogurt with cucumber, mint, garlic, and remaining ¼ teaspoon salt. Add burger mixture and toss gently to combine.

3. Cut 1-inch slice from each pita to make opening. Reserve cut-off pitas for another use. Spoon one-fourth of burger mixture into each pita. Sprinkle with tomato and feta.

EACH SANDWICH: About 390 calories (30 percent calories from fat), 24g protein, 45g carbohydrate, 13g total fat (3g saturated), 6g fiber, 9mg cholesterol, 945mg sodium

BBQ Tofu Sandwiches

Here's a quick and easy way to flavor tofu.

ACTIVE TIME: 20 minutes
TOTAL TIME: 25 minutes
MAKES: 4 sandwiches

1	package (16 ounces) extra-firm tofu
¼	cup ketchup
2	tablespoons Dijon mustard
2	tablespoons reduced-sodium soy sauce
1	tablespoon molasses
1	tablespoon grated, peeled fresh ginger
⅛	teaspoon cayenne (ground red) pepper
2	garlic cloves, crushed with garlic press
2	teaspoons sesame seeds
8	slices whole-grain bread, toasted

sliced ripe tomatoes, sliced red onion, and
  lettuce leaves (optional)

1. Drain tofu; wrap in clean dish towel. Place wrapped tofu in pie plate; top with a dinner plate. Place 1 to 2 heavy cans on top of plate to weight down tofu to extract excess water; set aside about 15 minutes.

2. Meanwhile, preheat broiler. Coat rack in broiling pan with nonstick cooking spray.

3. In small bowl, combine ketchup, mustard, soy sauce, molasses, ginger, cayenne, and garlic, stirring until blended.

4. Remove plate and cans, unwrap tofu, and place on cutting board. Cut tofu lengthwise into 8 slices.

5. Place slices on rack in broiling pan; brush with half of ketchup mixture. Place in broiler about 5 inches from source of heat and broil tofu until ketchup mixture looks dry, about 3 minutes. With metal spatula, turn slices over; brush with remaining ketchup mixture and sprinkle with sesame seeds. Broil tofu 3 minutes longer.

6. To serve, place 2 tofu slices on 1 slice of toasted bread. Top with tomato, onion, and lettuce, if you like. Top with another slice of bread. Repeat with remaining tofu and bread.

EACH SANDWICH: About 230 calories (8 percent calories from fat), 14g protein, 35g carbohydrate, 5g total fat (0g saturated), 2g fiber, 0mg cholesterol, 975mg sodium

Black-Bean Burgers

Spicy cumin and coriander flavor these healthy meat-free black-bean burgers.

ACTIVE TIME: 15 minutes
TOTAL TIME: 20 minutes
MAKES: 4 main-dish servings

¼	cup dried bread crumbs
¼	teaspoon ground cumin
¼	teaspoon ground coriander
2	cans (15 ounces each) low-sodium black beans, rinsed and drained, or 3 cups cooked black beans
4	tablespoons light mayonnaise
¼	teaspoon salt
¼	teaspoon ground black pepper
2	large stalks celery, finely chopped
1	chipotle chile in adobo, finely chopped
4	green-leaf lettuce leaves
4	whole-wheat hamburger buns, toasted
4	slices ripe tomato

1. In food processor with knife blade attached, pulse bread crumbs, cumin, coriander, two-thirds of beans, 2 tablespoons mayonnaise, salt, and pepper until well blended. Transfer to large bowl. Stir in celery and remaining whole beans until well combined. Divide into 4 portions and shape into patties.

2. Lightly coat nonstick 12-inch skillet with nonstick cooking spray. Heat on medium 1 minute, then add patties. Cook 10 to 12 minutes or until browned on both sides, turning once.

3. Meanwhile, in small bowl, combine chipotle chile and remaining 2 tablespoons mayonnaise until well mixed. Place 1 lettuce leaf on bottom of each bun; top with patty, then tomato slice. Divide chipotle mayonnaise among burgers and replace tops of buns to serve.

EACH SERVING: About 370 calories (19 percent calories from fat), 18g protein, 59g carbohydrate, 8g total fat (1g saturated), 14g fiber, 5mg cholesterol, 725mg sodium ● ●

Polenta with Garlicky Greens

This is a nutritious meal of soft cornmeal, with a tasty topping of sautéed Swiss chard, raisins, and pine nuts. We simplified and reduced the total prep time by microwaving the polenta. (Stir just once instead of constantly.)

ACTIVE TIME: 30 minutes
TOTAL TIME: 50 minutes
MAKES: 4 main-dish servings

2	bunches Swiss chard (3½ pounds)
1	tablespoon olive oil
3	garlic cloves, thinly sliced
¼	teaspoon crushed red pepper
1	teaspoon salt
⅓	cup plus 4½ cups water
¼	cup golden raisins
1½	cups yellow cornmeal
2	cups skim milk
2	tablespoons freshly grated Parmesan or Romano cheese, plus additional for serving
1	tablespoon pine nuts (pignoli), toasted and chopped

1. Cut off and discard bottom 3 inches of Swiss-chard stems. Cut remaining stems into ½-inch-thick slices; coarsely chop leaves. Rinse stems and leaves separately and dry with paper towels; place in separate bowls.

2. In nonstick 12-inch skillet, heat oil, garlic, and crushed red pepper over medium heat until garlic is lightly golden, about 2 minutes, stirring occasionally.

3. Add sliced chard stems to skillet and cook 8 minutes, stirring occasionally. Gradually add chard leaves and ½ teaspoon salt, stirring until leaves wilt; stir in ⅓ cup water. Cover skillet and simmer until stems and leaves are tender, about 5 minutes; stir in raisins and set aside.

4. Meanwhile, prepare polenta in microwave oven: In 4-quart microwave-safe bowl or casserole, combine cornmeal, remaining ½ teaspoon salt, milk, and remaining 4½ cups water. Cover and cook on High 12 to 15 minutes, until thickened, stirring once.

5. To serve, stir Parmesan into polenta. Spoon polenta onto platter; top with Swiss-chard mixture and sprinkle with pine nuts. Serve with additional Parmesan to sprinkle over each serving, if you like.

EACH SERVING: About 415 calories (15 percent calories from fat), 16g protein, 76g carbohydrate, 7g total fat (1g saturated), 10g fiber, 5mg cholesterol, 995mg sodium ☻

Broccoli-Cheese Polenta Pizza

Here's a different take on pizza, made with the toothsome corn goodness of ready-made polenta. Using part-skim ricotta helps keep the calories and fat low.

ACTIVE TIME: 20 minutes
TOTAL TIME: 25 minutes

MAKES: 4 main-dish servings

olive oil nonstick cooking spray

1	log (16 ounces) precooked plain polenta, cut into ¼-inch-thick slices
1	bag (12 ounces) broccoli flowerets
¾	cup part-skim ricotta cheese
¼	cup freshly grated Parmesan cheese
1	teaspoon freshly grated lemon peel
⅛	teaspoon ground black pepper
1	large ripe plum tomato (4 ounces), chopped

1. Preheat broiler.

2. Coat 12-inch pizza pan or large cookie sheet with cooking spray. In center of pizza pan, place 1 slice polenta; arrange remaining slices in two concentric circles around first slice, overlapping slightly to form a 10-inch round. Generously coat polenta with cooking spray. Place pan in oven about 4 inches from heat source; broil polenta until heated through, about 5 minutes. Do not turn broiler off.

3. Meanwhile, in microwave-safe medium bowl, combine broccoli and *2 tablespoons water*. Cover with plastic wrap, turning back one section to vent. Heat broccoli in microwave oven on High 3 minutes or just until tender. Drain.

4. In small bowl, combine ricotta, Parmesan, lemon peel, and pepper.

5. Arrange broccoli evenly over polenta. Drop cheese mixture by tablespoons over polenta and broccoli; sprinkle with tomato. Broil pizza until topping is hot, 3 to 5 minutes.

EACH SERVING: About 200 calories (27 percent calories from fat), 12g protein, 25g carbohydrate, 6g total fat (3g saturated), 4g fiber, 18mg cholesterol, 530mg sodium

Moroccan Sweet-Potato Stew

This fragrant stew, served on top of couscous, is loaded with vegetables and spices.

ACTIVE TIME: 15 minutes
TOTAL TIME: 45 minutes
MAKES: 4 main-dish servings

2	teaspoons olive oil
1	yellow onion, chopped
3	garlic cloves, crushed with garlic press
1½	teaspoons curry powder
1½	teaspoons ground cumin
¼	teaspoon ground allspice
1	can (14½ ounces) diced tomatoes
1	can (14½ ounces) reduced-sodium vegetable broth
1	cup no-salt-added canned garbanzo beans, rinsed and drained
1	large sweet potato (1 pound), peeled and cut into ¾-inch chunks
2	small zucchini (6 ounces each), cut into ¾-inch chunks
1	cup whole-grain couscous (Moroccan pasta)
¼	cup loosely packed fresh mint leaves, chopped

1. In nonstick 12-inch skillet, heat oil over medium heat until hot. Add onion and cook until tender and lightly browned, 8 to 10 minutes, stirring occasionally. Stir in garlic, curry powder, cumin, and allspice; cook 30 seconds.

2. Add tomatoes, broth, beans, and sweet potato; cover and heat to boiling over medium-high heat. Reduce heat to medium and cook 10 minutes.

3. Stir in zucchini, cover, and cook until vegetables are tender, about 10 minutes.

4. Meanwhile, prepare couscous as label directs.

5. Just before serving, stir mint into stew. Serve stew with couscous.

EACH SERVING: About 360 calories (13 percent calories from fat), 14g protein, 70g carbohydrate, 5g total fat (1g saturated), 13g fiber, 0mg cholesterol, 670mg sodium ♥ ⏱

Spiced Couscous with Vegetables

A blend of cumin, curry powder, and paprika complements this tasty Moroccan-style dish.

ACTIVE TIME: 15 minutes
TOTAL TIME: 30 minutes

MAKES: 4 main-dish servings

1	package (10 ounces) whole-wheat couscous (Moroccan pasta)
¼	teaspoon coarsely ground black pepper
2	tablespoons olive oil
1	teaspoon salt
2	carrots, peeled and cut into ¼-inch pieces
1	red onion, cut into ¼-inch pieces
1	zucchini, cut into ¼-inch pieces
3	ripe medium tomatoes, cut into ¼-inch pieces
1	tablespoon ground cumin
2	teaspoons curry powder
2	teaspoons paprika
¼	cup pine nuts (pignoli), toasted
¼	cup loosely packed fresh parsley leaves, chopped
¼	cup pitted prunes, cut into slivers

1. Prepare couscous as label directs, but instead of the salt or butter called for, stir in pepper, 1 tablespoon oil, and ½ teaspoon salt; cover and keep warm.

2. Meanwhile, in nonstick 12-inch skillet, heat remaining 1 tablespoon oil over medium heat until hot. Add carrots and onion; cook 5 minutes, stirring occasionally. Add zucchini and cook until vegetables are tender, about 5 minutes longer. Stir in tomatoes, cumin, curry, paprika, and remaining ½ teaspoon salt; cook 2 minutes.

3. Stir vegetable mixture into couscous; sprinkle with pine nuts, parsley, and prunes.

EACH SERVING: About 450 calories (24 percent calories from fat), 14g protein, 76g carbohydrate, 12g total fat (2g saturated), 14g fiber, 0mg cholesterol, 570mg sodium 🌱 🍽

GET YOUR GRAINS: COUSCOUS

Originally from North Africa, this grainlike pasta is made from semolina wheat flour. The packaged, precooked version is ready to eat in just 5 minutes and is widely available in supermarkets. Look for whole-wheat couscous, which is similar in taste and texture to regular couscous, but packs a whopping 8 grams of fiber per serving.

Farro Risotto with Butternut Squash

The firm, chewy texture of farro resembles Arborio rice but boasts the nutritional characteristics of spelt. Italians have enjoyed this grain since the days of the Roman Empire.

ACTIVE TIME: 20 minutes
TOTAL TIME: 55 minutes

MAKES: 4 main-dish servings

1   tablespoon olive oil
1   small onion, finely chopped
½   teaspoon salt
¼   teaspoon ground black pepper
1½ cups farro (emmer wheat)
½   cup dry white wine
1¼ cups water
1   can (14½ ounces) vegetable broth or 1¾ cups homemade (page 92)
⅛   teaspoon dried thyme
⅛   teaspoon dried rosemary, crushed
1   butternut squash (2 pounds), peeled and cut into ½-inch pieces
½   cup freshly grated Parmesan cheese, plus additional for serving
¼   cup loosely packed fresh parsley leaves, chopped

1. In deep nonstick 12-inch skillet, heat oil over medium heat until hot. Add onion, salt, and pepper, and cook 5 to 7 minutes or until onion is tender and lightly browned. Add farro and cook 2 to 3 minutes or until lightly browned, stirring constantly. Add wine and cook about 1 minute or until absorbed.

2. To farro mixture in skillet, add water, broth, thyme, and rosemary; cover skillet and heat to boiling over high heat. Stir in squash; reduce heat to medium-low. Cover and simmer about 20 minutes longer or until farro is just tender (mixture will still be soupy).

3. Uncover and cook 1 to 2 minutes longer over high heat, stirring constantly, until most liquid is absorbed. Remove skillet from heat and stir in Parmesan and parsley. Serve with additional Parmesan, if you like.

EACH SERVING: About 415 calories (20 percent calories from fat), 16g protein, 74g carbohydrate, 9g total fat (3g saturated), 6g fiber, 8mg cholesterol, 925mg sodium 🌱

BROWN RICE RISOTTO WITH BUTTERNUT SQUASH: Prepare recipe as above, substituting *1½ cups regular long-grain brown rice* for farro. In step 2, add *2½ cups water* and cook rice 45 minutes (instead of 20 minutes) on medium-low heat, once pot is covered and simmering.

EACH SERVING: About 445 calories (18 percent calories from fat), 13g protein, 80g carbohydrate, 9g total fat (3g saturated), 6g fiber, 8mg cholesterol, 930mg sodium 🌱

Wheat-Berry Pilaf with Green Beans

Make this tasty veggie-flecked combination of brown rice and wheat berries the centerpiece of a vegetarian meal.

ACTIVE TIME: 30 minutes
TOTAL TIME: 1 hour, 30 minutes
MAKES: 4 main-dish or 8 side-dish servings

1	cup wheat berries (whole-wheat kernels)
4	cups water
½	cup long-grain brown rice
3	teaspoons olive oil
4	carrots, peeled and cut into ½-inch dice
2	stalks celery, cut into ½-inch dice
1	large onion (12 ounces), cut into ½-inch dice
1	can (14½ ounces) vegetable broth or 1¾ cups homemade (page 92)
8	ounces green beans, trimmed and cut into 1½-inch pieces
¾	teaspoon salt
½	teaspoon freshly grated orange peel
¼	teaspoon coarsely ground black pepper
¼	teaspoon dried thyme
¾	cup dried cranberries

1. In 3-quart saucepan, heat wheat berries and water to boiling over high heat. Reduce heat to low; cover and simmer until wheat berries are firm to the bite but tender enough to eat, about 50 minutes; drain and set aside.

2. Meanwhile, in 2-quart saucepan, prepare brown rice as label directs, but do not add butter or salt.

GET YOUR GRAINS: WHEAT BERRIES

Whole wheat is a nutritional powerhouse, containing thirteen B vitamins, vitamin E, protein, and essential fatty acids. Wheat berries are unmilled kernels of wheat; they are chewy with a pleasant nutty taste that makes them a great choice for salads. The coarsely crushed kernels of wheat are sold as cracked wheat. Because the kernels have been split open, cracked wheat cooks more quickly than wheat berries, so use it when you need to get whole-grain goodness fast!

3. While wheat berries and brown rice are cooking, in deep 12-inch skillet, heat 2 teaspoons oil over medium heat until hot. Add carrots and celery; cook until almost tender, about 10 minutes, stirring occasionally. Add onion and remaining 1 teaspoon oil; cook until vegetables are lightly browned, 12 to 15 minutes longer, stirring occasionally.

4. Increase heat to high; add broth, green beans, salt, orange peel, pepper, and thyme, and heat to boiling. Reduce heat to medium-high; cook until green beans are just tender, about 5 minutes, stirring often.

5. Add cranberries, wheat berries, and brown rice to skillet; stir to combine.

EACH MAIN-DISH SERVING: About 425 calories (13 percent calories from fat), 14g protein, 84g carbohydrate, 6g total fat (1g saturated), 12g fiber, 0mg cholesterol, 790mg sodium ⓥ 🥫

Cabbage and Bulgur Casserole

We layered napa cabbage with gingery grain filling and topped it all with tangy-sweet tomatoes.

ACTIVE TIME: 45 minutes
TOTAL TIME: 1 hour 25 minutes
MAKES: 6 main-dish servings

2	cups water
1½	cups bulgur
1	tablespoon vegetable oil
2	carrots, peeled and diced
2	stalks celery, diced
1	red pepper, diced
½	small head napa cabbage (Chinese cabbage), cored and cut crosswise into 2-inch strips to equal about 12 cups
3	garlic cloves, crushed with garlic press
3	green onions, sliced
2	tablespoons minced, peeled fresh ginger
2	tablespoons plus 1 teaspoon soy sauce
2	tablespoons seasoned rice vinegar
1	can (14½ ounces) diced tomatoes
2	tablespoons brown sugar
2	tablespoons chopped fresh parsley for garnish

1. Preheat oven to 350°F.

2. In 2-quart saucepan, heat 1½ cups water to boiling over high heat; stir in bulgur. Remove saucepan from heat; cover and set aside.

3. In 5-quart Dutch oven, heat oil over medium-high heat. Add carrots, celery, and red pepper; cook 5 minutes. Add cabbage stems, and cook until vegetables are tender, 7 minutes longer. Reduce heat to low; add garlic, green onions, and ginger, and cook 1 minute longer, stirring.

4. Add remaining ½ cup water; heat to boiling over high heat. Reduce heat to low; simmer 1 minute, stirring. Remove Dutch oven from heat; stir in 2 tablespoons soy sauce, 1 tablespoon vinegar, and cooked bulgur.

5. In small bowl, combine tomatoes with their juice, brown sugar, and remaining 1 teaspoon soy sauce and 1 tablespoon vinegar.

6. In 3-quart casserole, place half of cabbage leaves; top with bulgur mixture, then remaining cabbage leaves. Spoon tomato mixture over top. Cover casserole and bake until hot in center and top layer of cabbage leaves is wilted, about 40 minutes. Sprinkle with parsley before serving.

EACH SERVING: About 220 calories (12 percent calories from fat), 7g protein, 43g carbohydrate, 3g total fat (0g saturated), 12g fiber, 0mg cholesterol, 800mg sodium ☘ 🍽

White-Bean and Tomatillo Chili

This spicy vegetarian chili is made with fresh tomatillos—the tart, green, tomatolike fruits (with papery husks) that are a staple of Southwestern cuisine. Serve with warm tortillas and a dollop of plain yogurt.

ACTIVE TIME: 25 minutes
TOTAL TIME: 45 minutes

MAKES: 4 main-dish servings

2 tablespoons olive oil

3 garlic cloves, crushed with garlic press

1 small onion, cut in half and thinly sliced

1 jalapeño chile, seeded and minced

1 teaspoon ground cumin

1 pound tomatillos, husked, rinsed, and coarsely chopped

1¼ teaspoons salt

½ teaspoon sugar

1 can (14½ ounces) low-sodium vegetable broth or 1¾ cups homemade (page 92)

1 can (4 ounces) chopped mild green chiles

1 cup water

2 cans (15 to 19 ounces each) low-sodium white kidney beans (cannellini), rinsed, drained, and coarsely mashed

1 cup loosely packed fresh cilantro leaves, chopped

1. In nonstick 10-inch skillet, heat oil over medium heat until hot. Add garlic, onion, jalapeño, and cumin, and cook until light golden, 7 to 10 minutes, stirring often.

2. Meanwhile, in 5- to 6-quart saucepot, heat tomatillos, salt, sugar, broth, green chiles and their liquid broth, and water to boiling over high heat. Reduce heat to low. Stir onion mixture into saucepot; cover and simmer 15 minutes.

3. Stir in beans and cilantro; heat through.

EACH SERVING: About 300 calories (29 percent calories from fat), 12g protein, 42g carbohydrate, 10g total fat (1g saturated), 12g fiber, 0mg cholesterol, 966mg sodium 🌱 🍲

Indian Cauliflower Curry Stew

This easy-to-make vegetarian stew owes its complex flavor to spicy, fresh ginger and traditional Indian curry powder.

ACTIVE TIME: 25 minutes
TOTAL TIME: 50 minutes
MAKES: 8 main-dish servings

1	tablespoon olive oil
3	carrots, peeled and chopped
1	onion, chopped
1½	cups brown rice
1	tablespoon finely chopped, peeled fresh ginger
1	tablespoon curry powder
¾	teaspoon salt
2½	cups canned or homemade vegetable broth (page 92)
1	medium (2-pound) head cauliflower, cut into small florets
2	cans (15 to 19 ounces each) garbanzo beans (chickpeas), rinsed and drained
½	cup loosely packed fresh cilantro leaves, chopped
¼	cup plain low-fat yogurt plus additional for serving

1. In 6-quart Dutch oven, heat oil on medium-high heat until hot. Add carrots and onion, and cook 10 to 12 minutes or until vegetables are lightly browned and tender, stirring frequently.

2. Meanwhile, prepare rice as label directs; keep warm.

3. Stir ginger, curry, and salt into carrot mixture; cook 3 minutes, stirring constantly. Add broth; cover and heat to boiling on high. Stir in cauliflower and garbanzo beans; cover and cook on medium 15 to 20 minutes longer, gently stirring every 5 minutes until cauliflower is tender.

4. To serve, stir chopped cilantro and ¼ cup yogurt into cauliflower stew. Spoon rice into serving bowls; top with stew. Serve cauliflower stew with additional yogurt to dollop on top.

EACH SERVING: About 360 calories (13 percent calories from fat), 12g protein, 68g carbohydrate, 5g total fat (1g saturated), 10g fiber, 1mg cholesterol, 650mg sodium 🌱 🍲

GET YOUR GRAINS: BROWN RICE

Consider making brown rice a staple in your diet. It has all its bran layers intact (only the inedible outer husk is removed) and therefore all its nutrients—including 3.5 grams of fiber per cup—are present and accounted for. It is an excellent source of manganese (a mineral that helps produce energy from protein and carbohydrates) and selenium (key to a healthy immune system). Experiment with long-, medium-, and short-grain options. Note: White rice has only a shadow of the nutritive value of brown rice. Even though it's often enriched, it's been stripped of its bran and germ.

Couscous-Stuffed Artichokes

Instead of topping your grains with veggies, fill your veggies with whole-grain goodness.

ACTIVE TIME: 1 hour
TOTAL TIME: 1 hour 15 minutes
MAKES: 4 main-dish servings or 8 side-dish servings

4	large artichokes
1	tablespoon lemon juice
3	tablespoons olive oil
2	carrots, peeled and diced
2	garlic cloves, minced
¼	cup chopped fresh mint
3	tablespoons chopped fresh parsley
1	cup whole-wheat couscous (Moroccan pasta)
1½	cups canned or homemade vegetable broth (page 92)
½	teaspoon salt
¼	teaspoon coarsely ground black pepper
1	lemon, cut into wedges
	parsley sprigs for garnish

1. Prepare and cook artichokes: With sharp knife, cut off 1 inch straight across top of each artichoke. Cut off stems; peel and reserve them. Pull off outer dark green leaves and trim any thorny tips. Spread artichokes open and carefully cut around and remove chokes. In a 5-quart saucepot, heat lemon juice and *1 inch water* to boiling over high heat. Set artichokes on stem ends in boiling water, along with peeled stems; heat to boiling. Reduce heat to low; cover and simmer until a knife inserted in center goes though bottom easily, 30 to 40 minutes. Drain.

2. Meanwhile, preheat oven to 400°F.

3. In nonstick 10-inch skillet, heat 1 tablespoon oil over medium heat until hot. Add carrots and cook until tender, about 10 minutes, stirring occasionally. Stir in garlic; cook 1 minute longer. Remove to medium bowl. Dice artichoke stems; add to carrot mixture with mint and parsley.

4. Prepare couscous as label directs but use 1 cup broth in place of 1 cup of water called for. When couscous is done, stir in salt, pepper, carrot mixture, and remaining 2 tablespoons oil.

5. Pour remaining ½ cup broth into shallow baking dish large enough to hold all artichokes (13″ by 9″); arrange cooked artichokes in dish. Spoon couscous mixture between artichoke leaves and into center cavities. Bake until artichokes are heated through, 15 to 20 minutes.

6. Serve artichokes with lemon wedges and garnish with parsley sprigs.

EACH MAIN-DISH SERVING: About 350 calories (28 percent calories from fat), 11g protein, 54g carbohydrate, 11g total fat (2g saturated), 12g fiber, 4mg cholesterol, 600mg sodium ☘

Family Vegetarian Lasagna

This low-cal lasagna is meat-free and loaded with veggies. It tastes great as a leftover, so you can make it over the weekend and serve it later in the week, on a busy night.

ACTIVE TIME: 25 minutes
TOTAL TIME: 1 hour 15 minutes
MAKES: 4 main-dish servings

2	zucchini or yellow summer squash, thinly sliced
2	teaspoons olive oil
¼	teaspoon salt
1	bunch Swiss chard, tough stems discarded, thinly sliced
1	small onion (4 to 6 ounces), finely chopped
2	garlic cloves, crushed with press
1	teaspoon fresh thyme leaves, chopped
1	pound plum tomatoes, cored and thinly sliced
4	no-boil lasagna noodles, rinsed with cold water
2	carrots, peeled and shredded
1	cup part-skim ricotta cheese
1	ounce provolone cheese, finely shredded (¼ cup)

1. Arrange one oven rack 4 inches from broiler heat source and place second rack in center. Preheat broiler.

2. In large bowl, toss zucchini with 1 teaspoon oil and ⅛ teaspoon salt. Arrange on 18″ by 12″ jelly-roll pan in single layer. Broil 6 minutes or until golden brown, turning over once. Set aside. Reset oven control to 425°F.

3. Rinse chard in cold water; drain, leaving some water clinging to leaves.

4. In 12-inch skillet, heat remaining 1 teaspoon oil over medium heat. Add onion and cook 3 minutes or until soft, stirring occasionally. Add chard, garlic, thyme, and remaining ⅛ teaspoon salt. Cook 6 to 7 minutes or until chard is very soft, stirring frequently. Remove from heat and set aside.

5. In 8-inch square baking dish, layer half of tomatoes, lasagna noodles, Swiss chard, shredded carrots, zucchini slices, and ricotta, in that order. Repeat layering once. Top with provolone. Cover with foil. (Lasagna can be prepared to this point and refrigerated overnight.) Bake 30 minutes, covered. (If refrigerated, bake 10 minutes longer.) Uncover and bake 20 minutes longer or until golden brown and bubbling.

EACH SERVING: About 275 calories (29 percent calories from fat), 16g protein, 33g carbohydrate, 9g total fat (5g saturated), 6g fiber, 29mg cholesterol, 541mg sodium 🌿 🍽

Healthy Makeover Macaroni and Cheese

Predictable: Our classic mac and cheese, with its 1¼ pounds of cheese, has 640 calories and 30 fat grams per serving. Surprising: Our revamped version, with reduced-fat cheese and low-fat milk, is still creamy and flavorful but has only 420 calories and 12 fat grams for the same serving size.

ACTIVE TIME: 15 minutes
TOTAL TIME: 30 minutes

MAKES: 4 main-dish servings

8	ounces whole-wheat rotini pasta (2½ cups)
4	teaspoons cornstarch
2	cups low-fat (1%) milk
½	teaspoon Dijon mustard
¼	teaspoon salt
¼	teaspoon ground black pepper
4	ounces reduced-fat (2%) pasteurized process cheese spread, cut into ½-inch cubes
2	ounces extra-sharp Cheddar cheese, shredded (½ cup)
⅓	cup freshly grated Pecorino-Romano cheese
2	tablespoons plain dried bread crumbs
1	medium tomato, thinly sliced

1. Cook pasta as label directs.

2. Meanwhile, in 2-quart saucepan, whisk cornstarch into milk; heat to boiling over medium heat, whisking occasionally. Boil 1 minute. Remove saucepan from heat; whisk in mustard, salt, and pepper. Stir in pasteurized process cheese, Cheddar, and ¼ cup Romano. (Cheese does not need to melt completely.) In small bowl, combine bread crumbs with remaining Romano.

3. Preheat broiler. Spray shallow 1½-quart broiler-safe baking dish with nonstick cooking spray.

4. When pasta is done, drain and return to saucepot. Stir cheese sauce into pasta; spoon into prepared baking dish. Arrange tomato slices on top; sprinkle with crumb mixture.

5. Place baking dish in broiler about 6 inches from source of heat. Broil macaroni mixture 2 to 3 minutes or until top is lightly browned. Let macaroni and cheese stand 5 minutes to set slightly for easier serving.

EACH SERVING: About 420 calories (26 percent calories from fat), 23g protein, 59g carbohydrate, 12g total fat (7g saturated), 5g fiber, 37mg cholesterol, 920mg sodium 🟢 ⚘ ▦

Ratatouille Rigatoni

Traditional vegetables for French ratatouille (eggplant, yellow summer squash, peppers and onions) are roasted and turned into a healthy vegetarian sauce for rigatoni pasta. For photo, see page 212.

ACTIVE TIME: 15 minutes
TOTAL TIME: 1 hour

MAKES: 6 main-dish servings

1	large eggplant (15 ounces), trimmed and cut into ½-inch cubes
1	small onion (6 to 8 ounces), cut into ½-inch pieces
3	tablespoons extra-virgin olive oil
½	teaspoon salt
½	teaspoon ground black pepper
1	package (16 ounces) rigatoni pasta
2	yellow summer squash, cut into ½-inch pieces
1	medium red pepper (4 to 6 ounces), cut into ½-inch pieces
1	can (14½ ounces) crushed tomatoes
1	garlic clove, crushed with press
½	cup fresh basil leaves, very thinly sliced
½	cup freshly grated Parmesan cheese

1. Preheat oven to 450°F. In 18" by 12" jelly-roll pan, combine eggplant, onion, 2 tablespoons oil, ¼ teaspoon salt, and ¼ teaspoon black pepper until well mixed. Spread in even layer. Roast vegetables 15 minutes.

2. Meanwhile, in saucepot, cook pasta as label directs. To pan with eggplant, add squash, red pepper, remaining 1 tablespoon oil and remaining ¼ teaspoon each salt and black pepper. Stir gently until well mixed, then spread vegetables in even layer. Roast 25 to 30 minutes longer or until vegetables are very tender.

3. When pasta is done, drain and set aside. In same saucepot, heat tomatoes with their juice and garlic to boiling over medium-high heat; cook 4 minutes or until slightly thickened. Remove from heat; add pasta and roasted vegetables and basil; toss together until well combined.

4. Divide pasta and vegetable mixture among warm serving bowls. Sprinkle with grated Parmesan to serve.

EACH SERVING: About 445 calories (22 percent calories from fat), 16g protein, 72g carbohydrate, 11g total fat (3g saturated), 7g fiber, 7mg cholesterol, 670mg sodium

EAT YOUR EGGPLANT

It's worth the effort to learn to like eggplant: That bitter taste comes, in part, from chlorogenic acid, which helps prevent cancer and can also keep heart-threatening plaque from building up. What's more, lab studies show that eating eggplant lowers LDL cholesterol and helps artery walls relax, which can cut your risk for high blood pressure. To mellow eggplant's flavor, try grilling or slow-roasting it. (Salting it and letting it stand for 30 minutes also helps draw out some of the bitterness. Rinse off the salt before proceeding with your recipe.)

Pasta with Broccoli Rabe and Garbanzos

Bitter greens are paired with sweet golden raisins and tossed with pasta and beans. High in protein and fiber, this is a great meatless meal.

ACTIVE TIME: 20 minutes
TOTAL TIME: 30 minutes

MAKES: 6 main-dish servings

1	package (16 ounces) penne or ziti
1	gallon water
2	bunches broccoli rabe (about 12 ounces each), tough stems trimmed
2	tablespoons olive oil
3	garlic cloves, crushed with side of chef's knife
¼	teaspoon crushed red pepper
1	can (15 to 19 ounces) garbanzo beans, rinsed and drained
¼	cup golden raisins
1¼	teaspoons salt
	grated Parmesan cheese (optional)

1. In large saucepot, cook pasta as label directs. When pasta has reached desired doneness, remove ⅔ cup *pasta cooking water* and reserve. Drain pasta.

2. Meanwhile, in another large saucepot, heat gallon of water to boiling. Add broccoli rabe and cook 3 to 5 minutes or until thickest parts of stems are tender. Drain broccoli rabe and cool slightly. Cut into 2-inch pieces.

3. Wipe saucepot dry. Add oil, and heat over medium-high heat until hot. Add garlic and crushed red pepper, and cook 1 minute, stirring. Add broccoli rabe, garbanzo beans, and raisins, and cook about 3 minutes to heat through, stirring often. Remove saucepot from heat.

4. Add pasta, reserved cooking water, and salt to broccoli rabe mixture; toss well. Serve with Parmesan, if you like.

EACH SERVING: About 445 calories (14 percent calories from fat), 17g protein, 79g carbohydrate, 7g total fat (1g saturated), 6g fiber, 0mg cholesterol, 773mg sodium ✔ ✔

Whole-Wheat Penne Genovese

An onion-flecked white bean sauté adds heft to this fresh and healthy pesto pasta dish, making it light yet satisfying.

ACTIVE TIME: 15 minutes
TOTAL TIME: 30 minutes
MAKES: 6 main-dish servings

12	ounces whole-wheat penne or rotini
1½	cups packed fresh basil leaves
1	garlic clove, peeled
3	tablespoons water
3	tablespoons extra-virgin olive oil
¼	teaspoon salt
¼	teaspoon ground black pepper
½	cup grated Parmesan cheese
1	small onion (4 to 6 ounces), chopped
1	can (15 to 19 ounces) white kidney beans (cannellini), rinsed and drained
1	pint grape tomatoes (red, yellow, and orange mix if available), cut into quarters

1. In large saucepot, cook pasta as label directs.

2. Meanwhile, make pesto: In food processor with knife blade attached, blend basil, garlic, water, 2 tablespoons oil, salt, and pepper until pureed, stopping processor occasionally and scraping bowl with rubber spatula. Add Parmesan; pulse to combine. Set aside.

3. In 12-inch skillet, heat remaining 1 tablespoon oil over medium heat until very hot; add onion and cook 5 to 7 minutes or until beginning to soften. Stir in white beans, and cook 5 minutes longer, stirring occasionally.

4. Reserve *¼ cup pasta cooking water*. Drain pasta and return to saucepot; stir in white bean mixture, pesto, tomatoes, and reserved cooking water. Toss to coat.

EACH SERVING: About 375 calories (24 percent calories from fat), 15g protein, 59g carbohydrate, 10g total fat (2g saturated), 9g fiber, 5mg cholesterol, 435mg sodium ♥ ♥ ♥

Soba Noodles Primavera with Miso

This is a quick and easy Asian-inspired pasta primavera made with packaged broccoli flowerets and shredded carrots. For a nutritional boost, we used soba noodles and miso (concentrated soybean paste).

ACTIVE TIME: 20 minutes
TOTAL TIME: 40 minutes

MAKES: 4 main-dish servings

1	package (8 ounces) soba noodles
1	tablespoon olive oil
1	medium red pepper (4 to 6 ounces), thinly sliced
1	large onion (12 ounces), sliced
2	garlic cloves, crushed with garlic press
1	tablespoon grated, peeled fresh ginger
¼	teaspoon crushed red pepper
1	package (16 ounces) extra-firm tofu, drained, patted dry and cut into 1-inch chunks
1	bag (16 ounces) broccoli flowerets, cut into 1½-inch pieces
1	bag (10 ounces) shredded carrots
¼	cup water
¼	cup red (dark) miso paste
2	green onions, thinly sliced

1. In large saucepot, prepare noodles as label directs.

2. Meanwhile, in nonstick 5- to 6-quart Dutch oven, heat oil over medium heat until hot. Add red pepper and onion; cook until golden, about 10 minutes, stirring occasionally. Add garlic, ginger, crushed red pepper, and tofu; cook 1 minute, stirring. Add broccoli, carrots, and water; heat to boiling over medium-high heat. Reduce heat to medium; cover and cook until vegetables are tender, about 7 minutes.

3. When noodles have cooked to desired doneness, drain, reserving *¾ cup cooking water*. Return noodles to saucepot.

4. With wire whisk, mix miso paste into reserved noodle cooking water until blended.

5. To serve, toss noodles with tofu mixture, green onions, and miso-paste mixture.

EACH SERVING: About 450 calories (28 percent calories from fat), 26g protein, 68g carbohydrate, 11g total fat (2g saturated), 11g fiber, 0mg cholesterol, 1,290mg sodium ◉

On the Side

We've provided recipes for all our favorite light and healthy mains; now it's time to share some simple, healthy sides to pair with them. Hearty recipes for whole grains and many low-cal, low-fat ways to prepare everyone's favorite—the potato—are all there. And we've also tackled less popular vegetables—think beets—that you or your family members may be reluctant to eat.

If you're looking for an easy way to prepare veggies, try microwave-steaming; we provide instructions for a range of veggies along with a selection of flavorful low-fat dressings to top them off. Looking for creative ways to get beets, kale, or broccoli on the menu? Try our basil and balsamic roasted beets, our creamy broccoli gratin, or kale "chips"—simply spray the leaves with nonstick cooking spray, sprinkle with sea salt, and bake for a healthy alternative to potato chips even your kids will embrace. Or tempt them with our sweet maple-roasted butternut squash.

If your main dish doesn't include grains, serve up our brown rice or wild rice pilaf, or prepare one of our sweet and savory stuffings: There's pear with cornbread, wheat berries with dried apricots, and then some. And, as mentioned above, we have not forgotten the potatoes: Try them herb-roasted in a foil packet, smashed, or oven-baked, so you can enjoy French "fries" without all the fat. Healthy makeovers of cornbread and pumpkin bread round out the offerings.

Mashed Sweet Potatoes (recipe page 259)

Apple Cider Braised Greens

Our easy Apple Cider Braised Greens make an excellent side dish for holidays or any day.

ACTIVE TIME: 30 minutes
TOTAL TIME: 1 hour 5 minutes
MAKES: 8 cups or 16 side-dish servings

1½ pounds mustard greens
1½ pounds collard greens
1½ pounds Swiss chard
2 tablespoons olive oil
3 large garlic cloves, thinly sliced
1¼ cups apple cider
1 tablespoon cider vinegar
1½ teaspoons salt
2 red cooking apples such as Gala or Rome Beauty, unpeeled and cut into ¾-inch chunks

1. Remove stems from mustard greens; discard stems. Trim stem ends from collard greens and Swiss chard; remove stems from leaves. Cut stems into 1-inch pieces; cut leaves into 2-inch pieces. Rinse leaves and stems; drain well.

2. In 8-quart saucepot, heat oil over high heat until hot. Add garlic and cook 30 seconds to 1 minute or until golden, stirring constantly. Add as many leaves and stems as possible, cider, vinegar, and salt, stirring to wilt greens. Add remaining greens in batches.

3. Reduce heat to medium. Cover saucepot and cook greens 15 minutes. Stir in apples; cook, partially covered, 10 minutes longer or until stems are very tender and most of liquid evaporates, stirring occasionally. With slotted spoon, transfer to serving bowl.

EACH SERVING: About 60 calories (30 percent calories from fat), 2g protein, 10g carbohydrate, 2g total fat (0g saturated), 3g fiber, 0mg cholesterol, 310mg sodium ♥ ▤

TIP: *To make this dish ahead, spoon cooked greens into microwave-safe bowl; cover with plastic wrap and refrigerate up to 2 days. When ready to serve, vent plastic wrap and microwave on High 8 minutes or until hot, stirring halfway through.*

Sautéed Swiss Chard with Golden Raisins and Capers

This simple side also makes a delicious pasta partner. Toss with a pound of your favorite pasta and ½ cup pasta-cooking water for a spectacular main course.

ACTIVE TIME: 30 minutes
TOTAL TIME: 50 minutes

MAKES: 4 side-dish servings

2	pounds Swiss chard
1	tablespoon olive oil
1	small onion, chopped
⅓	cup golden raisins
2	tablespoons capers, drained

1. Trim tough stem ends from Swiss chard. Cut stems crosswise into 1-inch pieces; cut leaves into 2-inch pieces, keeping stems and leaves separate. Rinse leaves and stems; drain well.

2. In nonstick 12-inch skillet, heat oil over medium heat. Add onion and cook about 6 minutes or until onion begins to brown. Add chard stems and cook, covered, 5 to 7 minutes or until tender. Stir in raisins. Add leaves and stems in batches, covering skillet after each batch; cook 7 to 10 minutes total or until leaves are tender and wilted and most of liquid evaporates, stirring often. Remove from heat; stir in capers.

EACH SERVING: About 120 calories (30 percent calories from fat), 4g protein, 20g carbohydrate, 4g total fat (1g saturated), 5g fiber, 0mg cholesterol, 555mg sodium 🌿

Kale "Chips"

Our crisp kale "chips" are virtually fat free— perfect for guilt-free snacking.

ACTIVE TIME: 10 minutes
TOTAL TIME: 22 minutes

MAKES: 6 side-dish servings

1	bunch kale (10 ounces), rinsed and dried well
	nonstick cooking spray
½	teaspoon kosher salt

Preheat oven to 350°F. From kale, remove and discard thick stems, and tear leaves into large pieces. Spread leaves in single layer on 2 large cookie sheets. Spray leaves with nonstick cooking spray to coat lightly; sprinkle with salt. Bake 12 to 15 minutes or just until crisp but not browned. Cool on cookie sheets on wire racks.

EACH 1-CUP SERVING: About 15 calories (0 percent calories from fat), 1g protein, 3g carbohydrate, 0g total fat, 1g fiber, 0mg cholesterol, 175mg sodium 🌿 ❤️ 🧺

Tarragon Peas and Pearl Onions

Fresh tarragon adds a perky licorice flavor to these lightly cooked peas and pearl onions.

ACTIVE TIME: 6 minutes
TOTAL TIME: 16 minutes

MAKES: 8 side-dish servings

1	tablespoon margarine or butter
1	bag (16 ounces) frozen pearl onions
1	bag (16 ounces) frozen peas
¼	cup water
½	teaspoon salt
¼	teaspoon ground black pepper
1	tablespoon chopped fresh tarragon leaves

1. In nonstick 12-inch skillet, heat margarine over medium heat until melted. Add frozen pearl onions and cook 7 to 9 minutes or until browned.

2. Add frozen peas, water, salt, and pepper to skillet; stir to combine. Cover and cook 3 to 4 minutes longer or until onions and peas are tender. Stir tarragon into vegetables and spoon into serving bowl.

EACH SERVING: About 75 calories (20 percent calories from fat), 3g protein, 12g carbohydrate, 2g total fat (0g saturated), 4g fiber, 0mg cholesterol, 202mg sodium 🌿 ♥

Sesame Green Beans

These Asian-inspired green beans are delicious served hot or at room temperature.

ACTIVE TIME: 15 minutes
TOTAL TIME: 20 minutes

MAKES: 4 side-dish servings

1	teaspoon salt
1	pound green beans, trimmed
1	tablespoon soy sauce
½	teaspoon Asian sesame oil
1½	teaspoons minced, peeled fresh ginger or ¾ teaspoon ground ginger
1½	teaspoons sesame seeds, toasted

1. In 4-quart saucepan, combine *7 cups water* and salt; heat to boiling over high heat. Add green beans; heat to boiling. Cover and cook until just tender-crisp, 6 to 8 minutes. Drain; return green beans to saucepan.

2. Add soy sauce, sesame oil, and ginger to green beans in saucepan. Cook over low heat, stirring occasionally, until flavors have blended, about 3 minutes. Transfer to serving bowl and sprinkle with sesame seeds.

EACH SERVING: About 45 calories (20 percent calories from fat), 2g protein, 8g carbohydrate, 1g total fat (0g saturated), 3g fiber, 0mg cholesterol, 553mg sodium 🌿 🍴

Green Beans with Caramelized Onions

Caramelized onions make everything better. And this green-bean side dish—a lighter take on a beloved holiday casserole—is no exception.

ACTIVE TIME: 30 minutes
TOTAL TIME: 1 hour 10 minutes

MAKES: 14 cups or 16 side-dish servings

3   pounds green beans, trimmed
1½   pounds red onions (about 3 medium), each cut in half, then sliced
3   tablespoons margarine or butter
1   tablespoon fresh thyme leaves, chopped
1½   teaspoons salt
½   teaspoon ground black pepper

1. Fill large bowl with *ice water* to cool beans quickly after cooking; set aside. Heat 6- to 8-quart saucepot of *salted water* to boiling over high heat. Add beans in 2 batches and cook each batch 4 minutes or until beans are tender-crisp, making sure water returns to boiling before adding each batch of beans. With slotted spoon or sieve, transfer beans to bowl of ice water. Drain beans thoroughly.

2. In nonstick 12-inch skillet, combine onions, margarine, thyme, salt, and pepper. Cook over medium heat 15 minutes or until onions start to brown, stirring occasionally. Reduce heat to medium-low and cook 5 to 7 minutes longer or until onions turn dark brown, stirring frequently. Stir beans into onion mixture; heat through before serving.

EACH SERVING: About 60 calories (30 percent calories from fat), 2g protein, 9g carbohydrate, 2g total fat (0g saturated), 3g fiber, 0mg cholesterol, 250mg sodium ♥ 🥘

TIP: *If you'd like to make this dish ahead of time, up to two days in advance, blanch, cool, and drain beans. Cook onion mixture and cool. Refrigerate each component separately in sealed plastic bags. To reheat, toss beans and onion mixture into 4-quart microwave-safe glass bowl. Microwave on High about 8 minutes, stirring halfway through heating.*

LOW-FAT WAYS TO DRESS YOUR VEGGIES

Boost the flavor—without loading on the fat—with these simple alternatives to classic butter, cheese, and cream sauces.

FOR GREEN BEANS OR BROCCOLI

+ Thin orange marmalade with a little water; whisk in some ground ginger and heat over low. Stir sauce into hot green beans or broccoli flowerets.
+ Blend prepared horseradish, Dijon mustard, and light mayonnaise; drizzle over steamed green beans.
+ Whisk together seasoned rice vinegar, soy sauce, and grated fresh ginger to taste. Use as a dipping sauce for tender-crisp broccoli.

FOR YELLOW SQUASH OR ZUCCHINI

+ Toast bread crumbs with chopped garlic in 1 teaspoon of olive oil. Sprinkle over steamed yellow squash along with some chopped parsley.
+ Flavor cooked zucchini with a dusting of freshly grated Parmesan cheese (a little goes a long way) and cracked black pepper.

FOR DARK, LEAFY GREENS (SPINACH, SWISS CHARD, COLLARDS)

+ Sauté minced garlic and a pinch of crushed red pepper in 1 teaspoon of olive oil until fragrant. Add fresh spinach or Swiss chard to pan and cook until wilted.
+ Slice a piece of Canadian bacon (it's surprisingly low fat) into thin strips and cook in a nonstick skillet until crisp. Toss with boiled collard greens or steamed spinach.
+ Add a handful of yellow raisins to steamed bitter greens, such as Swiss chard.

FOR ASPARAGUS OR CAULIFLOWER

+ Prepare a mock hollandaise by mixing light mayonnaise with Dijon mustard, fresh lemon juice, and a pinch of ground pepper. Drizzle the cool sauce over steamed cauliflower, broccoli, or—the classic hollandaise partner—asparagus spears.
+ Chop some mango chutney (available in the gourmet or international section of most supermarkets) and toss it with steamed cauliflower or asparagus.

FOR EGGPLANT

+ Heat chopped fresh tomato with crushed fennel seeds in a skillet until hot. Spoon over baked or broiled eggplant slices.

FOR NEW POTATOES

+ Toss chopped mixed fresh herbs (such as basil, mint, rosemary, or oregano) and grated lemon zest with boiled new potato halves. Season with salt to taste.

Broccoli Gratin

We've trimmed the fat from a family favorite by using creamy Yukon Gold potatoes as the base of this dish, making the traditional use of heavy cream and milk unnecessary.

ACTIVE TIME: 10 minutes
TOTAL TIME: 30 minutes
MAKES: 8 side-dish servings

1   pound broccoli flowerets
1   pound Yukon Gold potatoes, peeled and cut into 1-inch chunks
2   cups water
pinch ground nutmeg
¾   cup freshly grated Parmesan cheese
½   teaspoon salt
¼   teaspoon coarsely ground black pepper

1. In 4-quart saucepan, place broccoli, potatoes, and water. Cover and heat to boiling over high heat. Reduce heat to medium-low; cover and cook until vegetables are very tender, 17 to 20 minutes, stirring once halfway through cooking.

2. Meanwhile, preheat broiler and set oven rack 6 inches from source of heat.

3. Drain vegetables in colander set over large bowl, reserving *¼ cup cooking water*. Return vegetables to saucepan. With potato masher or slotted spoon, coarsely mash vegetables, adding some reserved vegetable cooking water if mixture seems dry. Stir in nutmeg, ¼ cup Parmesan, salt, and pepper.

4. In shallow, broiler-safe 1- to 1½-quart baking dish, spread vegetable mixture; sprinkle with remaining ½ cup Parmesan. Place dish in oven and broil until Parmesan is browned, 2 to 3 minutes.

EACH SERVING: About 95 calories (28 percent calories from fat), 6g protein, 13g carbohydrate, 3g total fat (2g saturated), 2g fiber, 6mg cholesterol, 305mg sodium 🌿 ❤ 🍲

TIP: *The unbaked casserole can be refrigerated up to 1 day. Bake 10 minutes longer than directed if casserole has been chilled.*

Cracked Wheat with Greens

Cracked wheat combines what's best about wheat berries and bulgur. It's less refined than bulgur, so you get more nutrition and a nuttier, chewier texture, but because the grains have been cracked open, you have a much shorter cooking time than for wheat berries.

ACTIVE TIME: 20 minutes
TOTAL TIME: 45 minutes

MAKES: 6 side-dish servings

1	small bunch (10 ounces) kale, stems and tough ribs removed
1	small bunch (10 ounces) Swiss chard, stems trimmed
2	tablespoons olive oil
1	medium onion, chopped
1	medium red bell pepper, chopped
3	large garlic cloves, minced
¾	teaspoon salt
¼	teaspoon crushed red pepper
¼	teaspoon ground black pepper
1	cup coarse cracked wheat
1½	cups water
1	lemon, cut into wedges

1. Cut kale and Swiss chard into ¼-inch-wide ribbons.

2. In 8-quart pot over medium heat, heat oil until hot. Add onion and bell pepper; cook, stirring occasionally, until vegetables soften, about 5 minutes. Stir in garlic, salt, crushed red pepper, black pepper, and cracked wheat. Cook, stirring, for 3 minutes. Stir in kale, Swiss chard, and water. Bring to a boil. Reduce heat; cover and simmer, stirring occasionally, especially towards end of cooking time, until cracked wheat and greens are tender, 15 to 20 minutes.

3. Serve with lemon wedges.

EACH SERVING: About 150 calories (30 percent calories from fat), 5g protein, 24g carbohydrate, 5g total fat (1g saturated), 5g fiber, 0mg cholesterol, 395 mg sodium ♥

Mixed Pea Pod Stir-Fry

This sweet and tender-crisp medley celebrates the glorious flavor of fresh green vegetables.

ACTIVE TIME: 15 minutes
TOTAL TIME: 16 minutes
MAKES: 4 side-dish servings

1	teaspoon salt
8	ounces green beans, trimmed
2	teaspoons vegetable oil
4	ounces snow peas, trimmed and strings removed
4	ounces sugar snap peas, trimmed and strings removed
1	garlic clove, finely chopped
1	tablespoon soy sauce

1. In 12-inch skillet, combine *4 cups water* and salt; heat to boiling over high heat. Add green beans and cook 3 minutes. Drain; wipe skillet dry with paper towels.

2. In same skillet, heat oil over high heat. Add green beans and cook, stirring frequently (stir-frying), until they begin to brown, 2 to 3 minutes. Add snow peas, sugar snap peas, and garlic; stir-fry until snow peas and sugar snap peas are tender-crisp, about 1 minute longer. Stir in soy sauce and remove from heat.

EACH SERVING: About 65 calories (28 percent calories from fat), 3g protein, 8g carbohydrate, 2g total fat (0g saturated), 3g fiber, 0mg cholesterol, 844mg sodium ☺

EASY MICROWAVE-STEAMED VEGETABLES

Want tasty vegetables fast? Follow these simple instructions and the cook-time chart opposite to microwave-steam perfect veggies every time. In microwave cooking, vegetables retain more vitamins and minerals because they cook quickly with little or no water. And greasing a bowl or dish with oil or butter isn't necessary, since the microwave's moist heat prevents sticking.

In a covered, microwave-safe dish, cook one pound vegetables (or amount specified opposite) with ¼ cup water on High until tender, stirring once halfway through cooking time. Take care not to overcook; the finished veggies should be crisp and brightly colored, never mushy. Season with salt and pepper and serve.

VEGETABLE	MINUTES TO COOK
Asparagus	4 to 6
Beans, green or yellow wax	4 to 7
Beets, whole (remove the greens)	10 to 14
Bell peppers, cut into strips	5 to 7
Broccoli flowerets	5 to 6
Carrots, peeled and sliced	5 to 8
Cauliflower flowerets	5 to 6
Peas, shelled (1 cup)	4 to 5
Spinach (10 ounces)	30 to 90 seconds
Zucchini or yellow squash, sliced	4 to 7

Millet with Corn and Green Chiles

Millet has a mild flavor that is greatly enhanced by pan-toasting it first. For an extra shot of flavor, serve this topped with a dollop of reduced-fat sour cream and your favorite salsa.

ACTIVE TIME: 25 minutes
TOTAL TIME: 50 minutes

MAKES: 8 side-dish servings

1   cup millet
2   cups fresh (cut from 4 ears) or frozen corn kernels
2   teaspoons vegetable oil
1   medium onion, chopped
1   garlic clove, crushed with garlic press
1   teaspoon ground cumin
3½ cups water
1   can (4½ ounces) diced green chiles, drained
½   teaspoon salt
¼   cup lightly packed fresh cilantro leaves, chopped (optional)

1. In large skillet, cook millet over medium heat until toasted, about 5 minutes, stirring frequently. Pour millet into bowl and set aside.

2. Add corn to dry skillet and cook over high heat until corn browns, about 5 minutes, stirring frequently. Transfer corn to plate.

3. In same skillet, heat oil over medium heat. Add onion; cook until softened, about 5 minutes. Stir in garlic and cumin and cook until fragrant, about 1 minute. Add water, green chiles, and salt. Bring to boiling. Stir in millet. Reduce heat; cover and simmer until millet is tender and water is absorbed, 25 to 30 minutes.

4. Remove skillet from heat, stir in corn; cover and let stand 5 minutes to heat through. Stir in cilantro if using.

EACH SERVING: About 150 calories (30 percent calories from fat), 4g protein, 29g carbohydrate, 3g total fat (0g saturated), 4g fiber, 0mg cholesterol, 200mg sodium ♥ ⟱

GET YOUR GRAINS: MILLET

A staple in Asia and Africa, millet is best toasted, then prepared like rice by boiling it in water to make hot cereal or seasoned pilafs. Of all the cereal grains, this gluten-free grain has the richest amino-acid protein profile and the highest iron content. It is also rich in B vitamins.

Basic Couscous

Couscous is the perfect side for a busy weekday meal, taking all of 10 minutes to put together. Pair any of these variations with a simple vegetable stew or stir-fry and your meal will come in under 450 calories total.

ACTIVE TIME: 5 minutes
TOTAL TIME: 10 minutes plus standing
MAKES: 4 side-dish servings

1	cup whole-wheat couscous (Moroccan pasta)
1¼	cups water
½	teaspoon salt

Prepare couscous as the label directs, adding seasoning to the water before boiling. Do not add butter or margarine.

EACH SERVING: About 105 calories (0 percent calories from fat), 4g protein, 23g carbohydrate, 0g total fat, 4g fiber, 0mg cholesterol, 405mg sodium

LIME COUSCOUS: Add *1 tablespoon fresh lime juice* and *1 teaspoon freshly grated lime peel* to water when preparing couscous.

EACH SERVING: About 110 calories (0 percent calories from fat), 4g protein, 23g carbohydrate, 0g total fat, 4g fiber, 0mg cholesterol, 405mg sodium

MOROCCAN COUSCOUS: Add *¼ cup golden raisins, ¼ teaspoon ground cinnamon, ¼ teaspoon ground turmeric,* and *¼ teaspoon ground cumin* to water when preparing couscous.

EACH SERVING: About 200 calories (0 percent calories from fat), 6g protein, 43g carbohydrate, 0g total fat, 4g fiber, 0mg cholesterol, 405mg sodium

SUN-DRIED TOMATO AND GREEN ONION COUSCOUS: Add *1 medium green onion,* sliced, and *5 sun-dried tomato halves,* chopped, to water when preparing couscous.

EACH SERVING: About 185 calories (0 percent calories from fat), 7g protein, 38g carbohydrate, 0g total fat, 4g fiber, 0mg cholesterol, 500mg sodium

Aromatic Brown Rice

Think of rice as a blank canvas that you can add any number of flavorings to for your own taste creation. Below is a basic recipe for brown rice, followed by three very different variations.

ACTIVE TIME: 5 minutes
TOTAL TIME: 25 minutes

MAKES: 4 side-dish servings

1   cup long-grain brown rice
1   cup canned or homemade chicken or vegetable broth (pages 92–93)
¾   cup water
¼   teaspoon salt

In a medium saucepan, combine rice, broth, water, and salt and bring to boiling, uncovered, over high heat. Cover and simmer over low heat until rice is tender and liquid is absorbed, 18 to 20 minutes.

EACH SERVING: About 175 calories (10 percent calories from fat), 4g protein, 36g carbohydrate, 2g total fat (0g saturated), 3g fiber, 0mg cholesterol, 295mg sodium ☺ ▭

ORANGE-CILANTRO BROWN RICE: After rice has cooked, stir in *2 tablespoons chopped fresh cilantro* and *½ teaspoon freshly grated orange peel.*

EACH SERVING: About 175 calories (5 percent calories from fat), 4g protein, 37g carbohydrate, 1g total fat (0g saturated), 3g fiber, 3mg cholesterol, 295mg sodium ☺ ▭

ASIAN BROWN RICE: Omit salt when cooking rice. After rice has cooked, stir in *2 green onions,* chopped, *2 teaspoons soy sauce,* and *¼ teaspoon Asian sesame oil.*

EACH SERVING: About 180 calories (5 percent calories from fat), 4g protein, 38g carbohydrate, 1g total fat (0g saturated), 3g fiber, 3mg cholesterol, 380mg sodium ☺ ▭

LEMON-PARSLEY BROWN RICE: After rice has cooked, stir in *2 tablespoons chopped fresh parsley* and *1 teaspoon freshly grated lemon peel.*

EACH SERVING: About 175 calories (5 percent calories from fat), 4g protein, 37g carbohydrate, 1g total fat (0g saturated), 3g fiber, 3mg cholesterol, 295mg sodium ☺ ▭

Brown Rice and Vegetable Pilaf

Add beans, rotisserie chicken, or shrimp to this versatile pilaf and dinner is served.

ACTIVE TIME: 15 minutes
TOTAL TIME: 1 hour 25 minutes
MAKES: 6 side-dish servings

1   tablespoon olive or vegetable oil
1   medium onion, finely chopped
1   stalk celery, finely chopped
1   package (8 ounces) mushrooms, trimmed and sliced
1   garlic clove, finely chopped
1   cup long-grain brown rice
2¼ cups water
2   carrots, peeled and chopped
1¼ teaspoons salt
⅛   teaspoon dried thyme
⅛   teaspoon ground black pepper
pinch dried sage

1. In 10-inch skillet, heat oil over medium heat. Add onion and celery; cook until onion is tender, about 5 minutes, stirring frequently. Stir in mushrooms; increase heat to medium-high and cook until mushrooms begin to brown and liquid has evaporated. Stir in garlic. Add rice; cook, stirring, 30 seconds. Stir in water, carrots, salt, thyme, pepper, and sage; heat to boiling.

2. Reduce heat; cover and simmer until rice is tender and all liquid has been absorbed, about 45 minutes. Fluff with fork.

EACH SERVING: About 165 calories (16 percent calories from fat), 4g protein, 31g carbohydrate, 3g total fat (0g saturated), 3g fiber, 0mg cholesterol, 503mg sodium ▦

Brown Rice and Cranberry Stuffing

Here's a flavorful low-fat alternative to ordinary bread stuffing.

ACTIVE TIME: 45 minutes
TOTAL TIME: 2 hours
MAKES: 11 cups or 22 side-dish servings

2   tablespoons olive oil
3   medium carrots, peeled and cut into ½-inch pieces
2   medium fennel bulbs, trimmed and cut into ¼-inch pieces
2   stalks celery, cut into ¼-inch pieces
1   medium onion, chopped
3   cups long-grain brown rice
1   can (14½ ounces) chicken broth or 1¾ cups homemade (page 93)
¾   cup dried cranberries
1¾ teaspoons salt
½   teaspoon dried thyme
¼   teaspoon coarsely ground black pepper
4½ cups water

1. Preheat oven to 325°F.

2. In 12-inch skillet, heat oil over medium heat until hot. Add carrots, fennel, celery, and onion and cook until vegetables are tender and lightly browned, about 20 minutes, stirring frequently.

3. Stir in rice, broth, cranberries, salt, thyme, pepper, and water. Cover and heat to boiling. Pour rice mixture into 13" by 9" baking dish; cover with foil and bake until liquid is absorbed and rice is tender, about 1 hour 15 minutes.

EACH SERVING: About 135 calories (13 percent calories from fat), 3g protein, 26g carbohydrate, 2g total fat (0g saturated), 3g fiber, 0mg cholesterol, 265mg sodium ♥ ▦

Wild Rice and Orzo Pilaf

You can prepare this and refrigerate it for up to 2 days, then bake just before serving.

ACTIVE TIME: 25 minutes
TOTAL TIME: 1 hour 10 minutes
MAKES: 9 cups or 12 side-dish servings

1¼ cups orzo pasta (8 ounces)
1 cup wild rice (6 ounces)
3 tablespoons margarine or butter
1 small onion, finely chopped
1 stalk celery, finely chopped
1 pound mushrooms, trimmed and sliced
2 teaspoons chopped fresh thyme leaves
1 teaspoon salt
¼ teaspoon coarsely ground black pepper

1. Prepare orzo and wild rice, separately, as labels direct.

2. Meanwhile, in 12-inch skillet, melt margarine over medium heat. Add onion and celery and cook, stirring occasionally, until tender, about 10 minutes. Add mushrooms, thyme, salt, and pepper; cook, stirring occasionally, until mushrooms are tender and liquid evaporates, about 10 minutes longer.

3. Preheat oven to 350°F. In shallow 2 ½-quart baking dish, stir orzo, rice, and mushroom mixture until blended. Cover and bake until heated through, about 35 minutes.

EACH SERVING: About 150 calories (17 percent calories from fat), 5g protein, 26g carbohydrate, 3g total fat (1g saturated), 2g fiber, 0mg cholesterol, 220mg sodium ♥ ▣

EAT WILD RICE

Wild rice isn't really a rice; it's the seed of a marsh grass native to the Great Lakes region of the U.S. Wild rice contains twice the protein and fiber of brown rice but less iron and calcium. The rice grains vary in length and color and have a slightly smoky, earthy flavor and chewy texture. Because of this chewiness (and high cost), it is often prepared in tandem with brown or white rice, or try it with orzo, as in the recipe here.

Savory Pear and Cornbread Stuffing

Spruce up packaged cornbread stuffing mix with Bartlett pears, green onions, and fresh parsley.

ACTIVE TIME: 10 minutes
TOTAL TIME: 40 minutes

MAKES: 8 cups or 16 side-dish servings

1	tablespoon olive oil
2	stalks celery, chopped
2	large ripe Bartlett pears
4	green onions
½	cup loosely packed fresh parsley leaves
3	cups water
1	package (12 ounces) cornbread stuffing mix

1. Preheat oven to 425°F.

2. In 4-quart saucepan, heat oil over medium-high heat until hot. Add celery and cook 5 minutes, stirring occasionally. Meanwhile, cut pears into ½-inch chunks, slice green onions, and chop parsley.

3. Add water to celery in saucepan; cover and heat to boiling over high heat. Remove from heat; stir in stuffing mix, pears, green onions, and parsley until combined. Spoon stuffing into shallow 3- to 3½-quart casserole; cover with foil. Bake 20 minutes; uncover and bake 10 minutes longer.

EACH ½ CUP: About 110 calories (25 percent calories from fat), 3g protein, 19g carbohydrate, 3g total fat (0g saturated), 2g fiber, 0mg cholesterol, 385mg sodium

Double Cornbread

Frozen corn and jalapeños enhance the texture and flavor of hearty cornbread.

ACTIVE TIME: 20 minutes
TOTAL TIME: 30 minutes

MAKES: 24 pieces

1½	cups all-purpose flour
1½	cups yellow cornmeal
¼	cup sugar
4	teaspoons baking powder
½	teaspoon baking soda
1	teaspoon salt
2½	cups buttermilk
3	large eggs
1	package (10 ounces) frozen corn, thawed
6	tablespoons butter or margarine, melted
2	jalapeño chiles, seeds and membranes discarded, finely chopped

1. Preheat oven to 450°F. Grease 13" by 9" baking pan. In large bowl, combine flour, cornmeal, sugar, baking powder, baking soda, and salt. In medium bowl, with wire whisk or fork, beat buttermilk and eggs until blended.

2. Add corn, melted butter, and jalapeños to buttermilk mixture, then add to flour mixture. Stir until ingredients are just mixed.

3. Pour batter into prepared pan. Bake 22 to 25 minutes or until golden at edges and toothpick inserted in center comes out clean. Cut lengthwise into 4 strips, then cut each strip crosswise into 6 pieces. Serve warm.

EACH SERVING: About 125 calories (29 percent calories from fat), 4g protein, 19g carbohydrate, 4g total fat (2g saturated), 1g fiber, 36mg cholesterol, 255mg sodium

Wild Rice and Mushroom Stuffing

This recipe makes an elegant alternative to ordinary bread stuffing. It's richly flavored with two kinds of mushrooms and other vegetables.

ACTIVE TIME: 45 minutes
TOTAL TIME: 1 hour 5 minutes
MAKES: 13 cups or 26 side-dish servings

1	cup wild rice (about 6 ounces), rinsed
3¾	cups water
1	cup dried cranberries or dark seedless raisins
4	tablespoons margarine or butter
3	medium carrots, peeled and cut into ¼-inch pieces
2	stalks celery, cut into ¼-inch pieces
1	medium onion, cut into ¼-inch pieces
1	teaspoon salt
½	teaspoon dried thyme
¼	teaspoon coarsely ground black pepper
8	ounces shiitake mushrooms, stems discarded, caps sliced
10	ounces white mushrooms, trimmed and sliced
2	cups long-grain brown rice
1	can (14½ ounces) chicken broth or 1¾ cups homemade (page 93)

1. In 2-quart saucepan, heat wild rice and 2 cups water to boiling over high heat. Reduce heat to low; cover and simmer until wild rice is tender, 35 to 40 minutes. Stir in cranberries; heat 1 minute. Drain wild rice mixture if necessary.

2. Meanwhile, in nonstick 5- to 6-quart Dutch oven, melt 2 tablespoons margarine over medium heat. Add carrots, celery, and onion and cook until tender and golden, 12 to 15 minutes. Stir in salt, thyme, and pepper and cook 1 minute; transfer to medium bowl.

3. In same Dutch oven, melt remaining 2 tablespoons margarine over medium heat. Add shiitake and white mushrooms and cook until tender and golden and liquid evaporates, about 12 minutes; transfer to bowl with vegetables.

4. Preheat oven to 325°F.

5. In same Dutch oven, heat brown rice, broth, and remaining 1¾ cups water to boiling over high heat. Reduce heat to low; cover and simmer until tender, 18 to 20 minutes. Stir wild-rice and vegetable mixtures into brown rice.

6. Spoon stuffing into 13" by 9" glass baking dish or shallow 3½-quart casserole. Cover with foil and bake until stuffing is heated through, about 20 minutes.

EACH SERVING: About 120 calories (15 percent calories from fat), 3g protein, 23g carbohydrate, 2g total fat (0g saturated), 2g fiber, 0mg cholesterol, 190mg sodium ♥ ▦

TIP: *To cut down on last-minute cooking, prepare the components of this dish up to 2 days before serving and refrigerate. Increase the baking time by 10 minutes.*

Wheat-Berry Stuffing with Apricots

Our wholesome stuffing—made with grains, veggies, and dried fruit—will quickly become a family favorite. It's a good choice to make ahead. Just allow 10 minutes more time to bake if cold.

ACTIVE TIME: 1 hour 15 minutes
TOTAL TIME: 1 hour 35 minutes

MAKES: about 10 cups or 20 side-dish servings

1½ cups wheat berries (whole-wheat kernels)
6½ cups water
1 cup long-grain brown rice
1 tablespoon olive oil
3 carrots, peeled and cut into ¼-inch pieces
3 stalks celery, cut into ¼-inch pieces
2 red onions, cut into ¼-inch pieces
2 strips (3" by 1" each) orange peel
⅛ teaspoon ground allspice
¾ cup dried apricots, sliced
¾ cup pitted prunes, coarsely chopped
1 can (14½ ounces) chicken or vegetable broth or 1¾ cups homemade (pages 92-93)
1½ teaspoons salt
½ teaspoon coarsely ground black pepper
½ cup loosely packed fresh parsley leaves, chopped

1. In 4-quart saucepan, heat wheat berries and 6 cups water to boiling over high heat. Reduce heat to low; cover and simmer until wheat berries are firm to the bite but tender enough to eat, about 1 hour; drain and set aside.

2. Preheat oven to 350°F.

3. Meanwhile, prepare rice in 5- to 6-quart saucepan as label directs. Transfer to medium bowl; cover and set aside. Wash and dry saucepan.

4. In same saucepan, heat oil over medium heat until hot. Add carrots, celery, and onions and cook until tender and lightly browned, about 15 minutes, stirring often. Add orange peel and allspice and cook 2 minutes longer. Add apricots, prunes, broth, salt, pepper, and remaining ½ cup water; heat to boiling over high heat. Reduce heat to low; simmer, uncovered, 5 minutes to blend flavors. Discard orange peel.

5. Add wheat berries, rice, and parsley to vegetable mixture, stirring to combine. Spoon wheat berry mixture into 13" by 9" baking dish. Cover with foil and bake stuffing until heated through, about 20 minutes.

EACH SERVING: About 125 calories (14 percent calories from fat), 4g protein, 27g carbohydrate, 1g total fat (0g saturated), 3g fiber, 0mg cholesterol, 235mg sodium ♥ ▤

Cranberry-Apple Chutney

Try this recipe in place of regular cranberry sauce. This chutney combines sweet, savory, and sour flavors for a great accompaniment to turkey and stuffing.

ACTIVE TIME: 10 minutes
TOTAL TIME: 45 minutes plus cooling
MAKES: about 4 cups or 16 servings

5 ounces pearl onions (1½ cups)
8 dried Calimyrna figs, chopped
1½ cups water
1 cup sugar
2 tablespoons cider vinegar
1 teaspoon coriander seeds
2 medium Pink Lady or Gala apples, peeled and chopped (2¼ cups)
1 bag (12 ounces) cranberries (3 cups), picked over

1. Fill 3-quart saucepan with *water;* cover and heat to boiling over high. Add onions and cook, uncovered, 2 minutes. Drain onions and add to bowl of *ice water* to stop cooking; drain again. When cool enough to handle, slice off and discard root end of onion; squeeze from opposite end. Onion will slip out of skin; discard skin. Repeat with remaining onions.

2. In 5-quart saucepot, stir together figs, water, sugar, vinegar, and coriander seeds until sugar dissolves. Heat to boiling, then add onions and apples. Reduce heat to medium-low; simmer 25 minutes or until apples are tender. Add cranberries and simmer 10 minutes or until a few cranberries pop, stirring occasionally. Spoon chutney into serving bowl; cover and refrigerate 3 hours or up to 4 days.

EACH ¼ CUP: About 100 calories (0 percent calories from fat), 1g protein, 26g carbohydrate, 0g total fat, 4g fiber, 0mg cholesterol, 2mg sodium ♥ ▤

Basil and Balsamic Beets

Fresh chopped basil is a cool counterpart to sweet, roasted beets in this easy-to-prepare side dish. Serve with roasted chicken for a delicious, diet-friendly dinner.

ACTIVE TIME: 5 minutes
TOTAL TIME: 1 hour 5 minutes plus cooling
MAKES: 4 side-dish servings

2	pounds beets
1	tablespoon olive oil
2	tablespoons chopped fresh basil
2	tablespoons balsamic vinegar
1	tablespoon brown sugar
¼	teaspoon salt

1. Preheat oven to 450°F. In 13" by 9" roasting pan, toss beets with oil. Roast 1 hour or until tender. Cool beets; peel and discard skins.

2. Cut beets into ¼-inch pieces; toss with basil, vinegar, brown sugar, and salt.

EACH SERVING: About 120 calories (30 percent calories from fat), 2g protein, 19g carbohydrate, 4g total fat (0.5g saturated), 4g fiber, 0mg cholesterol, 260mg sodium ♥

Maple-Roasted Squash

In the vegetable department, nothing says "fall" like butternut squash. Tossed with a mix of maple syrup and spices that give it a hint of heat and smoke flavor, it's roasted to concentrate its own natural sweetness.

ACTIVE TIME: 5 minutes
TOTAL TIME: 35 minutes
MAKES: 10 side-dish servings

1	package (2 pounds) peeled and cubed butternut squash
1	tablespoon olive oil
¼	teaspoon salt
⅓	cup maple syrup
½	teaspoon pumpkin-pie spice
	pinch cayenne (hot red) pepper

1. Preheat oven to 425°F. Line 15½" by 10½" jelly-roll pan with foil. Place squash in pan; drizzle with oil, sprinkle with salt, and toss to combine. Roast squash 15 minutes.

2. Meanwhile, in cup, stir maple syrup with pumpkin-pie spice and cayenne pepper.

3. Toss squash with maple syrup mixture. Roast until fork-tender, 15 to 20 minutes longer. Spoon squash, along with pan juices, into serving dish.

EACH SERVING: About 100 calories (18 percent calories from fat), 1g protein, 22g carbohydrate, 2g total fat (0g saturated), 2g fiber, 0mg cholesterol, 80mg sodium ☻ ♥

Light Mashed Potatoes

Fat-free half-and-half gives these potatoes the same silky texture you'd get with heavy cream but without the fat and cholesterol.

ACTIVE TIME: 15 minutes
TOTAL TIME: 30 minutes

MAKES: 6 side-dish servings

2	pounds Yukon Gold potatoes, peeled and cut into 1-inch pieces
1	tablespoon butter or margarine
¾	teaspoon salt
½	cup fat-free half-and-half, warmed

1. In 4-quart saucepan, combine potatoes and enough *water* to cover; heat to boiling over high heat. Reduce heat to low; cover and simmer 8 to 10 minutes or until potatoes are fork-tender. Reserve *¼ cup cooking water;* drain potatoes.

2. Return potatoes to saucepan. Mash with butter and salt. Gradually add warm half-and-half, continuing to mash potatoes until smooth and well blended; add reserved cooking water if necessary.

EACH SERVING: About 145 calories (12 percent calories from fat), 3g protein, 29g carbohydrate, 2g total fat (0g saturated), 2g fiber, 0mg cholesterol, 345mg sodium ♥ ♥ ≡

Mashed Sweet Potatoes

You don't have to wait until the holidays to enjoy this delectable side dish. A few tablespoons of soy sauce add a salty, earthy flavor to our rendition of this favorite. For photo, see page 236.

ACTIVE TIME: 10 minutes
TOTAL TIME: 20 minutes

MAKES: 12 side-dish servings

4	pounds sweet potatoes (5 medium), peeled and cut into 1½-inch chunks
4	tablespoons butter or margarine
3	tablespoons soy sauce
1	green onion, thinly sliced

1. In 5- or 6-quart saucepot, place sweet potatoes and enough *water* to cover; heat to boiling over high heat. Reduce heat to medium-low; cover and cook 10 to 12 minutes or until potatoes are tender. Drain well and set potatoes aside.

2. In same saucepot, melt butter over medium heat. Remove saucepot from heat; add soy sauce and potatoes. With potato masher, mash potatoes until almost smooth. Transfer to serving bowl and sprinkle with green onion.

EACH SERVING: About 150 calories (24 percent calories from fat), 2g protein, 27g carbohydrate, 4g total fat (1g saturated), 3g fiber, 0mg cholesterol, 310mg sodium ♥ ♥ ≡

Herb-Roasted Potatoes

Potato chunks tossed with parsley and butter cook into tender morsels when foil-wrapped. For photo, see page 12.

ACTIVE TIME: 15 minutes
TOTAL TIME: 45 minutes

MAKES: 6 side-dish servings

2   tablespoons butter or margarine
1   tablespoon chopped fresh parsley
½   teaspoon freshly grated lemon peel
½   teaspoon salt
⅛   teaspoon coarsely ground black pepper
1½   pounds small red potatoes, each cut in half

1. Preheat oven to 450°F. In 3-quart saucepan, melt butter with parsley, lemon peel, salt, and pepper over medium-low heat. Remove saucepan from heat; add potatoes and toss well to coat.

2. Place potato mixture in center of 24″ by 18″ sheet of heavy-duty foil. Fold edges over and pinch to seal tightly.

3. Place package in jelly-roll pan and bake until potatoes are tender when potatoes are pierced (through foil) with knife, about 30 minutes.

EACH SERVING: About 125 calories (29 percent calories from fat), 2g protein, 20g carbohydrate, 4g total fat (2g saturated), 1g fiber, 10mg cholesterol, 241mg sodium ♥

Oven Fries

You won't miss the fat in these hand-cut "fries." They bake beautifully in a jelly-roll pan with a spritz of nonstick cooking spray and a sprinkle of salt and pepper.

ACTIVE TIME: 10 minutes
TOTAL TIME: 30 minutes

MAKES: 4 side-dish servings

nonstick cooking spray
3   medium baking potatoes (8 ounces each)
½   teaspoon salt
¼   teaspoon coarsely ground black pepper

1. Preheat oven to 500°F. Spray two 15½″ by 10½″ jelly-roll pans or 2 large cookie sheets with nonstick cooking spray.

2. Scrub unpeeled potatoes well, but do not peel. Cut each potato lengthwise in half. With each potato half cut side down, cut lengthwise into ¼-inch-thick slices. Place potatoes in medium bowl and toss with salt and pepper.

3. Divide potato slices between pans and spray potatoes with nonstick cooking spray. Roast potatoes until tender and lightly browned, about 20 minutes, rotating pans between upper and lower racks halfway through roasting time.

EACH SERVING: About 130 calories (7 percent calories from fat), 4g protein, 28g carbohydrate, 1g total fat (0g saturated), 3g fiber, 0mg cholesterol, 280mg sodium ◔ ♥

ROSEMARY AND GARLIC OVEN FRIES: Prepare Oven Fries as above, but in step 3 add *½ teaspoon dried rosemary, crumbled,* and *2 garlic cloves, crushed with garlic press.*

Oven-Browned Carrots and Parsnips

A duet of sweet root vegetables is subtly accented by the flavor of fresh lemon peel and orange liqueur. Use two pans—overcrowding will keep vegetables from roasting properly.

ACTIVE TIME: 20 minutes
TOTAL TIME: 1 hour 20 minutes
MAKES: 10 side-dish servings

2	pounds carrots, peeled and cut into 3" by ½" sticks
2	pounds parsnips, peeled and cut into 3" by ½" sticks
4	strips fresh lemon peel (3" by 1" each)
2	tablespoons orange-flavored liqueur
1	teaspoon sugar
½	teaspoon salt
¼	teaspoon coarsely ground black pepper
3	tablespoons butter or margarine, cut into pieces

1. Preheat oven to 425°F. In large bowl, toss carrots and parsnips with lemon peel, liqueur, sugar, salt, and pepper.

2. Divide mixture between two 15½" by 10½" jelly-roll pans (or use 1 jelly-roll pan and 1 shallow large roasting pan) and dot with butter. Roast vegetables until tender and browned, about 1 hour, stirring occasionally and rotating pans between upper and lower racks halfway through roasting time.

EACH SERVING: About 135 calories (27 percent calories from fat), 2g protein, 24g carbohydrate, 4g total fat (3g saturated), 6g fiber, 9mg cholesterol, 190mg sodium 🌱 🧺

Healthy Makeover Pumpkin Bread

Treat family and friends to our slimmed-down quick bread. Gone are the traditional version's saturated fat and cholesterol (thanks to egg whites and a blend of low-fat yogurt and canola oil). No one will suspect you've tinkered—this bread is that good!

ACTIVE TIME: 20 minutes
TOTAL TIME: 1 hour 10 minutes
MAKES: 1 loaf, 16 slices

1	cup packed light brown sugar
2	large egg whites
1	cup solid pack pumpkin (not pumpkin pie mix)
¼	cup canola oil
⅓	cup low-fat plain yogurt
1	teaspoon vanilla extract
1	cup all-purpose flour
¾	cup whole-wheat flour
1½	teaspoons baking powder
1	teaspoon ground cinnamon
½	teaspoon ground nutmeg
½	teaspoon baking soda
½	teaspoon salt

1. Preheat oven to 350°F. Spray 8½" by 4½" metal loaf pan with nonstick cooking spray with flour.

2. In large bowl, with wire whisk, combine brown sugar and egg whites. Add pumpkin, oil, yogurt, and vanilla; stir to combine.

3. In medium bowl, combine all-purpose flour, whole-wheat flour, baking powder, cinnamon, nutmeg, baking soda, and salt. Add flour mixture to pumpkin mixture; stir until just combined. Do not overmix.

4. Pour batter into prepared pan. Bake 45 to 50 minutes or until toothpick inserted in center of loaf comes out clean. Cool in pan 10 minutes. Invert pumpkin bread onto wire rack; cool completely before slicing.

EACH SLICE: About 140 calories (26 percent calories from fat), 2g protein, 25g carbohydrate, 4g total fat (0g saturated), 1g fiber, 0mg cholesterol, 165mg sodium ♥ ▭

10

Sweet Finales

If you're worried that eating light and healthy means you have to pass on sweet treats, take heart! We've collected 25 recipes for scrumptious cookies, cakes, puddings, and fruity and frozen desserts sure to satisfy your hankerings. Most are less than 200 calories per serving (and many come in under 100 calories) and all are low-fat, so you can dip in, guilt-free.

We open with fruit desserts: From pears steeped in wine sauce and a classic strawberry rhubarb crisp to a sweet and fruity salsa served with cinnamon sugar tortilla chips, we make use of an entire fruit basket of options. We even include a mixed fruit salad you can prepare on your grill, gilded with a delectable honey glaze.

Then it's onto the baked goods: Enjoy a warm chocolate banana cake and even a slimmed-down take on carrot cake (the light cream cheese frosting, made with reduced-fat cream cheese and low-fat mik, is so satisfying, you'd never know the difference). Or fill your cookie jar with our reduced-fat oatmeal raisin cookies, butterscotch blondies, or brownie bites, which are topped with a chocolatey frosting for the chocolate lovers in the house. If you're trying to get more grains into your diet (and who isn't?), whip up a batch of whole-wheat sugar cookies; you can use a white whole-wheat flour for a more traditional look and texture.

Last, but certainly not least, we offer creamy puddings and icy treats, like our dinner-party-worthy panna cotta drizzled with a pretty blackberry sauce or our colorful sorbet terrine finished with a warm plum compote.

Sgroppino Sorbet with Prosecco and Mint (recipe page 289)

Chianti-Roasted Pears

This is a super-easy dessert for company. Bosc pears become tender and caramelized on the outside when baked with a butter-and-sugar coating and basted with red wine.

ACTIVE TIME: 15 minutes
TOTAL TIME: 1 hour plus cooling
MAKES: 6 servings

1	large navel orange (12 to 14 ounces)
6	Bosc pears (8 ounces each)
½	cup hearty red wine (such as Chianti)
¼	cup water
¼	cup sugar
1	tablespoon butter or margarine, melted

1. Preheat oven to 450°F. With vegetable peeler, remove peel from orange in 2″ by ½″ strips. Reserve orange for another use.

2. With melon baller or small knife, remove cores and seeds from pears by cutting through blossom end (bottom) of unpeeled pears (do not remove stems from pears).

3. In shallow 1½- to 2-quart glass or ceramic baking dish, combine orange peel, wine, and water. Place sugar in medium bowl. Hold pears, one at a time, over bowl of sugar with one hand (keep other hand dry). With dry hand, use pastry brush to brush pears with melted butter, then sprinkle pears with sugar until coated. Stand pears in baking dish. Sprinkle any remaining sugar into baking dish around pears.

4. Bake pears 35 to 40 minutes or until tender when pierced with tip of small knife, basting occasionally with syrup in baking dish.

5. Cool pears slightly, about 30 minutes, to serve warm. Or cool completely; cover and refrigerate up to 1 day. Reheat to serve warm if you like.

EACH SERVING: About 135 calories (20 percent calories from fat), 1g protein, 29g carbohydrate, 3 total fat (1g saturated), 4g fiber, 5mg cholesterol, 20mg sodium ♥ ▭

Three-Fruit Salad with Vanilla Bean Syrup

If you don't have a vanilla bean, stir one-half teaspoon vanilla extract into the chilled syrup.

ACTIVE TIME: 30 minutes
TOTAL TIME: 40 minutes plus chilling
MAKES: 12 servings

2	large lemons
1	vanilla bean
¾	cup water
¾	cup sugar
3	ripe mangoes, peeled and cut into 1-inch pieces
2	pints strawberries, hulled and each cut in half, or into quarters if large
1	medium honeydew melon, peeled and cut into 1-inch pieces

1. From 1 lemon, with vegetable peeler, remove strips of yellow outer peel; from lemons, squeeze ¼ cup juice. Cut vanilla bean lengthwise in half. With small knife, scrape seeds from vanilla bean; reserve seeds and pod.

2. In 1-quart saucepan, combine lemon peel, vanilla seeds and pod, water, and sugar; heat to boiling over high heat. Reduce heat to medium; cook until syrup has thickened, about 5 minutes. Pour syrup mixture through sieve into bowl; stir in lemon juice. Cover and refrigerate syrup until chilled, about 2 hours.

3. Place mangoes, strawberries, and melon in large bowl; add syrup and toss.

EACH SERVING: About 140 calories (0 percent calories from fat), 3g fiber, 1g protein, 35g carbohydrate, 0g total fat, 0mg cholesterol, 13mg sodium ♥ ▭

Broiled Brown-Sugar Bananas

A sweet, satisfying dessert with just four basic ingredients.

ACTIVE TIME: 5 minutes
TOTAL TIME: 10 minutes
MAKES: 4 servings

4	ripe medium bananas, unpeeled
2	tablespoons brown sugar
1	tablespoon lower-fat margarine
⅛	teaspoon ground cinnamon

1. Preheat broiler.

2. Cut each unpeeled banana lengthwise almost in half, being careful not to cut all the way through and leaving 1 inch uncut at banana end.

3. In cup, with fork, blend together brown sugar, margarine, and cinnamon. Place bananas, cut side up, on rack in broiling pan. Spoon brown-sugar mixture over split bananas.

4. Place pan in broiler at closest position to source of heat; broil until bananas are browned, about 5 minutes.

5. Serve bananas in skins and use spoon to scoop out fruit.

EACH SERVING: About 150 calories (12 percent calories from fat), 1g protein, 34g carbohydrate, 2g total fat (1g saturated), 3g fiber, 0mg cholesterol, 20mg sodium ◔ ♥

Fresh Fruit
with Raspberry Dip

Try this refreshing dip with any seasonal fruit.

TOTAL TIME: 20 minutes

MAKES: 2 cups or 8 servings

1   cup raspberries
1   lime
1½ cups reduced-fat (2%) Greek yogurt
¼   cup packed light brown sugar
assorted fresh fruit for dipping (such as
    strawberries, grapes, kiwifruit slices, and
    plum, peach, and/or apricot wedges)

1. Place raspberries in sieve set over bowl. With back of spoon, press berries through sieve into bowl; discard seeds. From lime, grate 1 teaspoon peel and squeeze 1 tablespoon juice.

2. Add lime peel and juice, yogurt, and brown sugar to bowl with raspberry puree and stir to combine. Transfer to airtight container and refrigerate up to 1 day.

3. Spoon sauce into serving bowl and place on large platter. Arrange fruit on same platter.

EACH ¼ CUP SAUCE: About 55 calories (16 percent calories from fat), 3g protein, 10g carbohydrate, 1g total fat (1g saturated), 1g fiber, 2mg cholesterol, 15mg sodium ♥ ♥ ▤

EAT YOUR BERRIES

They're not only delicious, they're berry, berry nutritious!

+ **BLUEBERRIES** contain powerful antioxidant compounds that may improve memory and coordination.
+ **RASPBERRIES** are loaded with 4 grams of fiber per half cup, and they boast high levels of antioxidants (although not the stratospheric levels found in blueberries).
+ **STRAWBERRIES** are rich in ellagic acid, a cancer fighter. One half cup provides 57 percent of your daily requirement for vitamin C.
+ **BLACKBERRIES** are rich in a compound that helps fight cancer and inflammation and may also reduce the risk of heart disease.

They're also a good source of fiber, at 4 grams per half cup.

+ **ELDERBERRIES, BLACK CURRANTS, AND CHOKEBERRIES** are still scarce in the marketplace, but that may change as consumers learn about their high antioxidant content— they may have 50 percent higher antioxidant levels than the more common berries!

TIP: These days, fresh berries are found in stores year-round, but they can be expensive off-season, so it pays to freeze them. Do it when the berries are at their peak to preserve nutrients. Here's how: Rinse the berries in a colander, and if necessary, hull them. Freeze in zip-tight plastic bags and you'll have fresh berries year-round.

Honeyed Hot Fruit Salad

A few turns on the grill transform fresh fruit into a sumptuous finale. For photo, see page 8.

ACTIVE TIME: 15 minutes
TOTAL TIME: 25 minutes
MAKES: 6 servings

½   cup honey
1   tablespoon fresh lemon juice
¼   cup loosely packed fresh mint leaves, thinly sliced
1   medium pineapple, cut lengthwise into 6 wedges, with leaves attached
2   large bananas, peeled and each cut diagonally into thirds
3   medium plums, each cut in half and pitted
2   medium nectarines or peaches, each cut into quarters and pitted

1. Prepare outdoor grill for direct grilling over medium heat.

2. In cup, stir honey, lemon juice, and 1 tablespoon sliced mint.

3. With tongs, place fruit pieces on hot grill rack over medium heat and grill, turning fruit occasionally and brushing it with honey mixture during last 3 minutes of cooking, until browned and tender, 10 to 15 minutes.

4. To serve, arrange grilled fruit on large platter; drizzle with any remaining honey mixture. Sprinkle with remaining mint.

EACH SERVING: About 215 calories (4 percent calories from fat), 2g protein, 55g carbohydrate, 1g total fat (0g saturated), 5g fiber, 0mg cholesterol, 5mg sodium ● ❋

Grilled Angel Food Cake with Strawberries

Store-bought angel food cake goes gourmet when it's grilled and topped with sweetened balsamic-soaked strawberries.

TOTAL TIME: 15 minutes plus standing
MAKES: 6 servings

1½   pounds strawberries, hulled and each cut in half, or into quarters if large
2   tablespoons balsamic vinegar
1   tablespoon sugar
1   (9-ounce) store-bought angel food cake
Whipped cream (optional)

1. In medium bowl, toss strawberries with vinegar and sugar. Let stand at room temperature until sugar dissolves, at least 30 minutes, stirring occasionally.

2. Meanwhile, prepare outdoor grill for direct grilling over medium heat. Cut cake into 6 wedges.

3. Place cake on hot grill rack and grill 3 to 4 minutes or until lightly toasted on both sides, turning over once. Spoon strawberries with their juice onto 6 dessert plates. Place grilled cake on plates with strawberries; serve with whipped cream, if you like.

EACH SERVING: 155 calories (27 percent calories from fat), 3g protein, 35g carbohydrate, 1g total fat (0g saturated), 3g fiber, 0mg cholesterol, 320mg sodium

Sweet Summer Salsa with Tortilla Chips

Here's a sweet take on a typically savory classic. The salsa is best made just before serving, but the homemade chips can be baked up to one week ahead.

ACTIVE TIME: 25 minutes
TOTAL TIME: 35 minutes
MAKES: 3½ cups or 8 servings

SWEET TORTILLA CHIPS

4   (8-inch) flour tortillas
1   tablespoon butter or margarine, melted
1   tablespoon sugar
pinch ground cinnamon

SUMMER SALSA

1   lime
1   tablespoon sugar
1   large ripe peach, pitted and chopped
1   large ripe red or purple plum, pitted and chopped
1   large ripe apricot, pitted and chopped
½   cup dark sweet cherries, pitted and chopped
½   cup seedless green grapes, chopped

1. Prepare Sweet Tortilla Chips: Preheat oven to 375°F.

2. Brush tortillas with butter. In cup, combine sugar and cinnamon. Sprinkle 1 side of each tortilla with cinnamon-sugar. Stack tortillas and cut into 6 wedges, making 24 wedges in total. Arrange wedges, sugar side up, in single layer on 2 large cookie sheets. Place on 2 oven racks and bake chips until golden, 10 to 12 minutes, rotating cookie sheets between upper and lower racks halfway through baking.

3. Cool chips on cookie sheets on wire racks. Store in tightly covered container up to 1 week.

4. Just before serving, prepare Summer Salsa: From lime, grate ¼ teaspoon peel and squeeze 1 tablespoon juice. In medium bowl, stir lime and juice, sugar, and chopped fruit until combined.

5. To serve, spoon salsa into serving bowl. Use chips to scoop up salsa.

EACH SERVING: About 155 calories (23 percent calories from fat), 3g protein, 28g carbohydrate, 4g total fat (2g saturated), 2g fiber, 4mg cholesterol, 150mg sodium

Grapefruit-Meringue Nests with Berries

Grapefruit adds citrus appeal to these edible meringue berry baskets. Slices of other citrus and kiwi would also pair nicely with the grapefruit syrup.

ACTIVE TIME: 25 minutes
TOTAL TIME: 2 hours 25 minutes
MAKES: 8 servings

MERINGUE NESTS

3	large egg whites
⅛	teaspoon cream of tartar
½	cup sugar
1	teaspoon freshly grated Ruby Red grapefruit peel

MIXED BERRIES

1	container (4.4 ounces) blueberries
1	container (4.4 ounces) raspberries
2	pounds strawberries, hulled and each cut in half
¼	cup sugar
¼	cup fresh Ruby Red grapefruit juice

1. Prepare Meringue Nests: Preheat oven to 200°F. Line large cookie sheet with parchment paper or silicone baking mat. In large bowl, with mixer on high speed, beat egg whites and cream of tartar until soft peaks form. Sprinkle in sugar, 2 tablespoons at a time, beating until sugar dissolves and meringue stands in stiff, glossy peaks when beaters are lifted. With large rubber spatula, gently fold grapefruit peel into meringue until well combined.

2. Divide mixture into 8 even mounds (heaping ¼-cup measuring cup) on prepared sheet, spacing about 2 inches apart. Pressing back of spoon into center of each meringue, form mounds into 3-inch-round nests. Bake 2 hours or until firm. Turn off oven; leave meringues in oven 1 hour or overnight to dry. When meringues are dry, carefully remove from parchment. Meringues can be stored in tightly sealed container at room temperature up to 2 weeks.

3. Prepare Mixed Berries: In large bowl, combine blueberries, raspberries, and half of strawberries. In 12-inch skillet, combine sugar and grapefruit juice. Heat to boiling over medium heat, stirring occasionally. Boil 2 minutes or until sugar dissolves and mixture is clear pink. Add remaining strawberries and cook 1 to 3 minutes or until berries release their juices and have softened slightly. Pour mixture over uncooked berries. Stir gently until well combined.

4. Place meringue nests on serving plates. Divide berries among nests and drizzle grapefruit syrup all around. Serve immediately.

EACH SERVING: 130 calories (7 percent calories from fat), 30g carbohydrate, 2g protein, 1g total fat (0g saturated), 4g fiber, 0mg cholesterol, 25mg sodium
♥ ▭

Blueberry-Lemon Tiramisu

Impress your friends and family with this surprisingly low-fat tiramisu.

ACTIVE TIME: 20 minutes
TOTAL TIME: 25 minutes plus chilling overnight
MAKES: 9 servings

1 to 2 lemons
3¾ cups blueberries
¾ cup sugar
4   tablespoons water
1   container (17.6 ounces) nonfat Greek yogurt
1   package (3 ounces) ladyfingers (see Tip)
mint sprig for garnish

1. From lemon(s), grate 1½ teaspoons peel and squeeze ¼ cup juice.

2. In medium saucepan, combine 1½ cups blueberries, ¼ cup sugar, and 1 tablespoon water. Heat over medium heat 5 minutes or until blueberries soften and juices thicken, stirring occasionally. Transfer to medium bowl and stir in 1½ cups blueberries. Set aside.

3. Prepare lemon syrup: In microwave-safe small bowl, combine ¼ cup sugar and remaining 3 tablespoons water. Cook in microwave on High 1 minute. Stir in 3 tablespoons lemon juice and 1 teaspoon lemon peel.

4. In medium bowl, stir together yogurt and remaining ¼ cup sugar, 1 tablespoon lemon juice, and ½ teaspoon lemon peel.

5. In 8-inch square baking dish, arrange half of ladyfingers. Brush with half of lemon syrup. Spoon blueberry mixture over ladyfingers. Arrange remaining ladyfingers over blueberries. Brush with remaining lemon syrup. Spread yogurt mixture on top. Cover and refrigerate overnight. To serve, top tiramisu with ¾ cup blueberries and garnish with mint sprig.

EACH SERVING: 165 calories (5 percent calories from fat), 7g protein, 34g carbohydrate, 1g total fat (0g saturated), 2g fiber, 23mg cholesterol, 90mg sodium

TIP: *We tested this recipe with both soft and hard (Italian-style) ladyfingers and had good results with both types. For the best texture, let the tiramisu sit in the refrigerator overnight.*

Strawberry-Rhubarb Crisp

This sweet-tart confection is just as tasty as Grandma's strawberry-rhubarb pie—but with one-fifth the calories. By replacing the butter-laden crust with a whole-grain crumble, we've eliminated more than 30 grams of total fat and slashed the saturated fat by almost 90 percent. Got a spoon? Dig in!

ACTIVE TIME: 15 minutes
TOTAL TIME: 1 hour 5 minutes

MAKES: 8 servings

1	small orange
1	pound strawberries, hulled and each cut in half, or into quarters if large
10	ounces rhubarb, trimmed and cut into ½-inch-thick slices
¼	cup granulated sugar
1	tablespoon cornstarch
⅓	cup old-fashioned oats, uncooked
⅓	cup packed dark brown sugar
¼	cup whole-wheat flour
pinch salt	
3	tablespoons butter or margarine, slightly softened

1. Preheat oven to 375°F. From orange, grate peel and divide between 2 large bowls; squeeze ¼ cup orange juice into small bowl.

2. In one large bowl with peel, combine strawberries, rhubarb, and granulated sugar until well mixed. To small bowl with juice, add cornstarch; stir until well mixed. Stir juice mixture into fruit mixture to combine. Pour into 9-inch glass or ceramic pie plate; spread filling in an even layer.

3. In other large bowl with peel, combine oats, brown sugar, flour, and salt. With pastry blender or fingertips, blend in butter until mixture forms coarse crumbs with a few pea-size pieces.

4. Sprinkle oat mixture evenly over strawberry mixture. Place pie plate on foil-lined cookie sheet to catch any drips. Bake 45 minutes or until topping is golden brown and fruit filling is hot and bubbling.

5. Cool crisp on wire rack until filling is set but still slightly warm, at least 1 hour. Serve warm.

EACH SERVING: About 155 calories (29 percent calories from fat), 2g protein, 27g carbohydrate, 5g total fat (3g saturated), 3g fiber, 12mg cholesterol, 70mg sodium

Healthy Makeover Carrot Cake

A dessert with a vegetable in its name can't be that bad for you, right? Wrong. Good Housekeeping's *own classic carrot cake recipe weighs in at 640 calories and 20 fat grams per slice. Here's a greatly slimmed down version you can enjoy without guilt. For an even healthier treat, skip the icing altogether.*

ACTIVE TIME: 20 minutes
TOTAL TIME: 1 hour 5 minutes plus cooling
MAKES: 20 servings

CARROT CAKE

2¼ cups all-purpose flour
2   teaspoons baking soda
2   teaspoons ground cinnamon
1   teaspoon ground ginger
1   teaspoon baking powder
1   teaspoon salt
2   large eggs
2   large egg whites
1   cup granulated sugar
¾   cup packed dark brown sugar
1   can (8 to 8 ¼ ounces) crushed pineapple in juice
⅓   cup canola oil
1   tablespoon vanilla extract
1   bag (10 ounces) shredded carrots
½   cup dark seedless raisins.

CREAM-CHEESE ICING

2   ounces reduced-fat cream cheese
¾   cup confectioners' sugar
½   teaspoon low-fat milk
¼   teaspoon vanilla extract

1. Preheat oven to 350°F. Spray nonstick 12-cup Bundt-style pan with nonstick cooking spray with flour.

2. Prepare Carrot Cake: Combine flour, baking soda, cinnamon, ginger, baking powder, and salt.

3. In large bowl, with mixer on medium speed, beat eggs and egg whites until blended. Beat in granulated and dark brown sugars; beat 2 minutes. On low speed, beat in pineapple with juice, oil, and vanilla. Add flour mixture; beat 1 minute. Stir in carrots and raisins.

4. Pour batter into pan. Bake 45 to 50 minutes or until toothpick inserted in center comes out clean. Cool in pan 10 minutes. Invert cake onto rack; cool completely.

5. Prepare Cream-Cheese Icing: In bowl, stir cream cheese and ¼ cup confectioners' sugar until smooth. Add milk, vanilla, and remaining confectioners' sugar; stir to a drizzling consistency. Drizzle icing over cake.

EACH SERVING: 210 calories (21 percent calories from fat), 3g protein, 40g carbohydrate, 5g total fat (1g saturated), 1g fiber, 23mg cholesterol, 295mg sodium

LIGHTEN UP YOUR FAVORITE DESSERTS

You don't have to kiss your favorite recipes good-bye because they call for high-fat ingredients. Just make these easy swaps.

- Replace the semisweet chocolate chips in treasured cookie classics with half the amount of *mini* semisweet chips (they'll scatter through more of the dough than big chips, but still add that authentic richness). Or try using the full amount of low-fat baking chips; the impostor effect is not quite as noticeable when the cookies are eaten warm from the oven.
- Omit up to half the butter, margarine, or oil in cakes, muffins, or quick breads, and substitute applesauce, prune puree, or a fruit-based fat replacement (such as Lighter Bake). These switches are especially successful in coffee cakes and bar cookies.
- Substitute plain nonfat or low-fat yogurt or reduced-fat sour cream for regular sour cream. The flavor comes very close to the original in muffins and cakes.
- Eliminate the bottom crust in fruit pies to significantly reduce calories and fat—spoon the filling into a pie plate, add the top crust, and serve cobbler-style. (You don't even need to grease the plate—the saucy fruit will spoon right out.)
- Cut back the amount of nuts in a recipe to a few tablespoons, finely chop, and sprinkle on *top* of cookies, brownies, cakes, and breads before baking—they'll get a nice toasty flavor in the oven, and you'll see and taste them first.

- Slip light cream cheese (Neufchâtel) into cheesecakes rather than using full-fat cheese—you'll save about 6 grams of fat and 60 calories per slice.
- Use ¼ cup no-cholesterol egg substitute in place of each whole egg in quick breads, muffins, and cakes. Or substitute 2 whites for each egg up to 2 eggs (too many whites can make the texture a bit rubbery).
- Count on lower-fat dairy products. Instead of whole or 2 percent milk, use 1 percent or skim. Rather than heavy cream (unless it must be whipped), pour in light cream or half-and-half—either will perform perfectly in most frostings, glazes, and doughs. If a pie or cookie calls for canned evaporated or sweetened condensed milk, get the fat-free or low-fat kind.
- For mock whipped cream, beat evaporated skim milk. Chill the milk, bowl, and beaters in your freezer for at least 15 minutes; beat in 1 tablespoon lemon juice to stabilize the mixture, and sweeten the taste. Serve immediately because it collapses quickly. We won't lie to you—it's no double for the real thing—but it *is* creamy-looking, white, and fluffy.
- Don't grease baking pans with butter or margarine—try new nonstick pan liners, kitchen parchment, or a spritz of cooking spray with flour.

Warm Chocolate Banana Cake

Chocolate lovers won't feel deprived when they dig into this low-fat brownie-like cake with a fudgy texture. Serve with fat-free vanilla ice cream, if you like.

ACTIVE TIME: 15 minutes
TOTAL TIME: 50 minutes

MAKES: 8 servings

1	cup all-purpose flour
1	cup unsweetened cocoa
½	cup granulated sugar
1	teaspoon baking powder
½	teaspoon salt
¼	teaspoon ground cinnamon
1	ripe large banana, mashed (½ cup)
1	large egg, beaten
¼	cup cold water, plus 1¼ cups boiling water
2	tablespoons butter or margarine, melted
1	teaspoon vanilla extract
½	cup packed dark brown sugar

1. Preheat oven to 350°F. In large bowl, combine flour, ¾ cup cocoa, granulated sugar, baking powder, salt, and cinnamon.

2. In medium bowl, with wooden spoon, stir banana, egg, cold water, melted butter, and vanilla until blended.

3. Stir banana mixture into flour mixture just until blended (batter will be thick). Spoon into ungreased 8-inch square baking dish; spread evenly in pan.

4. In same large bowl, with wire whisk, beat brown sugar, remaining ¼ cup cocoa, and boiling water until blended. Pour over chocolate batter in baking dish; do not stir.

5. Bake 35 minutes (dessert should have some fudgy sauce on top). Cool in pan on wire rack 5 minutes. Serve warm.

EACH SERVING: 235 calories (19 percent calories from fat), 5g protein, 47g carbohydrate, 5g total fat (3g saturated), 4g fiber, 35mg cholesterol, 240mg sodium

Oatmeal-Raisin Cookies

If you thought the words "delicious" and "low-fat" could never be used to describe the same cookie, think again. This one's chewy and sweet, yet it has only 2 grams of fat per cookie.

ACTIVE TIME: 15 minutes
TOTAL TIME: 35 minutes
MAKES: about 48 cookies

2	cups all-purpose flour
1	teaspoon baking soda
½	teaspoon salt
½	cup light corn-oil spread (1 stick) (56 to 60% fat)
¾	cup packed dark brown sugar
½	cup granulated sugar
2	large egg whites
1	large egg
2	teaspoons vanilla extract
1	cup quick-cooking oats, uncooked
½	cup dark seedless raisins

1. Preheat oven to 375°F. Grease two large cookie sheets. In medium bowl, combine flour, baking soda, and salt.

2. In large bowl, with mixer at low speed, beat corn-oil spread and brown and granulated sugars until well combined. Increase speed to high; beat until mixture is light and fluffy. Add egg whites, whole egg, and vanilla; beat until blended. With wooden spoon, stir in flour mixture, oats, and raisins until combined.

3. Drop dough by level tablespoons, 2 inches apart, on prepared cookie sheets. Bake until golden, 10 to 12 minutes, rotating cookie sheets between upper and lower oven racks halfway through baking. With wide spatula, transfer cookies to wire racks to cool completely.

4. Repeat with remaining dough.

EACH COOKIE: About 65 calories (27 percent calories from fat), 1g protein, 12g carbohydrate, 2g total fat (0g saturated), 0g fiber, 4mg cholesterol, 72mg sodium ♥ 🍴

Whole-Wheat Sugar Cookies

We snuck some whole-wheat flour into these sugar cookies with tasty results. The photo at right shows Berry-Orange Linzer Jewels, a pretty variation filled with raspberry jam, and Brownie Bites, recipe page 284.

ACTIVE TIME: 1 hour
TOTAL TIME: 2 hours plus chilling
MAKES: about 72 cookies

1	cup all-purpose flour
1	cup white whole-wheat flour
½	teaspoon baking powder
¼	teaspoon salt
1	cup sugar
½	cup trans-fat-free vegetable-oil spread (1 stick) (60 to 70% oil)
1	large egg
2	teaspoons vanilla extract

1. On sheet of waxed paper, combine all-purpose and whole-wheat flours, baking powder, and salt.

2. In large bowl, with mixer on low speed, beat sugar and vegetable-oil spread until blended. Increase speed to high; beat until light and creamy, about 3 minutes, occasionally scraping down bowl with rubber spatula. Reduce speed to low; beat in egg and vanilla, then beat in flour mixture just until blended.

3. Divide dough in half; flatten each half into a disk. Wrap each disk with plastic wrap and refrigerate until dough is firm enough to roll, about 2 hours.

4. Preheat oven to 375°F.

5. On lightly floured surface, with floured rolling pin, roll one piece of dough ⅛ inch thick. With 2-inch cookie cutters, cut out as many cookies as possible; wrap and refrigerate trimmings. With lightly floured spatula, place cookies, 1 inch apart, on ungreased cookie sheet.

6. Bake cookies until lightly browned, 10 to 12 minutes. With thin metal spatula, transfer cookies to wire rack to cool. Repeat with remaining dough and trimmings.

EACH COOKIE: About 35 calories (27 percent calories from fat), 1g protein, 5g carbohydrate, 1g total fat (0g saturated), 0g fiber, 3mg cholesterol, 20mg sodium ♥ ▣

BERRY-ORANGE LINZER JEWELS: Prepare Whole-Wheat Sugar Cookies as directed, but in step 2, add *1 teaspoon freshly grated orange peel* with egg and vanilla. Chill, roll, and cut as directed in steps 3 and 5, but use scalloped 2-inch square or round cookie cutter to cut out centers of half the cookies. Bake and cool as directed in steps 5 and 6. When cookies are cool, if you like sprinkle *confectioners' sugar* through sieve over cookies with cutout centers. From *¼ cup seedless red raspberry jam*, spread scant ½ teaspoon jam on each whole cookie; top cookie with cutout center. Makes about 36 sandwich cookies.

EACH COOKIE: About 70 calories (26 percent calories from fat), 2g protein, 10g carbohydrate, 2g total fat (0g saturated), 0g fiber, 6mg cholesterol, 5mg sodium ♥ 🍽

WHOLE-WHEAT FLOUR THAT'S WHITE

Struggling to eat the recommended three servings of whole grains a day because you don't like the flavor and texture of whole wheat? Try baking with white whole-wheat flour. Milled from a variety of white wheat, it's as healthy as traditional whole wheat—with the same levels of fiber, nutrients, and minerals—but it lacks the heartier taste and grainy heft. It's ideal for all whole-grain recipes and can be substituted for up to half of the all-purpose flour in many baking goods without substantially changing the taste.

Low-Fat Butterscotch Blondies

These chewy treats are one of our test kitchen's favorites—there are only 3 grams of fat in each!

ACTIVE TIME: 15 minutes
TOTAL TIME: 50 minutes
MAKES: 16 blondies

1	cup all-purpose flour
½	teaspoon baking powder
¼	teaspoon salt
3	tablespoons butter or margarine
¾	cup packed dark brown sugar
2	large egg whites
⅓	cup dark corn syrup
2	teaspoons vanilla extract
2	tablespoons finely chopped pecans

1. Preheat oven to 350°F. Grease 8-inch square baking pan. In bowl, combine flour, baking powder, and salt.

2. In large bowl, with mixer at medium speed, beat butter and sugar until well blended, about 2 minutes. Reduce speed to low; beat in egg whites, corn syrup, and vanilla until smooth. Beat in flour mixture just until combined. Spread batter in prepared pan. Sprinkle with pecans.

3. Bake until toothpick inserted in center comes out clean and edges are lightly browned, 35 to 40 minutes. Cool completely in pan on wire rack.

4. When cool, cut into 4 strips, then cut each strip crosswise into 4 pieces.

EACH BLONDIE: About 115 calories (23 percent calories from fat), 1g protein, 21g carbohydrate, 3g total fat (1g saturated), 6mg cholesterol, 94mg sodium ♥ 🍽

Hermit Bars

Originating in New England in clipper-ship days, these spicy bars got their name because they keep so well. Sailors would stow them "like hermits" for snacking on long voyages.

ACTIVE TIME: 20 minutes
TOTAL TIME: 35 minutes plus cooling
MAKES: 32 bars

2	cups all-purpose flour
1	teaspoon ground cinnamon
½	teaspoon baking powder
½	teaspoon baking soda
½	teaspoon ground ginger
¼	teaspoon ground nutmeg
¼	teaspoon salt
⅛	teaspoon ground cloves
1	cup packed brown sugar
½	cup butter or margarine (1 stick), softened
⅓	cup dark molasses
1	large egg
1	cup dark seedless raisins
1	cup pecans (4 ounces), toasted and coarsely chopped (optional)

1. Preheat oven to 350°F. Grease and flour two large cookie sheets.

2. In large bowl, with wire whisk, mix flour, cinnamon, baking powder, baking soda, ginger, nutmeg, salt, and cloves.

3. In separate large bowl, with mixer at medium speed, beat brown sugar and butter until light and fluffy. Beat in molasses until well combined. Beat in egg. With mixer at low speed, beat in flour mixture just until blended, occasionally scraping bowl with rubber spatula. With spoon, stir in raisins and pecans if using.

4. Divide dough into quarters. With lightly floured hands, shape each quarter into 12" by 1½" log. On each prepared cookie sheet, place 2 logs, leaving about 3 inches in between.

5. Bake until logs flatten and edges are firm, 13 to 15 minutes, rotating cookie sheets between upper and lower oven racks halfway through baking. Cool logs on cookie sheets on wire racks 15 minutes.

6. Transfer logs to cutting board. Slice each log crosswise into 8 bars. Transfer to wire racks to cool completely.

EACH BAR: About 105 calories (26 percent calories from fat), 1g protein, 19g carbohydrate, 3g total fat (2g saturated), 1g fiber, 15mg cholesterol, 80mg sodium ♥ 🥬

Brownie Bites

Espresso powder gives these little brownies a nice flavor edge. The fudge frosting takes them over the top.

ACTIVE TIME: 30 minutes
TOTAL TIME: 38 minutes
MAKES: 28 cookies

BROWNIE BITES

1	teaspoon instant espresso coffee powder
1	teaspoon hot water
½	cup sweetened cocoa
⅓	cup all-purpose flour
⅓	cup whole-wheat flour
½	teaspoon baking powder
¼	teaspoon salt
⅛	teaspoon ground cinnamon
¾	cup sugar
3	tablespoons canola oil
2	tablespoons honey
1	teaspoon vanilla extract
1	large egg white

FROSTING

1	ounce unsweetened chocolate, coarsely chopped
3	tablespoons water
1	teaspoon trans-fat-free vegetable-oil spread (60 to 70% oil)
⅔	cup confectioners' sugar
½	teaspoon vanilla extract

1. Prepare Brownie Bites: Preheat oven to 350°F. Grease large cookie sheet. In cup, stir espresso powder into hot water until dissolved. Set aside.

2. In large bowl, combine cocoa, all-purpose and whole-wheat flours, baking powder, salt, and cinnamon. In medium bowl, whisk sugar, oil, honey, vanilla, egg white, and espresso mixture until mixed. With spoon, stir oil mixture into flour mixture, then with hands, press into a dough.

3. With lightly greased hands, shape dough by rolling heaping teaspoons into 1-inch balls and place on prepared cookie sheet, 2 inches apart; press to flatten slightly. Bake until brownies have cracked slightly, 7 to 8 minutes. Transfer to wire rack to cool. Repeat with remaining dough.

4. Prepare Frosting: In microwave-safe small bowl, heat chocolate and water in microwave oven on High 45 seconds; stir until smooth. Stir in vegetable oil spread, then confectioners' sugar and vanilla. Cool frosting slightly. Dip top of each cookie in frosting. Set aside to allow frosting to dry.

EACH COOKIE: About 100 calories (27 percent calories from fat), 1g protein, 19g carbohydrate, 3g total fat (1g saturated), 1g fiber, 0mg cholesterol, 74mg sodium ♥ 🍽

Healthy Makeover Brownies

The rich texture and chocolatey goodness of these bake-sale favorites speak of decadence, but compare each square's 95 calories, 3 grams of fat, and zero cholesterol to a regular brownie's doubly high calories, nearly quadrupled fat, and 60 milligrams of cholesterol, and you'll feel virtuous (and satisfied). Our cheats? Swapping nonfat cocoa for chocolate, and cholesterol-free spread for not-so-heart-healthy butter.

ACTIVE TIME: 15 minutes
TOTAL TIME: 35 minutes plus cooling

MAKES: 16 brownies

1	teaspoon instant coffee powder or granules
2	teaspoons vanilla extract
½	cup all-purpose flour
½	cup unsweetened cocoa
¼	teaspoon baking powder
¼	teaspoon salt
1	cup sugar
4	tablespoons trans-fat-free vegetable-oil spread (60 to 70% oil)
3	large egg whites

1. Preheat oven to 350°F. Line 8-inch square metal baking pan with foil; grease foil. In cup, dissolve coffee powder in vanilla extract.

2. On waxed paper, combine flour, cocoa, baking powder, and salt.

3. In medium bowl, whisk sugar, vegetable-oil spread, egg whites, and coffee mixture until well mixed, then blend in flour mixture. Spread in prepared pan.

4. Bake 22 to 24 minutes or until toothpick inserted in brownies 2 inches from edge comes out almost clean. Cool completely in pan on wire rack, about 2 hours.

5. When cool, lift foil, with brownie, out of pan; peel foil away from sides. Cut brownies into 4 strips, then cut each strip crosswise into 4 squares (see Tip).

EACH BROWNIE: About 95 calories (28 percent calories from fat), 2g protein, 17g carbohydrate, 3g total fat (1g saturated), 1g fiber, 0mg cholesterol, 75mg sodium ♥ 🍲

TIP: *If brownies are difficult to cut, dip knife in hot water; wipe dry, then cut. Repeat dipping and drying as necessary.*

Buttermilk Panna Cotta with Blackberry Sauce

This smooth and creamy dessert features antioxidant-rich blackberries.

ACTIVE TIME: 15 minutes
TOTAL TIME: 25 minutes plus chilling
MAKES: 8 servings

1   envelope unflavored gelatin
¼   cup plus 2 tablespoons water
2¾ cups buttermilk
½   cup plus 4 teaspoons sugar
10   ounces frozen blackberries, thawed
1   teaspoon fresh lemon juice

1. In cup, evenly sprinkle gelatin over ¼ cup water. Let stand 2 minutes to allow gelatin to absorb liquid and soften.

2. In 3-quart saucepan, heat ½ cup buttermilk and ½ cup sugar over medium heat 2 to 3 minutes or until sugar dissolves, stirring occasionally. Reduce heat to low; whisk in gelatin. Cook 1 to 2 minutes or until gelatin dissolves, stirring. Remove saucepan from heat; stir in remaining 2¼ cups buttermilk.

3. Pour buttermilk mixture into eight 4-ounce ramekins or 6-ounce custard cups. Place ramekins in jelly-roll pan for easier handling. Cover pan with plastic wrap and refrigerate panna cotta at least 4 hours or overnight, until well chilled and set.

4. Reserve ⅓ cup blackberries for garnish. In blender, puree remaining blackberries with lemon juice, remaining 2 tablespoons water, and 4 teaspoons sugar. Pour puree through sieve set over small bowl, stirring to press out fruit sauce; discard seeds. Cover and refrigerate sauce if not serving right away.

5. To unmold panna cotta, run tip of small knife around edge of ramekins. With hand, sharply tap side of each ramekin to break seal; invert onto 8 dessert plates. Spoon sauce around each panna cotta. Garnish with reserved berries.

EACH SERVING: 115 calories (8 percent calories from fat), 4g protein, 24g carbohydrate, 1g total fat (1g saturated), 1g fiber, 3mg cholesterol, 90mg sodium ♥ ⬛

Chocolate Pudding

Retro food at its best—and who doesn't love chocolate pudding? This clever version has only 2 grams of fat per serving and tastes divine warm or chilled.

ACTIVE TIME: 5 minutes
TOTAL TIME: 10 minutes
MAKES: 4 servings

⅓ cup sugar
¼ cup cornstarch
3 tablespoons unsweetened cocoa
pinch salt
2 cups fat-free milk
1 square (1 ounce) semisweet chocolate, finely chopped
1 teaspoon vanilla extract

1. In 2-quart saucepan, with wire whisk, mix sugar, cornstarch, cocoa, and salt until combined. Whisk in milk until blended. Heat mixture to boiling over medium heat, stirring constantly. Add chocolate; cook 1 minute, stirring, until chocolate has melted and pudding thickens slightly. Remove from heat; stir in vanilla.

2. Spoon pudding into custard cups. Serve warm or place plastic wrap directly on surface of pudding and refrigerate to serve cold later.

EACH SERVING: About 180 calories (10 percent calories from fat), 5g protein, 37g carbohydrate, 2g total fat (0g saturated), 1g fiber, 2mg cholesterol, 105mg sodium ♥ 🍽

Low-Fat Crème Caramel

Low-fat milk and a moderate number of eggs make this a guilt-free caramel custard.

ACTIVE TIME: 15 minutes
TOTAL TIME: 55 minutes plus cooling and chilling
MAKES: 8 servings

¾ cup sugar
1 large egg
2 large egg whites
2 cups low-fat (1%) milk
½ teaspoon vanilla extract

1. Preheat oven to 350°F. In heavy 1-quart saucepan, heat ½ cup sugar over medium heat, swirling pan occasionally, until sugar has melted and is amber in color. Immediately pour into eight 4- to 5-ounce ramekins.

2. In large bowl, with wire whisk, beat remaining ¼ cup sugar, whole egg, and egg whites until well blended. Beat in milk and vanilla; pour into ramekins. Skim off foam.

3. Place ramekins in medium roasting pan; cover loosely with foil. Place pan on rack in oven. Carefully pour enough very hot water into pan to come halfway up sides of ramekins. Bake until knife inserted 1 inch from center comes out clean, 40 to 45 minutes. Transfer ramekins to wire rack to cool. Refrigerate until well chilled, 3 hours or up to overnight.

4. To serve, run tip of small knife around edge of custards. Invert ramekins onto dessert plates, shaking cups gently until custards slip out, allowing caramel syrup to drip onto custards.

EACH SERVING: About 110 calories (8 percent calories from fat), 4g protein, 22g carbohydrate, 1g total fat (1g saturated), 0g fiber, 29mg cholesterol, 52mg sodium ♥ 🍽

Sgroppino Sorbet with Prosecco and Mint

Sgroppino is a classic after-dinner beverage from the Veneto region in northern Italy. It's usually made by whipping up lemon sorbet and Prosecco; a splash of vodka is sometimes added. Here we've left the sorbet intact as a light and refreshing float—a luscious and low-cal end to dinner. For photo, see page 264.

TOTAL TIME: 5 minutes

MAKES: 6 servings

1   pint lemon sorbet
2   cups Prosecco (Italian sparkling wine)
fresh mint sprigs

Evenly scoop sorbet into 6 wineglasses or dessert bowls. Pour ⅓ cup Prosecco into each glass; garnish with mint. Serve immediately.

EACH SERVING: 135 calories (0 percent calories from fat), 0g protein, 22g carbohydrate, 0g total fat (0g saturated), 0g fiber, 0mg cholesterol, 10mg sodium

Peachy Frozen Yogurt

Served as a fruity dessert or snack, our creamy Peachy Frozen Yogurt delivers a double dose of peach flavor and only 1 gram of fat per serving.

TOTAL TIME: 5 minutes

MAKES: 2½ cups or 4 servings

1   bag frozen sliced peaches (10 to 12 ounces)
2   containers (6 ounces each) low-fat peach yogurt
1   tablespoon sugar

In food processor with knife blade attached, process frozen peaches until finely shaved. Add yogurt and sugar. Process just until smooth. Serve immediately. If not serving right away, pour into 9-inch square baking pan; cover and freeze 1 hour for best texture.

EACH SERVING: 130 calories (7 percent calories from fat), 4g protein, 28g carbohydrate, 1g total fat (1g saturated), 2g fiber, 6mg cholesterol, 50mg sodium

Metric Equivalents

The recipes in this book use the standard United States method for measuring liquid and dry or solid ingredients (teaspoons, tablespoons, and cups). The information in these charts is provided to help cooks outside the U.S. successfully use these recipes. All equivalents are approximate.

METRIC EQUIVALENTS FOR DIFFERENT TYPES OF INGREDIENTS

A standard cup measure of a dry or solid ingredient will vary in weight depending on the type of ingredient. A standard cup of liquid is the same volume for any type of liquid. Use the following chart when converting standard cup measures to grams (weight) or milliliters (volume).

Standard Cup	Fine Powder (e.g., flour)	Grain (e.g., rice)	Granular (e.g., sugar)	Liquid Solids (e.g., butter)	Liquid (e.g., milk)
1	140 g	150 g	190 g	200 g	240 ml
3/4	105 g	113 g	143 g	150 g	180 ml
2/3	93 g	100 g	125 g	133 g	160 ml
1/2	70 g	75 g	95 g	100 g	120 ml
1/3	47 g	50 g	63 g	67 g	80 ml
1/4	35 g	38 g	48 g	50 g	60 ml
1/8	18 g	19 g	24 g	25 g	30 ml

USEFUL EQUIVALENTS FOR COOKING / OVEN TEMPERATURES

	Fahrenheit	Celsius	Gas Mark
Freeze water	32° F	0° C	
Room temperature	68° F	20° C	
Boil water	212° F	100° C	
Bake	325° F	160° C	3
	350° F	180° C	4
	375° F	190° C	5
	400° F	200° C	6
	425° F	220° C	7
	450° F	230° C	8
Broil			Grill

USEFUL EQUIVALENTS FOR LIQUID INGREDIENTS BY VOLUME

1/4 tsp	=					1 ml
1/2 tsp	=					2 ml
1 tsp	=					5 ml
3 tsp	=	1 tblsp	=	1/2 fl oz	=	15 ml
2 tblsp	=	1/8 cup	=	1 fl oz	=	30 ml
4 tblsp	=	1/4 cup	=	2 fl oz	=	60 ml
5 1/3 tblsp	=	1/3 cup	=	3 fl oz	=	80 ml
8 tblsp	=	1/2 cup	=	4 fl oz	=	120 ml
10 2/3 tblsp	=	2/3 cup	=	5 fl oz	=	160 ml
12 tblsp	=	3/4 cup	=	6 fl oz	=	180 ml
16 tblsp	=	1 cup	=	8 fl oz	=	240 ml
1 pt	=	2 cups	=	16 fl oz	=	480 ml
1 qt	=	4 cups	=	32 fl oz	=	960 ml
				33 fl oz	=	1000 ml

USEFUL EQUIVALENTS FOR DRY INGREDIENTS BY WEIGHT

(To convert ounces to grams, multiply the number of ounces by 30.)

1 oz	=	1/16 lb	=	30 g
4 oz	=	1/4 lb	=	120 g
8 oz	=	1/2 lb	=	240 g
12 oz	=	3/4 lb	=	360 g
16 oz	=	1 lb	=	480 g

USEFUL EQUIVALENTS FOR LENGTH

(To convert inches to centimeters, multiply the number of inches by 2.5.)

1 in	=				2.5 cm
6 in	=	1/2 ft	=		15 cm
12 in	=	1 ft	=		30 cm
36 in	=	3 ft	=	1 yd	=	90 cm
40 in	=				100 cm	= 1 m

Photography Credits

Index

Index of Recipes by Icon

This index makes it easy to search recipes by category, including 30 minutes or less, heart healthy, high fiber, and make ahead.

❤ HEART HEALTHY

If you're looking for heart-healthy options, here's a list of great choices for every meal. Each main dish contains 5 grams or less of saturated fat, 150 milligrams or less of cholesterol, and 480 milligrams or less of sodium. Each appetizer or side dish contains 2 grams or less of saturated fat, 50 milligrams or less of cholesterol, and 360 milligrams or less of sodium.

☻ HIGH FIBER

Want to get more fill-you-up fiber into your diet? Incorporate the following high fiber dishes into your regular repertoire. Each of these recipes contains 5 grams or more fiber per serving.

MAKE AHEAD

For convenience, you can make all (or a portion) of these recipes ahead of time. The individual recipes indicate which steps you can complete ahead of time, or indicate how long you can refrigerate or freeze the completed dish.

The Good Housekeeping
Triple-Test Promise

At *Good Housekeeping*, we want to make sure that every recipe we print works in any oven, with any brand of ingredient, no matter what. That's why, in our test kitchens at the **Good Housekeeping Research Institute**, we go all out: We test each recipe at least three times—and, often, several more times after that.

When a recipe is first developed, one member of our team prepares the dish and we judge it on these criteria: It must be **delicious, family-friendly, healthy,** and **easy to make**.

---

1 The recipe is then tested several more times to fine-tune the flavor and ease of preparation, always by the same team member, using the same equipment.

---

2 Next, another team member follows the recipe as written, **varying the brands of ingredients** and **kinds of equipment**. Even the types of stoves we use are changed.

---

3 A third team member repeats the whole process **using yet another set of equipment** and **alternative ingredients**. By the time the recipes appear on these pages, they are guaranteed to work in any kitchen, including yours. **We promise.**
